PRAISE FOR J. W. FREIE
FOUR SEASONS OF LONELINESS

"In this spellbinding book, J. W. Freiberg explores the vast territory of human loneliness with cases from his fascinating law practice. Beautifully written and impossible to put down, his stories range in theme from loneliness imposed by external events—such as world-shaking historical upheavals—to the limitations for rich social connections imposed by family structure, lack of educational opportunity, and poverty. As a lawyer, Freiberg eloquently describes how loneliness is played out in the ways people navigate through institutions and social relationships."

—Bessel van der Kolk, MD,
professor of psychiatry, Boston University School of Medicine,
New York Times bestselling author of *The Body Keeps the Score:
Brain, Mind, and Body in the Healing of Trauma*

"J. W. Freiberg's *Four Seasons of Loneliness* is a moving book that shares four compelling stories about four radically different people living very different lives. As the leader of the oldest child-welfare organization in the nation, I hear similar stories of sadness and heartache as state systems across the country fail to help sustain the adult and peer connections that children need to grow into healthy, resilient adults themselves. This book is a must read."

—Joan Wallace-Benjamin, PhD, president/CEO
of the Home for Little Wanderers

"J. W. Freiberg has written an amazing book. I was riveted by his style of writing and his humane approach to very extreme situations. Connections are most important to our well-being and to our self-esteem, and for those who have lost connections, it is clear that they have lost a part of themselves. Freiberg gives us a window into the souls of the perpetrators and the victims, and he does it with courage, care, and no condescension whatsoever. This is a book about and for humans who are grappling with their humanity and with understanding the challenges and diversity of others who live in our very same world. This is a magnificent book."

—Dr. Joyce Maguire Pavao, lecturer in psychiatry,
Harvard Medical School, CEO of Pavao Consulting and Coaching

"J. W. Freiberg has created a masterpiece of an unusual kind. The unique combination of legal and social-psychological perspective in exploring loneliness in the lives (and cases) of four very different individuals is at once compelling, disarming, and educational. The reader cannot help but walk away with new personal insights into the importance that loving connections play in his or her own life."

—Christopher F. Small, former executive director of the Italian
Home for Children in Boston, author of *The Italian Home for Children*

"Freiberg's posit, premise, research, observations, and lived experiences with isolation and its impacts are spellbinding and attention grabbing. There are so many clinical implications of this, especially in relation to the trauma work that I do as a professional clinician working with what we call 'attachment and attunement.' I love the premise that loneliness is not an emotion but a sensation. I can't even begin to wrap my clinical brain around where this could go in the future of trauma treatment. I loved it."

—Denise M. Hamilton, LICSW, chief operating officer
of Boston Youth Sanctuary

FOUR
SEASONS
OF
LONELINESS

FOUR
SEASONS
OF
LONELINESS

A LAWYER'S CASE STORIES

J. W. Freiberg

For my friends Pam
Bob – and this book
is all about how
important friendship
is in all our lives.

J. W. Freiberg

Published by Philia Books, Ltd., Boston, MA
www.jwfreiberg.com

Edited and Designed by Girl Friday Productions
www.girlfridayproductions.com
Editorial: Emilie Sandoz-Voyer, Shannon O'Neill, Amanda O'Brien, and Sue Franco
Interior Design: Rachel Christenson
Cover Design: Kathleen Lynch
Image Credits: cover © plainpicture/amanaimages

ISBN-13: 978-0-9975899-0-0
ISBN-10: 0-9975899-0-6
eISBN: 978-0-9975899-1-7
Library of Congress Control Number: 2016946984

First Edition

Printed in the United States of America

DEDICATION

As I understand it, what has held the moon and the Earth in a stable celestial state throughout the lives of all the poets who have looked skyward is the dynamic balance of gravity pulling the moon in and centrifugal force propelling it away.

And, as I understand it, what keeps each of us in a stable psychological state throughout our lives, as we each write our own poetry, are the connections to our family that hold us close in and the connections to our friends and colleagues that propel us outward into the world.

And so I dedicate this humble work to my family and to my friends:

Many years ago, my father gave me a photograph of my grandfather as a four-year-old, which was taken with *his* father and grandfather. When my son turned four, my father, my son, and I had a picture taken of the three of us in the same pose, with me holding that earlier photograph. So in the second photograph, there are six generations of my family, and at just about the time this book is published, a seventh will be born. We each have these family roots, and they serve to bind us in the passage of time just as gravity keeps the moon in the next poet's view. This book is dedicated especially to Justin and Sarah, and to Nini and Luke, and to Julie and Nina and their children, my wonderful family members who hold me so close.

This book is also dedicated to all the friends who have come on board during the seventy-two-year voyage I have been sailing. Some have left at earlier ports, and some have been buried at sea, but there has always been room for new shipmates to help hoist the sails and tend the tiller. We each have our own network of friends and colleagues, and this book is all about how important they are in our lives, and what happens to those among us who fail to make and nourish these connections.

TABLE OF
CONTENTS

PROLOGUE

Loneliness: The Perception of Inadequate Connections

This book is about loneliness, not solitude. By *solitude* I mean the state of mind of those few among us who, reportedly, can be alone without becoming lonely: the proverbial monastic in a cell abiding by a vow of silence, the Buddhist monk sitting in meditative repose year after year, or the recluse whose psychological makeup requires seclusion. Personally, I've never met such a person.

Loneliness, in contrast, is an unwelcome sensation familiar to the rest of us. We experience loneliness when we perceive detachment or separation from those we care about. This happens to us in all the phases—or seasons, as I call them—of our lives. Could there be anyone reading these words who has not, from time to time, felt lonely when sensing distance and disconnection from others?

Distinct from our personal moments of garden-variety lonesomeness is the devastating *chronic* loneliness of those who lead truly isolated, solitary lives, with no one to go home to, no one to call or be called by, no one to care for, and no one who cares. An ever-increasing percentage of the US population now lives alone. In 1970, only 17 percent of us did; by 2012 that number had grown to 27 percent.[1] Think about it: between a quarter and a third of American adults live alone, eat alone, and sleep alone.

Is there any way to know whether these forty-four million Americans are chronically lonely? Could it be that many of them are at peace with their solitude? Author Robert Putnam, former dean of the John F. Kennedy School of Government, takes a strong position on this issue in his aptly titled book, *Bowling Alone*, in which he presents research findings indicating that contemporary American society is producing extensive chronic loneliness, not tranquil solitude.[2] Is he correct? Can we know?

Well, it turns out we can know. Thanks to the UCLA Loneliness Scale 3, we actually have powerful statistics that address just this question.[3] Today, more than forty-four million American adults over age forty-five suffer from chronic loneliness as measured by the scale.[4] That number means that 35 percent of American adults reported in 2010 that they consider themselves to be chronically lonely. Perhaps the most frightening part of this statistic is that the figure was only 20 percent ten years earlier.[5]

Does it matter if an increasing percentage of us are chronically lonely? Is this a public health issue or merely a personal problem for the affected individuals? Psychiatrists Jacqueline Olds and Richard Schwartz tell us that it matters greatly.[6] Their research shows how profoundly isolated so many of us are: they write, for example, that one in four Americans report that they *spoke with no one about something*

---

1. Jonathan Vespa, Jamie M. Lewis, and Rose M. Kreider, *America's Families and Living Arrangements: 2012* (Washington, DC: US Census Bureau Report, 2013).
2. Robert Putnam, *Bowling Alone: The Collapse and Revival of American Community* (New York: Simon and Schuster, 2000).
3. Daniel W. Russell, "UCLA Loneliness Scale (Version 3): Reliability, validity, and factor structure," *Journal of Personality Assessment* 66, no. 3 (1996): 20–40. A copy of the scale is included as the appendix to this book.
4. Brad Edmondson, "All the Lonely People," *AARP The Magazine* November/December (2010).
5. Ibid.
6. Jacqueline Olds and Richard Schwartz, *The Lonely American: Drifting Apart in the Twenty-First Century* (Boston: Beacon Press, 2009).

important to them in the past six months. Add to this the findings of John T. Cacioppo, director of the Center for Cognitive and Social Neuroscience at the University of Chicago, whose work has concentrated on the lethality of loneliness.[7] His studies show that chronically lonely persons are significantly more likely to become diabetic, have sleep disorders, develop high blood pressure, acquire Alzheimer's, and have poorly functioning immune systems. It is certainly no surprise to learn that lonely persons die at a significantly younger age.[8]

So chronic loneliness is clearly important to study, given how ubiquitous it has become and how deleterious it is. But what could possibly be the connection between chronic loneliness and the legal profession? I spent decades at that intersection, and I briefly want to share with you how that came to be and then tell you four stories that convey what I observed.

Loneliness and the Law

I didn't set out to study loneliness. In my late thirties, I was just trying to get a law practice up and running. But Boston is a city in which attorneys routinely refer cases to one another based on areas of specialization, and because I had a PhD in the subject and had taught social psychology courses in the Department of Sociology at Boston University, fellow attorneys quickly labeled me "the psych lawyer." The more I referred out cases that I was unqualified to handle, the more they referred law cases to me that involved clients with psychological "issues." Within a two-year span, this unintended specialization had snowballed—whether I liked it or not. During this same period, I also began what would become thirty years of service as general counsel to five of the city's largest private social service agencies. Between them, these agencies employed over six hundred psychiatrists, psychologists, and clinical social workers, and part of my daily work was to be available for case consultations with clinical professionals. This meant I

---

7.   John T. Cacioppo and William Patrick, *Loneliness: Human Nature and the Need for Social Connection* (New York: W. W. Norton and Company, 2008).

8.   Ibid.

heard the details of hundreds and hundreds of psychological profiles. And while my legal mind provided what I hope was helpful counsel with respect to whatever legal problem was raised, my social psychology mind searched through these myriad cases to discern the archetypes and discover the recurring patterns.

For many years, more as an intellectual exercise than anything else, I made notes on the psychological motifs and regularities that cut across my case files. Over time, themes began to emerge, lessons garnered from the remarkably detailed life histories I had access to, a number of which provide the material for the stories that follow.

But why pick loneliness to write about when there are so many other discernible psychological patterns? Why didn't I write a book about *anger*, for example? I certainly worked on enough cases involving truly angry people: angry divorce litigants, angry cheated business partners, angry "falsely accused" criminal defendants, angry bilked investors, angry heirs excluded from wills, and oh so many others. But to me loneliness is a far more interesting topic than anger, *because you can't write about loneliness without writing about connections*—just as you can't write about hunger without writing about food. To me, loneliness is simply the perception of inadequate connections, in precisely the same way that hunger is the perception of inadequate food and thirst the perception of inadequate hydration. Loneliness is not an emotion; it is a sensation. And since it happens that studying how people make connections to each other—and to the social institutions in their lives—is *exactly* what social psychologists are trained to do, my cases involving lonely clients were the perfect subset for me to think and write about. And, on top of that, two of the clients you will meet in these pages actually extracted promises from me that I'd tell their stories by trying to write this book.

What follows is not a treatise on loneliness. On the contrary, it is simply a collection of the life histories of four clients, each of whom was chronically lonely, if for wildly dissimilar reasons. When these biographies are considered together, they shed light on different facets of the phenomenon of loneliness, which, the existentialists tell us, is an inescapable element of the human condition. While few among us are destined to suffer the chronic loneliness and hopeless isolation detailed in the following case histories, we all know what it is like to have important attachments disappear from our lives, and we have all experienced being disconnected from people we once cared deeply about. When parents die, when a spouse or lover departs, when children grow up and move out, when friends relocate far away, when a career ends, when the team disperses, when our community changes to the point where we no longer recognize it—the loss of connection is real, palpable, and undeniable. What matters, these cases show, is how we deal with such moments of loss and detachment. To be temporarily alone without succumbing to loneliness, to grieve loss and then move through it, and to dare to build new connections to replace those that have faded or vanished are strategies well known to each of us, but which play out so differently in the four lives chronicled in the case stories that follow.

Four Seasons of Loneliness

Loneliness is not reserved for the rejected seniors who populate nursing homes, sequestered from the younger generations of their families. Children, even babies, can feel terribly alone and disconnected. Each of you, thinking back on your own childhood, can probably remember moments when you felt cut off from the adults you depended on, like that dark feeling that overwhelmed you when you were the last child picked up from school—my eighty-year-old sister *still* has not forgiven our mother for committing this sin. And think of the sufferings of adolescence, when you were excluded from a clique or cast off by someone you thought was a friend. I have yet to meet a person who wants to relive their teenage years. At the other end of life, the elderly of our times no longer live in extended family situations, providing childcare for their grandchildren. Instead, they are statistically far more likely to await death in institutions that specialize in housing the terminally lonely. And those in between, who are still of working age, also increasingly fall prey to loneliness and disconnection because so many live alone, and so many must deal with the harshness of modern-day employment and its deskilled labor, income insecurity, elongated workdays, and arduous commutes.

Once I had determined to write about cases in which I represented chronically lonely clients, I still had a selection to make: Which cases shed the brightest light on the phenomenon of loneliness itself? Which life histories best revealed how connections are compromised or lost? Which best explained why some dare to establish new connections and others fail to even try? The choice of cases became clearer when it dawned on me that what most characterizes loneliness—like its fellow sensations hunger and thirst—is that it is experienced throughout our lives. Spring, summer, autumn, winter: in each season of our lives, we confront a different version of the same challenge, to find and live balanced lives in which we are both at peace with ourselves and simultaneously secure about our connections to others.

From the springtime of life, you will meet the loneliest boy I have ever known. But I forewarn you: to fathom the depth of his isolation, you will have to hear the details of the abuse he suffered in a home rife with incest and sexual exploitation—an upbringing that doomed him to a life of separation and seclusion.

From the glaring heat of revolutionary China, you will come to know the story of a remarkable client who spent much of the summer of his life—fifteen years of it—in solitary confinement. He has a great deal to tell us about what it means, what it feels like, to be so terrifyingly alone. The following words are his:

> Sitting on the low-slung bed, staring at the [prison cell] wall, I felt the room full of aloneness. It was not just the absence of other human life, but the presence of aloneness that seemed to fill the room, to shimmer between me and the wall, to weigh down the otherwise empty air until it seemed to press in and threaten to suffocate me.[9]

---

9. Sidney Rittenberg and Amanda Bennett, *The Man Who Stayed Behind* (Simon and Schuster, 1993), 414.

Then you will come to know an exceptionally lonely man in the autumn of his life, a man who created his own unendurable isolation by accomplishing intellectual achievements that separated him from everyone he met in the working-class setting of his life and then coupling this with a failure to reach out and make new connections with others from more educated strata.

And finally, as the winter snows of Boston blow sideways in the wind, you will meet a bachelor professor whose woeful loneliness as he lay dying was magnified a thousandfold precisely because he knew more about love than anyone else I've ever met.

*

Those who have read early drafts of these stories have inquired, almost to a person, if they are fact or fiction. These stories come from the files of law cases I actually worked on, and they contain a myriad of details about the lives of clients whom I counseled and represented. That being said, limits imposed by privilege and confidentiality requirements oblige me to modify identifying specifics of the cases from which these stories are drawn. I do this by changing names, altering identifying details, shifting locations, integrating elements from related law cases, and modifying some components of the actual cases I litigated, negotiated, and consulted on. But rest assured: the lessons about loneliness and connection that speak out from these stories come from very real law cases.

J. W. Freiberg
Boston, 2016

I

The Loneliest Boy

"Hi, Terry. Susan Sears here. Am I going to lose my house?" These were the first words I heard about a lawsuit that would stretch over three years and teach me more about loneliness than I ever wanted to learn. Ten minutes earlier my client had been served lawsuit papers, as she put it, "by the biggest goddamn sheriff I've ever seen. And he was out to scare me. Why would he do that?" Once I had calmed her down to the point where she could read me the heading to the lawsuit papers, I learned that she had indeed been sued, as had the small adoption agency she had run for over twenty years.

But allow me to step back a moment and explain how I got to one end of the phone line and Susan got to the other. In the fall of 1971, I became an assistant professor of sociology at Boston University, where I principally taught courses in social psychology. I was fascinated by the nature of the linkage between mind and society, how our perceptions and thoughts are colored and, to some extent, even structured by the era and social circumstances in which we live. I was ecstatic about my academic life in vibrant Boston, save for one problem: Boston University had an autocratic president who was so odious that he managed to provoke nearly the entire faculty to go on strike in 1975. I quickly became one of the leaders of the strike, and along with the other organizers, I appeared before the board of trustees—and the president—to present the junior faculty's view as to why his contract should not be renewed. As it turned out, the trustees determined to indeed renew the president's contract, and lo and behold, when my candidature for tenure came across his desk in 1978, it was *my* contract that was not renewed. Although a year later I was actually awarded tenure, I had in the interim applied to and been accepted to Harvard Law School, and since the problematic president was willing to pay my tuition in exchange for my resignation, off I went in 1980 to begin an entirely new career.

Little did I know that once I had learned the basics of practicing law, I would be almost immediately typecast as the attorney to whom cases and clients involving any and all sundry psychological issues should be sent. I had envisioned myself as a constitutional lawyer arguing great legal theories before the Supreme Court. But no, that was not to be the case. On the contrary, I practiced law "in the trenches," as the saying goes. And while the nature of my practice meant that neither fame nor fortune would come my way, it also meant that I would, in effect, be doing social psychological research through practicing law. It was only in retirement, however, that I took the time to write about the observations I had made daily for more than thirty years.

So back to my client Susan Sears. She had retained my general counsel services about five years before this lawsuit because she had heard about my previous career, my sympathetic ear for social service agencies, and—not unimportantly—my modest fee schedule. I asked her to fax over the lawsuit documents, relax with a cup of tea, and give me an hour to read over the papers.

I could see almost at once that the complaint and its collateral documents were well drafted. That's actually a good thing: quality counsel on the plaintiff's side of a personal injury lawsuit greatly increases the odds of a timely resolution. That being said, the complaint was sparsely written, and about all I could discern from the papers was that Susan and her agency were being blamed for a failed adoption that had shattered the adoptive home, traumatizing everybody in the family—adults and children alike. Since children were involved, the adoptive parents were identified as John and Jane Doe, their adoptive daughter was called Ashley Doe, and their preadoptive foster son—Ashley's biological brother—was dubbed Seth Doe. One thing, however, was abundantly clear: the plaintiffs were seeking massive monetary damages.

It was also obvious that the plaintiffs had brought a "shotgun" lawsuit; that is, they were suing anybody and everybody involved in any way with the failed adoptive placement. Additional defendants included the Massachusetts Department of Social Services (DSS) and about a dozen psychiatrists and psychologists. The DSS was accused of negligently managing the adoptive placement, while the mental health professionals, all of whom had treated the two adoptive children at different times after their removal from their birth family, were accused of negligence in failing to warn the adoptive parents about how the children might behave once they were placed.

The multiparty nature of the lawsuit meant two things to me: first, it was unlikely to settle quickly, and second, it was going to cost a small fortune to defend. I called Sears back.

"There's good news," I began, "and bad news. The good news is, you don't need to worry about your house. The nature of the claims means that it will certainly be covered by your agency's professional liability insurance policy, and I reviewed that policy last spring, I know for a fact that it is in full force and effect. And by the way, your policy has no deductible, so neither the agency nor any of you will have to pay a penny out of pocket, so you can relax."

"Okay, great." She paused. "Wait a minute. You said there's bad news too."

"The bad news is that this kind of lawsuit is likely to drag on for two or three years."

"Years! How do we handle this mess and make a living? There's only three of us." I could hear distress in her voice.

For the next half hour, I walked Sears through what it means—in practical terms—to be sued. I explained how the legal discovery process works and told her that, absent a settlement, the case would not proceed to trial for at least three years.

"You'll be our attorney on this, won't you?" Sears pleaded.

"That's up to your insurance company," I explained. "But by all odds, they'll agree to that. Even if they don't, I can be involved as the agency's general counsel. One way or another, I'm going to hold your hand throughout this entire process."

"Thank you, thank you, Terry," she said with real emotion in her voice, audibly exhaling into the phone. I could tell she was tearing up.

*

Sure enough, when I called the agency's insurer, the company's senior claim agent, Rhonda Wilkins, gave me the case to defend. She knew from past cases we had done together that my training in social psychology would be useful, especially because this case would involve depositions of more than a score of mental health professionals, not to mention our need to locate and work with a forensic psychiatrist to serve as our expert witness.

The plaintiffs' attorney was Jeff O'Toole. He and I had once served together on a Massachusetts Bar Association committee, and I had formed the impression that he was a reasonably classy guy, especially for someone who practiced plaintiff-side personal injury law. Working with him, I thought, would be far better than what I could have drawn: a back-of-the-yellow-pages ambulance chaser. But reaching him was another matter. I called, but it took O'Toole more than a week to get back to me. Not a promising start.

In the meantime, Sears sent me three boxes' worth of the agency's case records from the Doe adoptive placement. They arrived on the Friday before a three-day weekend in the still-chilly early spring. I took the documents home, set up a card table in front of my living room fireplace, and spent all three of those days reading the record from front to back. There were five fireplaces in our old Civil War–era house, and we used them far too seldom in the rush of modern life. It was delightful to take the opportunity to sit by one for once. My son was about four years old at the time, and he essentially spent the entire three days playing under the table by my feet, enjoying both his fort, as he called it, and the wonderful warmth thrown off by the fire. He was just old enough to help put on the occasional new log, and as I interrupted my reading from time to time to join him under the table, I couldn't help but reflect on how much of one's life is determined by the happenstance of birth. Seth Doe and my boy were born into circumstances as different as could be: Seth's life chances were doomed before he could walk or talk, and there was nothing he could do about it. This, if I remember correctly from college English class, is the technical definition of a tragic flaw: when one's downfall and destruction are predetermined by an ineradicable flaw.

At the time I read the *Doe* case record, I was serving as general counsel to half a dozen children's social service agencies, and in this capacity, I worked closely with the Massachusetts DSS. Accordingly, I had encountered some extreme and deeply disturbing cases involving the sexual abuse of children. But none of this adequately prepared me for the *Doe* case. I was horrified by what I read in the massive written record.

The two children involved had been raised by a young single mother, and all three of them lived in the home of the children's grandmother and step-grandfather, as did the two siblings of the mother. The family rented a humble house in a town northwest of Boston, and they appeared perfectly normal to the neighbors. The children presented and behaved well in school and in the community, and the adults were polite and accepted in the neighborhood. Teacher and guidance counselor notations that I read in the record drew the same conclusions. All of them consistently indicated that the children were appropriate with their classmates, polite with adults, and diligent in their schoolwork. Other documentation showed that they played well with other children and that their performance on tests and homework was entirely acceptable. Ashley was consistently a strong B student, and Seth's grades averaged out to A–. The school nurse's report was no different: it stated that the children seemed properly fed and exhibited no health or dental problems.

Behind this façade, however, was a home life as abnormal as any of us who worked on the case had ever encountered. The step-grandfather turned out to be, in the words of the chief counsel of the commonwealth's DSS, "one of the most sexually abusive offenders on record in Massachusetts." He not only had sexual relations with his wife, but also with all three of her children—two daughters and one son. Moreover, he had sired the two Doe children by one of his stepdaughters, so he was both their step-grandfather and their father. Still more shocking, he sexually abused these children from the time they were toddlers. The grandmother was also sexually active with all of her children and involved in group sex practices with the toddlers. The young mother of the two children was no different: she likewise engaged in group sex with her siblings in various combinations. So far as I could tell, there were simply no sexual boundaries whatsoever in the children's biological home.

But by far the most peculiar thing about the household (and this may well be as hard for you to accept as it was for me and the ten additional attorneys who would soon be working on the case) was that, although there was unparalleled sexual exploitation of the young adults and constant sexual abuse of the two small children, in every other sphere of life, the family consistently exhibited nurturing and loving concern for each other's welfare. That, obviously, is why the children presented as well in public as they did. Among the score of legal and mental health professionals who worked on the *Doe* case, there were many hundreds of years of collective experience. And yet not one of us had *ever* seen or even heard of this fact pattern (as lawyers call the circumstances of a case) before. On the contrary, in the hundreds of cases involving sexually abused children with which we had collectively dealt, there had always also been physical or psychological abuse—often both. At the very least, children with sexually abusive home lives are typically threatened and frightened into silence: they're told that if they disclose to anyone what goes on at home, they will be permanently taken away from their family. Instilling this fear of separation in a young child is in and of itself psychologically abusive, and it's common to learn that such children are often also threatened with violence if they disclose the family's hidden secrets. But from what I could discern in a first reading of the voluminous Doe record, the method used by the children's family to achieve secrecy and mask their home life was unlike any other I had ever experienced. It was pretty clearly not based on threats.

At some point, I needed a break from reading the enormous and depressing record. I started sifting through the folders, looking for a snapshot, a Polaroid, or a photo of any kind. When I eventually found one in practically the last file I looked in, it absolutely startled me. These were no ordinary children. They were a matched set of stunningly beautiful, blond, blue-eyed kids with big smiles and perfectly straight, white teeth. They looked to be about eight and six years old in the photo, which seemed to have been taken at a playground or park; there was a slide and a swing visible beyond them. One thing seemed certain: the children clearly loved whoever took the photo. You could see it in the warmth of their smiles and the twinkles in their big, bright eyes. I say this because when I look back at old photos of my son, he has the same unabashed look of pure joy spreading across his face that says, "Oh boy, someone I love is paying attention to me." I couldn't help but contrast this with photos I'd seen in other cases of kids from backgrounds filled with abuse, fear, and pain, where typically there was no smile at all or only a forced-looking one.

Even now, nearly thirty years later, I remember with surprising clarity the weekend I first read through the *Doe* case record and came face to face with the horrific facts. I can even remember that, as I read through it with the fire crackling behind me, I was constantly contrasting the calm normality of my own childhood, and that of my son's, with the tumultuous, wild ride that life had given the Doe children. I can easily picture myself that first evening of reading the Doe case record, when I told my son yet another installment of the bedtime story he so loved, *The Elephant Trainer Boy*. The story was a tale I made up, chapter by chapter, relating the adventures of an Indian boy whose father trained elephants that the boy delivered across all of India, despite his youth. It was easy for the boy, you see, because unbeknownst to everybody, even his father, he had learned Pachydermese. Why was this night different from all other nights? Why was just another normal, loving bedtime with my son so etched into my mind? It took me years to understand that it was the sharpness of the contrast between his life and that of the Doe children.

No sooner was my boy asleep than I dove back into the Doe files. Remarkably, the disclosure of the rampant and abusive sexuality inside the family household had come to light only by accident. The children's mother, who was on public relief and had counseling available to her, voluntarily sought guidance about why she felt so insecure when applying for jobs. Ashley had tagged along with her mother, and in the corner of the waiting room she spotted a satchel that had a doll's hand protruding from it. But what she found when she opened the little bag were not just ordinary dolls. These were what social workers call anatomically correct dolls, which are used by mental health professionals as an aid in determining if very young children have seen or experienced sexualized interactions. When the social worker found Ashley playing all-too knowledgeably with the dolls, she immediately filed a report with the DSS.

The department investigated the household that very evening, which culminated in an emergency removal of the two children and their placement in separate, temporary foster homes. During the weeks that followed, the children were interviewed by a Sexual Assault Intervention Network team, specialized clinical social workers, DSS personnel, the police, and the prosecutorial authorities handling the criminal cases against the perpetrators. The department brought an emergency court proceeding to take legal custody of the children, which was allowed. That was the end of the family: the children would never see any of the adults again.

The police arrested the children's grandparents, their mother, their aunt, and their uncle. Within a matter of weeks, a plea bargain was negotiated with the mother, who was considered by the police to be as much a victim as a perpetrator. She was allowed to avoid criminal prosecution in exchange for permanently releasing legal custody of the two children to the commonwealth. I later learned that she also agreed to immediately move out of Massachusetts forever and to never again seek to have contact with her children. To the best of my knowledge, she was never heard from again. While there was arguably some justice to this outcome given her limited capacities and her own victimization, I could find no justice whatsoever in the disposition of the criminal charges against the grandmother and step-grandfather. Incredibly, they were allowed to plead guilty to several felony counts, and in exchange for their written covenant never to return and never to attempt to make contact with the children, they also were allowed to leave the state. As chance would have it, in the years that followed, I came to know the judge who had ruled on the matter, and I only barely refrained from bringing up the case and excoriating His Honor for such a blatant miscarriage of justice. The disposition of the criminal charges against the aunt and the uncle was never known to me, although I did come to understand that they too were barred from ever having contact with the children again.

In the normal course of things, the children were moved from their two temporary shelter foster homes to two different, long-term foster homes. Not surprisingly, they each languished. Seth's record indicated that from the day of his removal from his birth family, his affect became almost entirely flat. To quote his foster mother, "Seth has never smiled—not once."

Ashley's record showed that she seldom played or interacted in any way with the other children in her foster home. She reportedly spent most of her time "staring off into space." The record also indicated, sadly, that while visitation between the children was clinically indicated and favored by all, because of the overly heavy caseloads of their DSS social workers, only two brief visits between the children actually occurred in the fourteen months prior to their preadoptive placement with the plaintiffs. So during this difficult period in their lives, the children had not only lost the adults in their family—forever—but had also lost each other. They were both alone, terribly alone, for these critically important transition months.

Notwithstanding the circumstances described above, both children were still consistently described in the record as "intelligent" and "articulate" by the myriad of adult professionals with whom they now dealt. Each child openly and honestly answered questions put to them by mental health professionals and other adults, and they were able to describe their lives in their birth home with remarkable clarity. What particularly caught my eye, however, was that in each and every investigative report I read, whether written by the police, the district attorney, DSS social workers, or the psychologists who provided clinical counseling to the children after their removal from the birth home, the children were quoted as expressing *love and concern* for their birth family, including their grandparents. Understandably, even admirably, they also repeatedly expressed a great deal of worried concern about what would become of their hapless mother.

*

More than a year passed in long-term foster care, and the children, now eleven and nine, were rapidly deteriorating. Seth was beginning to show significant signs of clinical depression, and Ashley was increasingly despondent and removed. Both children appeared joyless and limpid; the notes of their respective clinicians indicated that the only spark of life either child exhibited in clinical sessions was when they fantasized about being reunited in an adoptive home. Fortunately for them, that was exactly what the DSS had in mind.

Susan Sears's agency specialized in the adoptive placement of older sibling groups, which was why DSS referred the Doe children to her. She almost immediately thought of a couple that her agency had pre-cleared to adopt a sibling group and gave them a call to ascertain their interest. From Sears's point of view, this couple seemed ideal: they were a two-income, upper-middle-class family whose large home could easily provide a separate bedroom for each child. And just as importantly in Sears's eyes, both the wife and husband had successfully completed graduate work. Sears felt that their advanced level of education would prove useful, given the massive amount of sensitive information they would need to read and absorb about the children's background prior to making their decision as to whether these were the right children for them to adopt.

And indeed, we know from the deposition testimony of the parents that Sears was correct: the couple actually did read the same written record I had pored through. They both later testified that they were stunned by what the siblings had endured—anyone would be. So stunned, apparently, that they felt very unsure about proceeding with the adoption. But in the midst of all their quite reasonable uncertainty, something short-circuited the careful deliberation and due diligence the parents had initially planned to undertake in thinking through the complexities of this potential sibling adoption. These were educated, thoughtful people who would by nature be cautious. I was convinced that there would be no way to directly probe the parents to find out what had interfered with the process that had been planned, since there was a high probability they themselves would not have been aware of exactly what had happened. All that we later learned was that the prospective adoptive parents stopped all serious balancing of the pros and cons the day they met the children. My own guess is that this was a product of how monumentally good-looking these two siblings were. On top of this, I don't find it at all hard to understand how the potential adoptive parents got caught up in the children's exuberance at being reunited. And thus the die was cast.

The lawsuit, of course, displaced the parents' aborted due diligence process onto my client. But in this effort, the parents' suit had a problem because the file held a copy of just the kind of letter that trial attorneys dream of finding: Sears had written to the potential adoptive parents advising the couple to retain the services of their own consulting psychologist to advise them about the complexities of adopting survivors of childhood sexual abuse. And in fact, the couple had done so. Better yet (for us), the record contained a copy of the report submitted to them by their consulting psychologist. It clearly stated that children from such a background can act out in severe and unpredictable ways—unpredictable being the operative word. They were told about the behavioral patterns that are the most prevalent in children who were sexually abused at a young age, the most typical one for girls being teenage promiscuity and for boys being sexual predation. They were, in sum, sternly warned by their own consulting psychologist.

The adoption fantasy—for both parents and the children—clearly snowballed the day of the children's first visit to the home of the potential adoptive couple. Ashley told us far later in the litigation that the day of the first visit "was like Dorothy getting taken by the hurricane [sic] to the land of Oz." I remember smiling when she testified using this term, but I knew exactly what she meant. Adoption in Massachusetts often means upward social mobility for a child, since it is frequently young women of modest means who choose to place a child for adoption, while it is mostly couples of significant means who experience infertility due to waiting longer to start their family. But this case was extreme. The children had grown up in a simple, prefabricated wooden rental house in a proper but humble neighborhood. In stark contrast, the Does' home was a striking central entrance colonial that sat just at the top of a sizable hill in a tony neighborhood town just outside of Boston. Running downhill from the house was a massive yard, which the children each described as a park. It was nearly an acre in size—a virtual sea of perfectly manicured lawn. Better still, the property backed up to a vast nature preserve, and there was talk that day of all manner of enticing ideas, including a discussion about the possibility of constructing a tree house in the massive oak that grew at one end of the lawn just before the woods began. What seemed crystal clear from all we learned was that during that first visit, the children fell in love with the concept of being reunited and living in a fairy-tale house on the top of a hill, while the parents fell in love with the concept of having two such stunningly beautiful children.

The placement went very well indeed. Ashley and Seth were remarkably intact and were thrilled to escape the depressing loneliness they had each endured in their foster homes. These bright children understood that they now had a chance for a very different type of life. Here were parents who knew how to prepare one to face the world, and something in these two children drove them to take advantage of this. The children excelled in every way in the local school, and, according to the parents' testimony, were a delight to have in the adoptive home. The one hiccup was that, at the end of the mandatory six-month trial period before the adoption could be legally finalized, Seth, who had just turned thirteen, asked the Does if he could postpone these legal formalities. He reported to his clinical social worker that, although he liked living with his new family, he remained anxious about the fate of his mother. He just felt he couldn't permanently cut his connection to her—not yet. Ashley, on the other hand, wanted legal finalization to happen as soon as possible, and she was enthusiastically in favor of proceeding. To the credit of the adoptive couple, they had no qualms about the older child's reluctance to finalize his adoption at that point and took no offense from his admirable loyalty to his vanished mother. Sears's notes in the record were clear on this point: the couple felt that sometimes only the passage of time can heal great wounds, and they were determined to be patient out of respect for Seth's needs. In the meantime, they finalized the adoption of Ashley, and the Doe story seemed to be on its way to a happy ending.

*

Ah, but a different fate awaited them. Late one night, about eighteen months after the placement, the parents discovered that their adopted daughter and her brother had a full and completely secret sex life. The couple was shocked and horrified, understandably. They were furious with Seth, again, understandably. But then Mrs. Doe lost it, screaming at Seth and calling him a rapist. But that was nothing compared with the precipitous action she took next—a decision that would have devastating consequences for everyone in the family: the police were summoned.

Barely an hour after the children had been discovered together, Seth was led away in handcuffs, with Ashley watching. By noon, the boy was irretrievably caught up in the machinery of the Massachusetts Juvenile Justice System, which would change his life forever. By late that afternoon, the parents had cut all ties with the mental health professionals who had been counseling Ashley throughout the adoption proceedings and replaced them with a new clinician who specialized in therapy for rape victims. Ashley was now branded and stigmatized— and bereft of the brother she so loved.

*

Once Attorney O'Toole returned my call, I was able to begin learning how he planned to present the case. From his point of view, the gravamen (that is, the grievance) of the lawsuit was simple and straightforward: the department, the mental health professionals, and most assuredly my adoption agency clients, had all been grossly negligent in failing to give the parents adequate warning that the children might act out sexually with one another. Moreover, O'Toole concluded, this negligence led directly to a state of total chaos in the adoptive household, causing great and irreparable injuries to the parents and to

Ashley. I remember well the summary line he added: "My case is simple. Elegantly so."

I also remember that I failed to find a way to contest this for quite some time. The case certainly had a unique and compelling fact pattern, with children who had first lost their birth home and then experienced still more loss with the adoption disruption.

Before I could find words to respond, O'Toole ominously quoted an old hymn: "Snow, on snow, on snow. That's what we have here: loss, on loss, on loss."

He was right. He had a case with significant damages and a powerful argument. If the plaintiffs' claim of professional negligence could be sold to a jury, there was definitely the potential here for punitive damages. And if a jury is out to make a point—to punish, to teach a lesson—they could mete out punitive damages in very large amounts. This was not at all what Rhonda Wilkins was hiring me to produce as an outcome, nor what Susan Sears could live with as a blight on her professional reputation. But I remained flummoxed.

I asked a number of questions, principally to gain time to think. O'Toole droned on, but I was no longer listening. I was racking my brain during his righteous monologue to find some argument—any argument—against his position. I had been taught as a fledgling defense attorney that it was critically important to put doubt in a plaintiff's attorney's mind from the very outset of a case. But I still didn't see a counterargument, as I focused in again on O'Toole's words. He was in the midst of boasting about how strong his liability case was because he had already located and retained an expert who would testify that my clients should have better trained and equipped the adoptive parents for the challenge they were taking on. Basically, although he refrained from saying it directly, he was arguing that Sears should have forewarned the parents that the children might act out sexually with each other.

Having thought of nothing clever, and being out of time, I played the only card I had in my hand: my previous career. "Jeff, you don't know my background, but the only reason the insurer gave me this case to defend is because I have a PhD in the field. I used to teach courses on children and trauma at Boston University. And I couldn't disagree more with your expert's view. If only we *did* know enough to foresee and predict human behavior with such clarity." O'Toole was silent; he had no doctorate to throw up against mine. "But we don't. We have no way of being able to predict whether and how children rescued from abusive backgrounds will act. There are a thousand different possible behavioral reactions, and your clients were told about the most common patterns."

Having retaken the initiative, I wasn't about to give it up. When he started to speak, I plowed right on, adlibbing as I went. "Don't you see? The jury is going to hate the knee-jerk reaction of your clients to the children's sexual acting out. As I understand it, they didn't even wait until the morning to garner the advice of their own consulting psychologist or any other mental health professional. How are you going to get around that?"

O'Toole stammered a bit, and then asked me what alternative reaction they could possibly have had—and it was in replying to this question that I found the argument that would later prove critical to the resolution of the case.

"If I had been consulted by your clients after their discovery, I would have told them that the *last* people they wanted to call were the police. I would have advised them to handle the sexuality as a family matter, exhibiting connection and commitment to both children. Personally, I would have counseled that, as strange as it may seem, in the very discovery of the intersibling sexuality, the adoptive parents had stumbled on an enormous opportunity to make these children their own. They could have initiated discussions about sexual boundaries the children had never been taught, and in doing so, they could have become the very parents the children needed. Everybody could have won, Jeff, instead of everybody losing."

It was working. O'Toole remained silent, so I took the opportunity to ask him how he felt about Ashley losing her brother—the last family member in her life—*all because his clients didn't take the time to consult professionals about how to react to what they had learned.* To O'Toole's credit, he regained his voice and replied, if in a considerably less assertive tone.

"Look, Terry, I feel terrible about Ashley's additional loss, of course, but I'm her attorney, not her social worker."

"Well, the jury is going to feel terrible about it too, and if I do my job decently, they're going to blame your clients for their precipitous reaction that cost Ashley her brother. They're going to hear my expert testify that, with patience and professional input, they could have developed an understanding as to why these children were so sexualized and come up with a strategy about how to proceed. And they're going to hear that with those insights and that strategy, they could have built a successful adoptive family. That's what I'm going to argue to the jury, Jeff, and I promise you, I'll find just the right forensic psychiatrist to support that argument."

O'Toole was silent now, the way a bull goes still when the matador puzzles him into tighter and tighter circles with good cape work. Damn, I enjoyed the chess-like games of trial work. Game on.

*

This initial telephone conference was the first step in what turned out to be the better part of three years of litigation in the case. Because the plaintiffs had sued so many parties, every legal step in the lawsuit involved thirteen law offices—a logistical nightmare from a scheduling point of view. During this period, every imaginable person having anything to do with the children was deposed under oath. The records produced by so many witnesses were prodigious: over ten thousand separate documents were formally numbered and entered into the record. The most important deponents were, of course, the children, followed by the adoptive parents. The depositions of these four principal parties to the action lasted for three full days—each. Susan Sears and her two agency employees were examined for two days each, and there were day-long depositions of every single clinician who had ever worked with the children after their removal from the birth home. But it didn't end there: additional full-day depositions were taken from all the children's teachers and guidance counselors, the four sets of foster parents who had kept Ashley and Seth before their placement with the adoptive parents, every member of the clinical and milieu staff who had worked with Seth in his sexual offender program, and all of the children's treating doctors.

As the months passed, I began to develop the theory of the case that had come to me in that first telephone call with Attorney O'Toole. More and more I came to believe that the best defense of the case would be to take the offensive. It was critical to blame the adoptive parents for so quickly jettisoning Seth and thereby branding Ashley. It was they who had placed stigmatizing labels on these lost children: one as a rapist, the other as a rape victim. It hadn't had to be that way.

Above and beyond that, the adoptive parents could also be faulted for causing Ashley to suffer through the agony of a lawsuit. These people didn't need the money; it would be easy to demonstrate that to the jury. The lawsuit as brought by the adoptive parents required Ashley to give detailed testimony in response to the probing questions of *eleven* opposing attorneys. Even more invasive, arguably, was the right the judge granted the defense to have Ashley examined by the defense's own expert psychiatrist. And this examination would not be designed to be clinically therapeutic: its goal would be to probe the psychological health of Ashley in order to try to ascertain how the adoption disruption had injured her—above and beyond how she had been injured by the incest in and the loss of her birth family.

Everything that was true for Ashley was true for Seth as well. As the boy had neither biological nor adoptive parents, the court had appointed a guardian ad litem to protect his interests in the matter, and the guardian had hired separate counsel to add Seth into the lawsuit as an additional plaintiff. So Seth was deposed and examined by the psychiatric expert witness just as Ashley was, and the jury would need to work through whether they saw him as a perpetrator or as another victim—or both.

Once I had settled on my working theory of the case—that the culprits in these children's lives were the adults, not each other—I could begin thinking through an appropriate trial strategy. It may seem counterintuitive, but trial planning begins at the end and works back. The very first things to identify are the principal themes of the closing argument you want to make to the jury. From there, the trial attorney works backward to discover the evidence and arrange for the expert opinion that would be needed to support the argument. Of course, one has to keep one's mind open to react appropriately to what is learned in the discovery process, but that being said, at any given time, an experienced trial attorney knows exactly what his argument to the jury would be if the trial were to begin the following morning. I once had a case where this principle saved the day: all counsel had appeared at a routine pretrial hearing to have the court rule on some pretrial motions, and the judge, who had just had a case settle that opened up a full week-long gap in her trial schedule, precipitously scheduled trial to begin at nine o'clock the following morning.

Anyway, in the *Doe* case, it was clear that success would turn on finding just the right forensic psychiatrist to argue that the parents' reaction to their revelation did as much or more harm to Ashley as whatever harm came from the intersibling sexuality. And something else that had been drilled into my head in my early trial law training: you have got to have the "alpha" expert in the case. In other words, your expert needs to trump the opposing side's expert—above and beyond the substance of whatever they may argue about your case. This is because many jurors, when overwhelmed by incompatible expert testimony, end up comparing the experts themselves rather than the conflicting explanatory models they present. Accordingly, you want your expert to have gone to Harvard not Podunk, to have worked on important real-world projects to which the jurors can relate, and to have arguably national or international renown, not merely local reputation. And you also want an expert who has a winning forensic presence—either because he or she is charismatic or good-looking—or because their presence *as a person* is alluring for some other reason.

Richard Putnam, MD, fit the bill. He was a board-certified psychiatrist connected to Harvard Medical School who had largely been responsible for founding the field of trauma psychiatry and who regularly lectured throughout the United States and, for that matter, around the world. And on top of all that, he was strikingly handsome, with a commanding presence in a courtroom derived in significant part from his bass-baritone voice: it filled a courtroom. There were only two problems with Putnam: first, he was famously reluctant to take on new forensic work, and second, he was enormously expensive.

It was time to bite the bullet and call Rhonda Wilkins, the insurance claim agent on the case, and therefore my boss. She would, after all, be the person in charge of approving Dr. Putnam's staggering bills. She answered in her patented New Jersey accent after only one ring, and once I talked her through my current theory of the case, her immediate reaction—interrupting me toward the end of my little presentation—was, and I quote (imagine the accent yourself), "That scares the fuck out of me. It's an all or nothing gamble. Either you bring a juror all the way over to blaming the adoptive parents for freaking out, or you royally piss them off by insulting the couple who opened their home to these wild kids and then got fucked for trying to help. And you wouldn't have a chance of arguing this unless you can find the right shrink to back you up. And even if you did, the approach could still blow up in your face at trial. Something about it I don't like." She went silent—a rare thing for Wilkins as she thought further. "Why do I think you already have someone in mind?"

"Ah, good question," I responded. "Remember Dr. Putnam? We used him two years ago in that suicide case?"

"Grab him," she interrupted. "I sure the fuck don't want him showing up on the other side. But do us both a favor here: be very, very sure Putnam's testimony will support your theory before you adopt that idea with finality. We'll be royally fucked if you try what you're talking about and the jury likes the parents more than they like Putnam." With that, she hung up—no good-bye, no anything.

I was armed with Dr. Putnam's home number from the previous case we had worked on together, but it still took me over a week to hear back from him. Almost the first words out of his mouth were about how extraordinarily busy he was and how he was only taking on forensic cases that were interesting to him from a research perspective. He asked point blank, "Be honest with me. Is there any research potential here? I'm asking Terry the PhD, not Terry the lawyer. Anything interesting here?"

"Rick," I shot back, trying to sound as confident as possible, "I have a theory of this case that you may or may not be able to support once you've examined the children. But if I've got it right, there is extremely significant research potential here."

I proceeded to relay the details of the boundaryless sexuality in the three-generational birth family, along with the highly unusual—maybe unique—fact that it took place in a framework of what otherwise seemed to be perfectly normal parental love and nurturing. And I filled him in on what had happened with the children since.

"Have you met the children?" Putnam asked.

"No," I responded. "But those who have report that they were remarkably intact at the time of their removal from the birth home. My own guess at this point—and of course, what will count will be your examination findings—is that these children were psychologically unscathed by the sexuality in their birth home because of the environment in which it took place. I have a feeling that the first truly traumatic event to occur to them was probably the loss and criminalization of their birth family. The children never saw them again after the evening of the discovery when the department removed the children on an emergency basis. And they'll never see any of them again, ever. It was part of all the plea bargains. One moment they had this big crazy family, and the next thing they knew, the family was gone forever."

I could tell it was working. "That's an amazing proposition," Putnam said in his basso profundo voice after a significant pause to think through what I had said. "You're right though. It would be a unique set of facts, if you've got it right. I've never heard of that pattern." There was another long pause. "I'll take the case, but only if I am allowed to perform a serious psychiatric examination of both children. I won't do it without that. And before that I'll need to read the entire written record of everything that's known about the kids, about their birth family, and about the circumstances in the adoptive family. And for the examination I'll need no fewer than three two-hour sessions with each of the children. If you can get me all that, I'll write a report and testify for you. But, will the insurer pay for me to do all that? It's going to take me a ton of time."

I assured Putnam that I already had insurance company preapproval and also a plan to arrange for his bills to be shared by the ten different insurance companies in the case for the multiple defendants.

There was no problem with the latter idea. Within a week, I had the agreement of each of the other defendants' attorneys to share the cost of the expert witness, since his testimony was in the interest of our entire side of the case. Within another week, I had a full copy of the records messengered over to Putnam's office.

The only problem arose elsewhere. Attorney O'Toole adamantly refused the examination request, taking the position that Dr. Putnam could learn what he needed to know from reading Ashley's existing psychiatric chart and speaking with her current treating clinicians. Adding another psychiatrist to the mix, he argued, could upset Ashley, who was fragile.

So ten days later, off to court went all dozen attorneys to put the matter before the trial judge. Every once in a while in court you can feel the judge hurrying along your argument because he or she already has the gist of what you're saying, and wants to take the matter up him- or herself with the other side. The trick as an attorney in these situations is to quickly conclude and get out of the line of fire. And sure enough, as it turned out, the judge had her own very strong reaction to Attorney O'Toole's argument.

"Then don't bring the lawsuit if you think it might harm the child," she told him. "Your clients are the ones who made the decision to put the girl through this. So here are your two options, Counselor: drop the suit, or submit her to the examination. Make a decision. Now."

It was either check or checkmate, and O'Toole chose the former. He replied forcefully that he was not withdrawing the lawsuit and agreed to work out an examination schedule with me. He also shot me an icy stare that spoke volumes about the likely degree of cooperation I would get in the case from that point on.

Roughly two months later, which was still well before when the first of Putnam's psychiatric examinations was scheduled, I received a twenty-four-page report from him summing up his reaction to the massive written record of the children's background. I was thrilled with the quality of work the report evidenced and immediately called Putnam's secretary to make an appointment.

Two weeks later, on a sunny and unusually warm day in late spring almost a year after I had first received the *Doe* case, I met with Putnam. In his private practice, he worked out of the basement of the century-old Boston brownstone in which he and his family lived. The office was a warm, friendly room with a working fireplace, and gently worn burgundy-colored leather chairs. Two of the walls were covered with floor-to-ceiling bookcases, and in one of them I could see the three main books Putnam had authored on trauma issues; each of these books was shelved next to its translations in five or six different foreign languages. I was still salivating at the thought of how easy it was going to be to sell Putnam's expertise to the jury when he entered, unseen, from a side room. Without pleasantries, he jumped right into the heart of the matter.

"Two things, Terry. First, how in the hell is the plaintiffs' attorney planning to argue damages from the adoption disruption, given what these children went through in their birth home? I don't even understand how he can do that. And second, and here's the good news for you, I don't think your clients were negligent or unprofessional. There is no way in hell they could have predicted this sexual acting out, I can assure you. But tell me how you think plaintiffs' counsel intends to argue his damages case. I just don't get what the logic of it can be, do you?"

"Actually, I do know what he has in mind," I responded. "He's going to tell the jury that the breakup of the adoptive home caused *new damages* to these vulnerable children. He said he's going to argue that there was additional harm through aggravation of the original harm. Tough argument to make, but not impossible."

"I still don't see how he's going to pull that off," Putnam shot back. "Especially because I buy your theory that to the extent the kids were harmed by the adoption disruption, the origin of any 'additional harm' more likely came from the heartless handling of the discovery of the sexuality. And by the way, I was horrified to read that Seth was adjudicated a sexual offender. That is a gross miscarriage of justice—at least from what I know at this point. And the other side of the coin, obviously, is that Ashley was certainly *not* a rape victim. Hell, she was as clear as she could be with the police that she co-initiated and willfully participated on an equal basis. And from what I read, I think there's every reason to believe her. So here's your takeaway: subject to what I learn in my examinations of the children, at this point I can give you some very strong testimony to back up your argument." Putnam paused after delivering this good news, thinking about something. "You know what I really want to learn about in the examinations?" he asked. "I want to dig into what feelings, what *emotions* the sexual behavior generated for each of the kids. I want to know what it *meant* to the two of them. I really think this may give us the key to understand what was really going on."

"And what about Seth?"

"Yeah, I've been thinking about him. I definitely want to learn what he experienced in the sexual offender program. I'd love to know whether or not the program personnel felt that he was an offender. I mean, above and beyond the fact that they were being paid to treat him as one."

"Actually, I know," I kicked in. "I was general counsel to that program for a decade, and I'm good pals with its clinical director. I ran into her at a seminar a few months ago and spoke with her about the kid—way off the record. And it's just what you would expect. She told me straight up that she doesn't think Seth is a good fit for their program. That's how she put it. She just doesn't see him as an offender acting out a compulsion disorder. But Rick, the kid is stuck in a crazy catch-twenty-two. The program is pure behavior modification. There are no exceptions, apparently, so Seth would need to admit a sexual aggression problem before the program's protocol would allow him to advance at all. He'll be on level one *forever* unless he lies about it. Sad stuff, no?"

Putnam shook his head. "Poor kid. He'll be branded for life, whatever the clinical director says off the record."

We spent an additional hour and a half going over documents in the record to prepare Putnam for his upcoming examinations of the children. It was obvious how focused and excited Putnam was about the exams. It was also pretty clear to me that what he learned from this one-off case would almost certainly be reported at some upcoming psychiatric meeting.

Needless to say, it was fabulous to learn that Putnam came out the same way I did about the impact of the adoptive parents' reaction to their discovery of the intersibling sexuality. This meant I could reassure Wilkins of the theory of the case I was promoting, and it was time to do so. She was easy to reach, as always; somehow I had the distinct impression the woman basically lived at her desk. "Rhonda, Terry Freiberg about the *Doe* case," I began.

"I know which fucking case you're on, Terry. I call it my 'nightmare case.' We've reserved two million for it. Two fucking million dollars. That's the policy limit. And this is completely dumping my department's numbers in the toilet. I'm holding you personally responsible for the looks my supervisor gives me in the hallway, and he was an unpleasant son of a bitch even before this damn case came along."

"Rhonda," I wedged in, "I've got good news. Putnam is on board with the theory that the biggest stressor the kids ever faced beyond what went on in their birth home was how the adoptive parents handled the intersibling sexuality. He'll give us just the testimony I need to pull this off."

She was silent for a moment, disappointed at being drawn into conversation and away from excoriating me.

"It still frightens me," she replied, in a quiet voice she must have borrowed from someone down the hall. "So do us both a favor: keep your mind open to finding an alternative approach. See if you can't create an option that isn't so high risk."

"Fair enough. Open minds are good things."

"Okay. Go for it." Dial tone. Goddamn it. Why couldn't the woman say good-bye or ciao or something? Everyone else does.

*

By this time in the case, each of the defendant agencies and individual mental health professionals had produced every document in their respective files on the children. While some of the documents appeared in more than one professional's file, and hence were redundant, the total number of stamped documents was just over ten thousand pages. That's a lot of trees. At this point, it was time to schedule depositions. On the defense side, we identified just over seventy people we wanted to depose, and of course, the plaintiffs would have their own list of deponents.

Soon after this, the seemingly endless series of Tuesday depositions began. It ended up taking more than eighteen months' worth of Tuesdays. I thought about shifting the responsibility for some of the depositions to an associate attorney who had been helping me with the written record, but Wilkins would not hear of it. As she phrased it, "I want you to know every one of these fucking witnesses personally. You take your own personal ass into that conference room, and don't give me some fucking associate who'll leave your firm before this case goes to trial. Understand?"

I remember answering her command with a sarcastic "Yes, sir," but it was to no avail—she never heard the "sir" part.

While the depositions were tedious and often duplicative from a legal point of view, they were absolutely fascinating from a social psychological research perspective. Let's face it, social scientists have trouble gathering good data; they are usually dependent on the acuity of perception and the accuracy of reporting of those they interview. And they can't interview everyone they want to; people don't have to submit to that. But lawyers have the force of the law to subpoena anyone they want to examine—and to question witnesses under oath after warning them that they are testifying subject to "the pains and penalties of perjury." What a sweet little research tool!

The depositions were designed to uncover everything that any adult who had known the children had ever observed or learned about them. We deposed each of the four sets of foster parents, every teacher or school counselor who had encountered one or both of the children, and every medical doctor, social worker, psychologist, and psychiatrist who had treated either child along the way. During this process, we learned the most minute of details about every aspect of the children's lives, beginning the first moment after their removal from the birth home. And, of course, we immersed ourselves in an equally detailed examination of what occurred to the children after the adoption disruption. We also spoke to four witnesses who described Seth's progressive deterioration after his delinquency adjudication and subsequent placement in the commonwealth's Department of Youth Services. We deposed every mental health and teaching professional who had worked clinically or educationally with either child. The witnesses varied between those who had no memories of the children, and who could therefore only interpret their written notes for us, and those whose memories of the children were vivid and fresh.

I will never forget the tearful sobbing of one young clinical social worker who testified that she had seen Ashley up to about six months before the date of her deposition. With tears running down her cheeks, she described to us what it was like to listen to Ashley struggle to define herself as a rape victim. This clinician was remarkably open with us. In her opinion, Ashley was using the term *rape victim* because she had been coached that it would benefit the cause of her lawsuit. I looked over at Attorney O'Toole when this little gem came out. Lo and behold, he was looking down at his notepad, furiously pretending to scribble away. The social worker concluded with another small bomb: when she had asked the adoptive parents to come in to discuss this ingenuous self-labeling, she had been summarily dismissed.

Among the more interesting depositions were those of the four sets of very experienced foster parents who had known the children, particularly the two couples who had observed the children the night they were taken from their birth family. All eight of these witnesses reported the same reaction to the two kids: they were horrifically sad at being ripped out of their home, and they showed no signs of relief at finding a safe environment, as abused children typically do. The foster parents also reported that they found the children remarkably intact and well behaved. And all eight of these highly experienced observers reported consistently with one another on another matter of central importance to my theory of the case. The four who had known Ashley reported that they had never seen her show the first sign of exhibiting what clinicians call sexually reactive behavior (that is, overly sexualized and/or abnormally sexually available). Likewise, the four who knew Seth confirmed that he had never acted in a sexually aggressive manner toward another foster child. The evidentiary quality of these observations was magnified nicely by the fact that I had two completely independent sets of highly experienced witnesses who corroborated one another on each child. And, of course, Putnam could testify that being sexually reactive or sexually aggressive cannot be turned on and off at will. We both felt strongly that these observations by the foster parents corroborated our suspicion that the intersibling sexuality that took place in the adoptive home was something other than garden-variety sexual contact. The key to the case, we were more certain than ever, lay in discerning just what the children's sexuality was all about *to them*. Could intercourse be about something other than sex?

There was, of course, one terribly important era from the children's past that was impossible to learn much about. What precisely had they experienced in their birth home? Of course, we read and reread the reports the children had given to the Sexual Assault Intervention Network and to the police right after their removal from the home. But these are about what happened, not what the home was like. And these were just the children's views of what went on. Additionally, search as I might, I never located a photo of the inside of the residence. There were no social services used by the family (remember, the kids were thriving at school), so no DSS files. And, of course, the adults in the family were all gone with the wind to parts unknown. I have to admit that part of my beef with the trial judge who let them off was that if he'd put the grandfather and grandmother in prison, where they belonged, in my opinion, I would have known where to find them to take their depositions. But now, no such luck. So as for learning what went on in the family home, Putnam in his examinations and I in my depositions would have to get the story from the children, and they would be our only source of information. We wanted to learn how they were nurtured, fed, medically cared for, bathed, clothed, supervised as they did homework, ferried to hobbies and sports, and so on. The problem, of course, was that children seldom notice the details of all of this parental work. All children are basically oblivious to the scores of things adults do to raise them and make a household work.

With the depositions and examinations of the children soon to come, Putnam and I decided to meet to think through the approach each of us would use in our respective spheres. As soon as his schedule allowed, we met one evening after work at his office and walked to a small French bistro he favored in Boston's South End. Entering into the stillness of the restaurant with its checkered tablecloths was a delight in and of itself—there were cool spring winds gusting about outside, and the walk over had been brisker than my suit jacket could handle.

Putnam ordered up a bottle of Argentinian Malbec and a cheese platter, and asked the waiter's indulgence while we spoke together before
ordering.

Putnam had come to work. Even before the wine arrived, he
announced that we were going to reason out *tonight* a theory about
what we thought the intersibling sexuality meant to the two children. This theory would need to account for the fact that the sexuality
occurred *despite* the fact that there was ample evidence that Seth was
not sexually aggressive and Ashley was not sexually reactive. In addition, our hypothesis would need to account for a new fact that had
just come to light: both children had been prepubescent at the time of
their sexual encounters in the adoptive home. We knew this new fact
with confidence because my private eye had finally located a clinical
professional who had moved out of state and been nearly impossible
to locate. This clinical social worker was in the habit of videotaping his
sessions with children, and he had filmed Seth during the era when he
lived in the adoptive home. When you looked at the tape, it was crystal clear that you were looking at a boy who had not yet been through
puberty. So what was taking place? Why would prepubescent, nonsex-
ually aggressive children be having sex?

Putnam leaned back in his chair and swirled the dark-red Malbec
around and around in his glass, staring intently at it. After a goodly
pause, he asked me to think about what touching—hugging and being
hugged—means to small children. Then, before I could answer, he
turned toward me and seemingly on a whim asked me how many hugs
and kisses I'd lavished on my son in his first five years. I remember my
response word for word: "Got to be a million. Definitely a million."

"Exactly," he responded with emphasis. "Exactly. Now imagine if
you and your wife just stopped one day, if suddenly there were no more
kisses, no more hugs. Think how absent all that touch and warmth
would be to your child, how he would *hunger* for it. Now think of what
the Doe children experienced. In their birth home, they had the million kisses—but it didn't end there: the touching knew no limits. Put
aside for the moment that from an outside perspective they were being
sexually abused. Just for a moment, think of what they experienced as
hyperintensified touching. Now think of this: these children went from

this hypertouching to absolutely zero touching. From the moment they were removed from their home, there was no more touching *at all* in their lives. The foster homes they went to were completely touch-free environments—because touching was strictly forbidden by DSS regulations. Can you imagine how the Doe kids must have been *starved* for physical soothing by the time they were placed together eighteen months later in the adoptive home? And while I need to confirm this with the kids in their examinations, let's assume the adoptive parents rarely touched these kids who they barely knew." Putnam paused to finally taste his well-swirled Malbec. "Who knows?" he mused. "Perhaps to these children the intersibling sexuality was just their substitute for the normal touching most children their age get on a daily basis from their parents. I wouldn't be surprised if the Doe kids didn't even conceive of what they were doing as sex. They may have just experienced it as mutual soothing and nothing more."

Putnam leaned forward in his chair to cut a slice of cheese. What he said made perfect sense. Whatever these children were experiencing, it was likely to be very different from how it looked to adults outside their circle who would immediately classify it as incestuous sex. We clearly had our work cut out for us in the upcoming depositions and examinations.

After we had eaten, Putnam and I agreed that a glass of port sounded like a good idea—especially when compared to heading out into the windy chill. Our conversation turned to what we needed to learn about the adoptive parents in their upcoming depositions. I described how I had designed questions intended to probe their upbringing, their education, their early careers in the Catholic Church, their decision to leave the Church, their secular careers, the origin of their decision to adopt a sibling group of older children, the adoption training they had (or didn't have), and of course, any and all details about what they had been told about how the children might behave. I also intended to fully probe what they had heard from their own consulting psychologist about the difficulties and risks involved in adopting older children from a sexually abusive background, and why and by what logic they had determined to override his warnings.

Putnam went on to list a number of areas of inquiry that really mattered to him, including one issue in particular that he emphasized as critical. Leaning forward and looking me straight in the eyes, he pleaded with me. "I need to know—I absolutely need to know—what exactly the Does were thinking that night when they called the police. Something's up here, something we don't know yet. It doesn't add up. And you may have to push. It's deep down, but it's there. Just promise me you'll try. I want to learn as much as I can from your deposition transcripts before I design my examinations."

I did promise, and after we shook hands outside the restaurant and I was heading up the street to the T stop, I kept thinking about how I should approach this issue. The only strategy I came up with was to be doggedly persistent. I would keep approaching the issue from different angles, hoping that one of my questions would somehow unlock the door to Putnam's mysterious "something."

And so the day arrived when it was time to depose John and Jane Doe. If I had to describe them in three words, they would be prim and proper. The two parents were entirely formal in dress and manner: upper-middle-class individuals who seemed to take their social status very seriously. Each was lean, with nary an extra pound. They both responded to questions in a terse, almost military manner. There were no wasted words, essentially zero body language, no moments of warmth, and never a single smile from either of them. Usually, I later told Putnam, in tense circumstances like a deposition or even at trial, witnesses search for at least one opportunity to smile. This often happens at a break in the drama, when the judge is called off the bench by a telephone call from his wife or some such. I had always thought witnesses did it to take a momentary break from the tension, but as the years went by, I began to think it had more to do with a witness just wanting to exhibit that there were pleasant facets to his or her personality not being displayed on the stand. In any case, there was not one single smile from either of the Does, not in six days of deposition. This, and everything else about them, gave me the distinct impression that what really mattered most to them was being in control.

Given that my tactic was to approach the topic of sexuality as indirectly as possible, I started the deposition of each parent with very general questions, and only on the second day did I even get close to the topics Putnam and I were actually most interested in. There were a number of interesting findings, but there was one particular response of Mrs. Doe's that absolutely floored me. To the question, "Did Seth otherwise ever breach your trust in any way prior to the night of your discovery?" she answered with an emphatic "no." I looked up at her to take in her expression, but all I found was an ice-cold blank stare.

We took a break at this point, and the conference room quickly emptied as everyone headed to the restrooms or the firm's coffee room. Only the court reporter stayed behind to fuss with a troublesome change of paper for her steno machine. I'd known her for years from scores of other depositions—in this and many other cases—and we typically spoke frankly with one another.

"I don't know about you, Ruth, but if my home life as a child had turned on one single infraction, I would have been booted out of the family a hundred times."

"What do you mean?" she asked without looking up, deeply involved in her struggles with the complicated-looking machine.

"Well, hell, when I was a boy, I misbehaved right, left, and center. I'm probably the only adult you know who remembers the name of his grammar school principal: Sandra Jenkins. I'd misbehave in a classroom and get sent to her office. Mrs. Jenkins would counsel me on how to handle myself, and I'd straighten out and fly right on whatever that particular issue was. But there were so many issues, so many ways to get in trouble. Childhood's not easy. I remember the time my dad found me lighting matches behind the garage. I had accidentally lit up a little pile of leaves. I must have been about six. He put the fire out, sat down, and took me in his arms. Sure he talked to me about matches and fires and being careful, but mostly he reassured me that everybody makes mistakes, and that the only thing you need to do in life is learn from your mistakes. Hell, this kid Seth didn't get that—you heard what the adoptive mother said. He hadn't given them any trouble on anything whatsoever for eighteen months. God, he must have been so careful and aware of what they wanted. And then he makes one false step—admittedly a serious one—and *BANG!* in an hour he's in a police squad car and his life ends. Poor kid."

"Ah, sorry," Ruth said, finally looking up, clearly relieved at having straightened out the problems with her equipment. "What were you saying?"

As if on cue, the dozen other attorneys began wandering back into the room, and O'Toole and his client were soon seated and the deposition resumed. Now it was time to approach the touchier topics, beginning with whether or not the Does felt comfortable talking about sexual matters with other adults. I questioned whether their long service in the Catholic Church had made them in any way ill at ease with sexuality in general, and even asked them about the pattern of sexuality in their own marriage. On and on I went, accomplishing nothing, with the exception of embarrassing the hell out of everybody in the room.

Then, in utter desperation, I suppose, I took a wild gamble at almost the very end of the second day of Mrs. Doe's deposition. My question, which wasn't even written in my outline, was based on nothing more than a statistic Putnam had once mentioned to me years before in a different law case: fully a quarter of women in the United States experienced some form of sexual mistreatment as children. As I said, completely on a whim, I quoted this statistic and simply asked the deponent if she was among that group. Twenty seconds of silence followed, during which Mrs. Doe's face became progressively more flushed and increasingly stranger sounds welled up from her throat. And then she suddenly exploded into a storm of tears and bawling. She struggled to regain her voice, and of course, we all waited patiently while she took one deep breath after another in her effort to regain her composure. Finally, she looked up, ready to proceed. Glances shot back and forth between the defense attorneys, several of whom had been borderline asleep before this turn of events.

"Yes, I was, actually," she said in a strong voice that was half an octave lower than we had heard in her previous testimony. I was fumbling for a follow-up question, but I didn't need one. She was off and running. "My older cousin touched me when I was just about Ashley's age. He did this repeatedly when our families were visiting my grandmother's house, which we did on Sundays every other week. He and I were supposed to be helping out by vacuuming, but he used the vacuum noise to cover up . . . to cover up his . . . his . . . abuse." Her words once again deteriorated into loud sobs and moans that came from deep down within her. I asked her if she wanted to take a break, but in response she held her right hand up and vehemently shook her head no. It took her a good two minutes to gain enough control over her voice to ask for a few more moments respite. Then, still without another question from me, out came the nugget that the panning gold miner finds after sifting through half a mountain of streambed soil. "That's why I knew the night I walked in on them how violated Ashley must have felt, and why we had to get Seth out of her life right then, that night, immediately, once and for all. That's why I called the police, and that's why I insisted that we end Ashley's misery *immediately*. That boy needed to be dead for her—gone forever. She didn't need to be tortured by his presence the way I was by my cousin until he finally moved to California years later when we were adults."

Complete silence filled the room when Mrs. Doe finished. I looked over at Attorney O'Toole, who was looking right at me. He had a small, sly smile on his face, and he almost imperceptibly nodded at me. Clearly he considered this surprise testimony helpful to his case, and I could only surmise that to him it seemed further evidence of how vulnerable and fragile Mrs. Doe had been and how much damage had been done to her by the defendants' negligence. I thought it ironic that I too was thinking about how my case would benefit from what had just been revealed. From my perspective, the testimony showed that the adoptive mother had been far more fixated on herself and her personal history that fateful night than on what was best for Ashley and Seth.

Later that evening, Putnam's booming voice filled the phone line when I told him what Mrs. Doe had disclosed. "I knew it! I fucking knew it!" he called out. "That explains so much to me. Hang on, I want to make a few notes in the record." A good three minutes of silence followed, and then he came back on the line. "So how good is this disclosure for you on the legal end of the case?"

"It's a gem. Trust me. It's a gem." I found myself smiling as I said this, not that I took lightly Mrs. Doe's trauma and suffering; not at all. She had every right to do what she needed to do for herself as a survivor of her cousin's sexual predation. But in my view, that needed to be distinguished from whether or not it was appropriate for her to make a rash decision that fateful night with Seth and Ashley, and to do so without any professional consultation as to what was best for the children.

We were now a year and a half into the case, and on a dazzling, sunny day, the first deposition of the children began. Each child was scheduled to be deposed over three full days, which meant the process would stretch over six consecutive Tuesdays.

At the end of each of these six days, after the stenographer had packed up and left the room, the eleven defense attorneys typically stayed for at least another half hour to confer on what had been learned and what it all meant and implied. Several things were universally agreed on by each and every one of us, and hence seem well worth reporting. First, we were enormously impressed with how bright and articulate the children were. These were extremely well-spoken, thoughtful teenagers, who seemed well beyond their years in many ways. But we were also struck by the depth of character of each child. They were captivating, even charming. Besides having remained as strikingly good-looking as ever, there was a warmth and a quiet strength to both personalities. We were really, truly impressed—all of us—and it's got to be hard to fool an entire room full of clever people.

But we also all commented on the fact that the children were beginning to show the effects of the constant wear and tear on them from everything they'd been through, including the stress of the litigation. And, not surprisingly, there was an element of underlying sadness in each of them. How could there not have been with all the loss and separation they had endured? But even here there was balance. Something had instilled in each of these children an element of brightness that somehow had not been extinguished—not yet anyways.

On the second day of Ashley's deposition, I began to inquire about what losing Seth meant to her. She was open and honest in answering. She told us that she had been completely devastated by the loss of her brother, which she testified her adoptive parents had told her was "necessary" and "permanent." When asked at what point she had heard them say this, she was very clear. They had told her this immediately after the police had marched Seth out of their house that calamitous night. She said she missed Seth terribly, even now, and, as she phrased it, "I know that somehow we will find each other later in life." When she said this, she crossed her arms over her chest and gave herself a little squeeze. This was body language I very much intended to communicate to Putnam.

When the defense team discussed Seth after his deposition, we all agreed that we perceived him as a disheartened boy run down by life. But again, it was not so simple, because we also found that there was still a remarkable warmth to this handsome boy and elements of resilience and optimism to his character. His remaining hopefulness, however, ran smack into the sad daily life he endured in the sexual offender program to which he'd been condemned. Living in a secure facility, he was, in effect, a prisoner, whose every movement was monitored and restricted. And his adjudication had formally branded him as a sexual offender. This meant his name was entered into the Massachusetts Sex Offender Registry, the consequences of which are staggering. It's nearly impossible for registered offenders to find a job or rent an apartment because employers and landlords have open access to the registry.

Seth testified that he was trapped between the horns of a terrible dilemma, given his refusal to admit to his clinician that he was a sex offender. Apparently nothing had changed since I had first heard about his life in the offender program. He confirmed that the consequences of insisting on this had been made clear to him prior to his decision. No admission meant he would be treated as being in denial of his compulsion disorder, which in turn meant he couldn't even *begin* climbing the behavior modification ladder that would have eventually led to his being trusted to live in an unlocked facility. And so, month after month, he remained at the bottom of the hierarchy, enjoying no privileges at all. When I probed the matter with additional questions, Seth testified that he would never make the required admission, no matter what the cost to him.

"I didn't rape my sister," he asserted. "That's not at all what we were doing together. They don't understand. I would rather stay as a level-one offender than to accept their definition of what I did, of who I am."

Seth described life in the birth home as isolated and insular. He reported that neither he nor Ashley had neighborhood friends of any consequence and that this was in significant part because of how adults in the household presented the world. Seth testified that his father (who was also his step-grandfather) repeatedly reminded the children that there was their "family and its ways, and there was the outside world and its ways." Both children stated that they had been brought up to never, ever talk to anyone outside the family about life inside their household. The children's father was apparently quite adamant about the importance of "keeping everything that happened in our house private, because other families would never understand, and because other families have their private ways too."

The details of the ritualized sexuality that was imposed on the children, especially by their father/step-grandfather but also by their grandmother, uncle, aunt, and mother, were well known to all counsel from the police report and prosecutorial record. These details were so shocking, in fact, that they made it nearly impossible for most of the defense attorneys listening to the testimony to grasp why the children still spoke with such affection for their birth family. But the truth is, there was complete consistency between the two siblings on the issue. Both still cared deeply about their birth family, notwithstanding all that had taken place in their home and the devastating consequences that ensued. The heart and soul of the testimony given by the two siblings on this issue can be summarized as follows:

First, both children made it clear that they now fully understood the criminality and gross impropriety of the sexual assaults of the adults in their home. It was obviously very important to each of them to articulate this point. Seth brought it up three different times.

Second, each child was literally pleading with us to try to understand that they had depended on their parents, just like any other child does. You literally could have heard a pin drop in the conference room when each child set out to convince us that while there was what they now understood to be illegal and impermissible sexuality, there was also an abundance of love and nurturing in the household. Seth, who was both older and more articulate than his sister, tried as hard as he could to get us to recognize how the family's physical touching—sometimes sexualized, sometimes not—was to him and his sister "simply life as we knew it" (his term).

"It wasn't like they were trying to hurt us," he told the attorneys. "You need to understand that. I've heard stories in my offender program about parents who intentionally hurt their children. There's nothing in common. One boy has dozens of round scars on his back from cigarette burns because that's how he was punished. Our parents never, ever hurt us. They just didn't know or care that you had to keep grown-up ways of sex away from your children. They got that part all wrong, completely wrong. But that's different from not loving us, and it's very different, totally different, from hurting us on purpose." Each time Seth finished these little lectures, which he would append to answers to my questions, he would look around the table of attorneys for approval, or at least acknowledgment of what he had said. But every time this happened, with the exception of yours truly, he only encountered blank stares or the tops of heads of attorneys madly writing in their note pads.

I asked Seth a series of questions aimed at trying to learn what regular games the children played inside their new home and what they did outside on the large grounds. He listed a dozen board and other games and described a number of imaginative outside games the siblings played together. But when I asked whether their sexual couplings were possibly a form of play for them, Seth adamantly rejected this characterization. So did Ashley in her deposition. I had to admire the strength of character it took for each of the children to refuse to buy into even a friendly effort to impose an external definition on their sexualized behavior. So if it wasn't sex, and it wasn't sex-play, what was it? It was time to learn the details.

I asked each of the children when and how they were together sexually, and both reported that it would only happen late at night when one would awaken and go quietly into the other's room. Then, while trying to be as delicate as possible, I elicited what the children actually did together. The response from both was given without hesitation or embarrassment. The sexuality amounted to hugging, kissing, stroking, and, indeed, vaginal penetration. As gingerly as one can, I asked Seth if he ejaculated at any time, and consistent with the fact that he had not yet been through puberty when he lived with the adoptive parents (and also consistent with Putnam's theories on the matter), he answered, "No, I was too young, and that just wasn't in my mind. That wasn't the point."

Ashley said the same thing in her deposition. When I inquired who went more often into the room of the other, they each reported that it didn't matter, that it could be either one of them. They both said this took place about two or three times a week.

Seth gave fascinating testimony in response to questions seeking to elicit *why* they had sex together if it wasn't sex and it wasn't sex-play—especially because after the destruction of the birth family home, they knew perfectly well that there were serious consequences to incest.

Seth gazed off into the distance while thinking about his answer, and then, after a good thirty seconds, he told us, "When I was holding Ashley, it was . . . how I got back to my family. It was as if I could actually feel and hear and smell the family all around me again, like when we had dinner with everyone sitting around the table eating and laughing. In the adoption house, everything was formal and dry. There wasn't any laughter, there wasn't any nonsense, and there weren't any smells—just the smell of soap and those spray cans. But at my parents' house, it was completely different. It was loud, and crazy, and funny, and it smelled good. Once my dad spilled spaghetti sauce on his clean shirt, and after he looked down at the mess, he looked up and said how stupid he felt. We always put on clean shirts for dinner, but you know what we did? Every one of us started smearing spaghetti sauce on our shirts too, and then all over our cheeks, and we all laughed so hard and so long that we all had tears running down our cheeks making tracks in the spaghetti sauce."

Telling this made Seth laugh out loud, and he looked around the table at the twelve attorneys to see if anyone would share the moment with him. He found only one big smile; with all my heart and soul I wanted to call out, "Hell, why don't I get invited to parties like that?" but with the stenographer taking down every word, I refrained. Now, of course, I wish I hadn't.

Anyway, Seth sighed and then turned his head away, looking off into space again, inner space probably, and continued his answer without another prompt from me. "Can you lawyers *possibly* understand what I'm saying?" With these words, another sad sigh came out, all on its own. "When I held Ashley in the adoption home, I could actually feel again how much my stomach hurt from laughing so hard on the spaghetti sauce night. I could see everyone around the table, real clearly. With my everyday memory, I was starting to lose the faces. I don't have any photographs, you know. I could smell my home again when I held Ashley, but I can't smell it usually. Anyway, that's what it was like at my real home. You were constantly bombarded with feelings and sights and sounds and smells. I know it must sound crazy to you, but when I held Ashley it was like a way back to all that. It wasn't just memories that came back to me when we were alone together; it was the feelings and the sounds and the smells *themselves*. And it was the same for Ashley, because when we were in bed together, we talked about how weird it was to have it all come back so clearly. Sometimes, we'd lie there holding each other, and we would share some memory that would crack us up, and we'd have to put the pillow over our faces so we wouldn't make noise."

I had no further questions for Seth, and this answer concluded his deposition. There is no way I can describe how profoundly silent the room was after Seth finished speaking. The sound of that silence has stayed with me ever since.

In Ashley's final day of deposition, when I asked her what the sexuality with Seth meant to her, she looked down at the table for a long time, and then began to answer in such a quiet voice that the court stenographer had to ask her to speak up. We were completely mesmerized. At one point, she used a metaphor I will never forget: "It was like drinking water when you're really, really thirsty." Ashley told us that as far back as she could remember, she had always been held and kissed and touched and loved by everyone in her family. She testified that, "Even though I learned that the sexual parts of the loving were very, very wrong and illegal for families to do together and for kids to be involved in, in some ways I missed it, and in some ways I was thirsty for it. Seth and I had this beautiful secret—a secret that came from our real family. And it was so powerful we couldn't resist it. And we couldn't resist it even though we knew our adoption parents would never, ever understand if they caught us. But when I woke up at night and was scared by things or sad at my mom being so gone, it was Seth I wanted to be with, not my adoption mom. I mean she tried hard back then to be a great mom, but she couldn't possibly understand. It was like Seth and I had a secret place to go to that only we knew about. And it was only when we were together in bed and touching each other that we ever talked about home. And it was more than just talk. It was like we were back there in our house." This final sentence of Ashley's deposition was spoken slowly, with her eyes closed, her head gently turning from side to side.

As I drove home that evening after the sixth and final day of those depositions, I ran into the single most colossal traffic jam I had ever been in. At one point, it actually took me an hour to go half a block. While I was as frustrated as everyone around me, the enforced time alone ended up being a blessing in disguise. It gave me the perfect opportunity to process what an amazing experience I had been through in deposing these two children. Each had testified so willingly and openly about everything he or she had been through, and each had done so without any evident shame or remorse. It was as if they realized that this would be one of the few times they would *ever* be able to speak so candidly about the details of their lives in their two homes.

Sitting there in that interminable traffic allowed my mind to wander, to try to summarize for myself what I thought about the children now that I had come to know them in person. Most importantly, I realized that I truly believed Seth and Ashley when they testified that their parents raised and nurtured them in a loving way. That's the only possible explanation Putnam and I could come up with as to why they survived so intact. But now, more was clear to me. I think for the first time I realized that love is not enough, not in this family, maybe not ever. These parents violated one of mankind's most universal norms— the incest taboo—and the consequences for these children were devastating. When you raise a child, it's not okay to live solely within the bubble of love between parents and child, to live as if your home were the world. If it were, then I suppose you could do it any way that works for you and the children. But it's not just about you and your child and your home. A parent's task is to raise a child so that they fit into the outside world, not just into the idiosyncrasies of their nuclear family. It follows that one of the principal duties of a parent is to teach their child the norms and proscriptions of the culture and society in which he or she will live. Loving parenting, I realized that day in traffic, cannot be selfish parenting, and that was one thing the Doe children surely suffered: massive parental selfishness.

About two weeks later, I received the final transcripts of the children's depositions from the court reporter. I immediately messengered copies of all six of them to Dr. Putnam, but, somewhat surprisingly, I didn't hear back from him. Just about a month later he began his psychiatric examinations of the children, which took place over a three-week period. Again, he didn't call. Then one day, roughly three months after I had sent the transcripts over, I received by messenger Putnam's final written report.

I needed to be alone with the report, so I left the office, as a busy law practice is essentially a series of incessant interruptions. And besides, it was only a short walk from my office to several benches set at the water's edge on Boston Harbor—exactly where the Tea Party events had occurred two hundred years earlier. It was a remarkably warm late spring day, just about two years out after the *Doe* case had arrived in the office. The sky was crystal clear, and the harbor water was as blue as a child would paint it. I plopped down on one of the benches and dove into the document; even the call of seagulls and the horns of passing ships failed to interrupt my concentration on Putnam's subtle and fascinating analysis.

It was the good doctor's opinion that there had been two principal moments of traumatic impact on the children. First, he reviewed what we knew about the birth home, along with the accidental disclosure and emergency removal of the children. During this first period, Putnam explained, based on the evidence in the written record and his corroboration of that evidence during his examination of the children, it was his considered opinion, "to a reasonable degree of medical certainty," that great and irreparable psychiatric harm was done to the children. But here was the unexpected twist: the psychiatric harm done during this period was, in his opinion, more a function of the sudden and final termination of the affective, emotional relationship between the children and their birth family than of the incest itself.

In parallel fashion, with respect to the period of time at the Does' house, Putnam's opinion was that the sudden disappearance of all that had been built between the children and the adoptive parents was a far more powerful stressor on the children than the prepubescent, mutual soothing these two siblings engaged in with their intersibling trysts. From the point of view of the children, Putnam wrote, the transition from their humble origins to the luxurious setting of the Doe household was like a Cinderella story. Imagine, Putnam implored, the psychological cost for a child to make this sociological transition and then to lose it all in an hour. And, the analysis continued, if Seth's loss of the new life he had come to know at the Does' palace was great, Ashley's loss of Seth's love and company was even greater.

In discussing the intersibling sexuality, Putnam developed a fascinating metaphor. Think of the children, he suggested, as if they were bilingual adopted siblings who, when they were alone together, spoke to each other in the language of their birth home. Actually, this would be expected, and it's hard to imagine that an adoptive parent would fail to respect this or tell the siblings to stop speaking in the second language. And, he pointed out, modern-day adoption protocol for parents in international adoptions strongly encourages adoptive parents to learn what they can of their adopted children's native tongue and to take the child to visit their country of origin, if feasible. With all this in mind, Putnam urged, think of the body language between Ashley and Seth as analogous. The sexualized touching they engaged in was a reproduction of the body language they had used in their birth home. His opinion went still further. He advocated that we see the late-night, prepubescent couplings in the adoptive home as more ritual than sexual. These children, he wrote, were desperately lonely and entirely adrift. They were cut off from their roots with devastating finality, and for purposes of dealing with this loss on an emotional level, they had only each other, and in these late night moments they spoke to each other in their native language—sexualized touching.

Putnam also wove into his analysis a series of additional potent stressors that he thought had done harm to the children. These included Ashley's anger with her adoptive parents for their abandonment of Seth, Ashley's guilt at seeing Seth criminalized for their mutually-initiated sexuality, and interestingly, Ashley's quiet rage over being forced to relive all of this in the process of the lawsuit itself. The last of these was something he had picked up in his psychiatric examinations that I had missed altogether in my deposition inquiries.

The conclusion, accordingly, was that by far the greatest stressors on the children were the two sudden and brutal losses of family connections. These psychological insults, Putnam summarized, were of an altogether different magnitude than were the sexual deviancy of the birth home and the intersibling sexuality of the adoptive home.

When I finished reading Putnam's report, I put it down on the bench beside me and just let the fresh air, the seaside sounds, and the beauty of the afternoon wash over me like a shower. I remember now that my mind wandered that day, for some inexplicable reason, to an image of my son's recent little league baseball game, during which he had slid headfirst into a very dusty home plate. He had been on first base when the next player hit a pretty hot grounder. These were just little guys, and at their age, this particular grounder, like most others, eluded both the shortstop and the left fielder. By the time the kid in left field had retrieved the ball and tossed it to the shortstop, my boy, having completely ignored his coach's signal to stop at third base, was heading full speed ahead for home plate. Six-year-old shortstops don't throw very hard, so the ball sailing home and my son could be seen racing each other at roughly the same speed. And they arrived at home plate at precisely the same moment. The commotion of the headfirst slide and the catcher's tag threw up such a huge cloud of dust that both kids were invisible for a few seconds. The parent serving as umpire stood over the tangled-up players waiting for the dust to settle, and I stood in the stands alongside my aged father who was visiting from out of state, hoping against all hope for the call to go my son's way. And it did! "SAFE!" yelled out the umpire for all to hear. My son, still lying with his chest on home plate, looked up at the stands for his visiting grandfather and proud father, and when he found us, his dust-covered face broke into the toothiest smile I've ever seen. All this family stuff, as unimportant as it is in the great arc of human history, is not at all unimportant to the family members who live it. And that's what was lost to Seth and Ashley, lost forever. By the way, the coach ended up giving the game ball to my son, who signed it in his childish scrawl and gave it to my father. It was on my father's coffee table for the rest of his life. I found it there years later when I went to clean out his modest little house after he died, and it made me cry. I cried for the beauty of intact intergenerational bonds that that baseball represented, and I cried for the tragic loss of family connections I had come to know in the *Doe* case.

*

About three weeks later, Putnam and I met at his office with the goal of beginning the process of selecting a line of argument to present to the jury. The massive amount of data we possessed on the children was a treasure trove from a research point of view but daunting from a trial strategy perspective.

Putnam launched right in. "I am prepared to testify that, from a mental health angle, both of these children currently exhibit intact mental health. That's the shocking fact here. They're really quite impressive. Somehow they've survived everything they've been through. I'm amazed, really. One thing's for sure: there doesn't appear to have been any fear generated by the children's father or by the boundaryless sexuality in the birth home, and I probed hard for that. On the contrary, there's *still* a deep attachment to the birth family, and a heartfelt concern about the fate of their mother."

We were both quiet as we considered this anomalous case. "Rick," I finally asked, "how in the hell are we going to explain our case to a jury?"

"Oh, I've got a theory all right," Putnam came back with. "I've been piecing it together, as best I can. The police and prosecutorial reports are clear: the birth mother was young, and also young for her age, pretty much a child herself. The children told me she was as dependent on the grandparents as they were. And from what I could tell, they don't blame her in any way for what took place in the household, nor for what this led to. So what we have here, I think, is a case of 'parentified' children: kids who perceive the vulnerability of their parent, and do whatever they can to care for their parent's welfare. So part of the explanation as to why these children are so intact may be that they saw themselves as *needing* to keep themselves intact so they would be strong enough to keep their mother safe. This parentified-child phenomenon is not all that rare; we see it all the time in war zones."

"Okay. But how does this play into what you said a few minutes ago about the absence of fear? Why wouldn't children forced into caring for their incompetent parent experience fear at having to play such an exaggerated role in navigating the adult world?"

"Good question," Putnam replied, pointing at me sharply with his index finger. "I think the answer to that lies in what their father-slash-step-grandfather was like as a person. I examined the kids about him as closely as I could and from every angle I could think of. But *not once* did they ever express any fear of him—none whatsoever. I can't exaggerate how atypical this is for intergenerational family sexual abuse. Somehow, despite the persistent sexuality that he visited on these children, and despite his instructions to keep the family secrets from the outside world, something about the framework of the overall experience kept it from traumatizing the children. Fear played no role; that, I can guarantee you. Did you pick up any signs of trauma reaction in the kids in your depositions?"

"No, and neither did the other defense counsel. The eleven of us discussed it over and over again. To a person, we agreed: these children were intact, intelligent, articulate, even charming. And when they talked about the sexuality in the household, there was nothing in their language or body language that reminded me of the scores of survivors of childhood sexual abuse their age who I've worked with in other cases. To me, frankly, other than the content of their story, I would have never picked these children out to be survivors."

"So that's a dozen of us with the same reaction. And I was looking for all sorts of collateral clues: whether or not their memories were expressed in somatic or intellectual terms, whether or not their body language conformed to what they were saying, whether or not there were inconsistencies in their two stories, and whether or not what they told me was consistent with what the record shows they told clinicians and police authorities early in the case. And, don't forget, there's important corroboration for this in the fact that *not one* of their teachers or doctors or any other adult picked up any clue of a problem in the birth home until the accidental disclosure with the anatomically correct dolls."

"Yes, and I've got something else for you," I broke in, somewhat excitedly. "We've now deposed every single teacher, school counselor, and doctor we could still locate and I asked each and every one of these professionals to look back with twenty-twenty hindsight and tell me if they could now think of *any* hint of the sexuality they had missed at the time. And every single one of them answered no. Every single one, Rick. Not *one* of them even dreamed of the incestuous sexuality in the birth family home. How in the hell do you explain that?"

"That, my friend," Putnam said in his stentorian voice, "is because there was, as I said earlier, *no fear involved*. This is in total contrast to the kids I normally see in my trauma center—many of them live in fear twenty-four-seven. One thing I feel sure about—and this I can sure as hell tell your jury—the critical difference with the Doe kids is that the participation of these children with the ritual sexuality and their total compliance in maintaining the wall of secrecy was certainly not fear based. I'm convinced of that. That's why they gave off no signs or signals; I'm sure of it."

"So if their complicity wasn't fear based, what was it? Why such perfect compliance?" I wondered aloud.

"I don't know, to be honest with you. But I expect it's because they loved their crazy family, and because they felt safe and connected. Those are the key words, Terry. Safe and connected. And let me add this. My research is showing that just as traumatic memories are stored somatically and not intellectually, love memories are as well. That's why when you hear a love song from your teenage years, you can immediately picture the girl you were dating at the time. So if my theory is right, just as fear-based abuse or trauma is linked in memory to body sensations— the war vet who hears a car backfire and re-experiences the trauma he endured in combat—so love-based memories are similarly linked to body sensations. I think that's why these kids brought up *sensations* when you probed them about their memories of home: the *tastes* of Grandma's cooking, the *sounds* of dining room laughter, the *sights* of the spaghetti stains. Fear-memory and love-memory are stored in the brain stem, and linked to perceptions, as opposed to rote memory— the list of US presidents or whatever—that are stored elsewhere in the brain. There are two very different kinds of memory involved. These kids experienced the family sexuality as an integral part of the pattern of how their crazy, deviant family loved and connected with each other. My guess is that these children did not experience the need for secrecy as a threat about their abandonment but as a confirmation of their inclusion. Their family was a secret society, and they saw themselves as full members. My guess is that these children probably grew up thinking very little about their family's sexuality. From the perspective of the children, since they felt safe, nurtured, and loved at home, and since they were never physically or emotionally mistreated, the entire topic may have had much less importance for them than we as adults are likely to conceive."

"Okay, assume you're right," I followed on. "What would have been the implications for the children's mental health if there had never been a disclosure? Where would all this have come out in the end?"

"Oh, another good question," Putnam said, once again pointing at me. "As they reached puberty, I imagine things might have changed pretty dramatically. But let's put this in perspective. Of the more than twenty percent of girls and fifteen percent of boys sexually abused as children in this country, the vast majority grow up to lead psychologically healthy, normal lives. Of course, it's true that a certain percentage of survivors lead lives that are enormously tormented by what happened to them as children. We know so little about why some children can tolerate such abuse while others are deeply traumatized. But I'm afraid the only honest answer to your question about where the Doe kids would fall on this spectrum is to tell you that the science of psychiatry would have to be a hell of a lot more advanced than it is today for me to do better than just take a guess. That's all it would be—an educated guess."

"All right. Let's move on then. What are you going to be able to tell the jury about the psychiatric implications for the children of how the adoptive family handled the discovery of the intersibling sexuality?" I asked.

"That's easier. My testimony will be that the psychiatric impact of the intersibling sexuality *itself* was minimal when compared to the parade of horrors that came to pass in the children's lives after the adoption disruption. In my opinion, the children meant no harm to each other and did no harm to each other. And I can tell your jury that, while the children are psychologically solid young people, the loss to the siblings of each other, on top of the loss of the rest of their family, will probably in the end be the single biggest stressor on their future mental health."

"It's that big?"

"It's that big."

"Wow. Okay. I hear you. Let me ask you another question, a hypothetical one. Say you were the family shrink to the adoptive parents the night of their discovery of the intersibling sexuality. Say you got a call in the middle of the night from your clients. They had just found these two kids in bed with each other, having sex. How would you have counseled them?"

"Oh man, I would have loved to have taken that call." Putnam leaned forward, rubbing his massive hands together. "To begin with, I would have insisted that the matter could not and should not be thought through in the middle of the night. Everybody needed to go to sleep in safe, separate rooms until the next day when we could all put our heads together and look at the options. That would have changed everything, in my view. If the adoptive couple had taken the time to look at the possibilities, it seems unlikely that they would have done what they did," Putnam asserted.

"How so? What would you have said to them the next morning?" I asked. "And remember, the adoptive mom had her own issues to deal with."

"I would have told them that I actually saw a wonderful opportunity for them. They could have used this discovery to become the emotional parents of the children. All they would have had to do was to handle the disclosure of the intersibling sexuality with love and tenderness. They had the perfect opportunity to help the kids get to normal—for which the kids would have been eternally grateful. Metaphorically speaking, those kids could have been sort of reborn into normal childhoods at that point, since everything would have come out into the open. And I'll tell you something else. I would have advised Mrs. Doe to get counseling to deal with her own abuse as a child. She clearly needs to work on her untreated trauma. But mostly, I would have stressed that what the children needed was education about when and with whom sex is appropriate. What the children clearly did *not* need in their lives were more police, more criminal courts, more loss, and more stigma. And finally, I would have bet the parents a bottle of wine—hell, a whole goddamn case of wine—that in the midst of this transition process, Seth on his own would have initiated a conversation about being ready to have his adoption legally finalized."

"So no police, no social service agencies?"

"Absolutely not. I would have advised them to handle this by themselves, as a family matter, supported by private clinical family therapy."

Putnam was silent for quite a while. Then he told me something he had neglected to say up to this point. "You know, each kid probed me to see if there was any way they could see each other, or even if they could learn about how the other was doing. The boy actually asked me if I couldn't make up a story about why I needed to see them together to better understand what went on between them. It was tempting—really tempting—to join him in a scheme. But I assumed the parents would have objected, and the whole thing would have been back in court. Not what the kids needed."

Putnam paused again, then started up, his honeyed, baritone voice spellbinding in its resonance. "One last thing that really moved me: after Ashley had described to me how much she missed her brother, I asked her *how* she missed him. She said, and I'm quoting from my notes, 'I try not to think about Seth, because when I miss him, I miss him with my whole body. It actually hurts, like when you have the flu and you ache all over.'" Putnam looked up at me for a response, but what was there to say?

It was time to leave, but I had one last, practical question. "Rick, we're facing a bit of a double-edged sword here. How are you going to reply on cross-examination if the plaintiffs' attorney says to you, 'Now, Dr. Putnam, for purposes of this question, let's assume you're right that the intersibling sexuality was driven not by sexual aggression on Seth's part, but by the two siblings seeking to nurture each other in the "language of their birth home," as you put it. If that's one way siblings from a sexually abusive home deal with the past, shouldn't the children's psychologists and social workers, and especially the adoption agency who placed the children, have warned the adoptive parents about this possibility?"

Putnam responded in the formal tone of voice he used in court when he testified. "Let me try to explain, ladies and gentlemen of the jury. Psychiatry and its allied mental health professions are fledgling sciences. We are just beginning to understand how human beings react to the stimuli in their environment. We all understand linear causality: hit a pool ball at the correct angle, and sure enough, the target ball will go in the pocket. But hit a boy, and it is not at all clear how he will react. He may act out by hitting smaller children, or he may become determined to be the type of adult who doesn't go around hitting people. So mental health professionals can never *predict* human behavioral reactions the way your question presupposes. All we can do is list past reactions that appear in the literature or that a clinician has seen. And intersibling sexuality is extraordinarily atypical. I've never run into it before in over thirty years of work in this field, nor have any of the colleagues with whom I've consulted about this case." He smiled over at me. "How's that for an answer?"

"Oh, that'll do; that'll do." I replied with a grin.

We spent another ten minutes on routine case logistics before the meeting ended. I thought more and more about what a tragedy it would be if this case didn't settle. On top of all her other issues, if the case went to trial, Ashley would have to hear Putnam's testimony on how her adoptive parents had let her down so terribly by their precipitous and self-centered decisions. She didn't need that.

*

The case dragged on almost another year, during which time Attorney O'Toole deposed Dr. Putnam and I deposed O'Toole's expert witness. The trial clerk of the court finally set a trial date, and I began the arduous process of preparing for trial. But then, out of the blue, just three weeks short of trial, O'Toole called and told me the plaintiffs wanted to make a serious effort to settle the matter. The settlement amount he proposed was shockingly modest. To this day, I have no idea exactly what motivated the plaintiff parents to take a very modest six-figure number and call it quits. But it was the right decision on their part, for numerous reasons.

Within a week, I had arranged a meeting with the other defense attorneys to discuss the settlement offer. My fellow defense counsel were elated. They almost universally felt the case was way too risky to try, given that it was completely dependent on Dr. Putnam's capacity to convince the jury of his interpretation of the meaning and impact of the intersibling sexuality. They feared that if the jury ended up being at all sympathetic to the adoptive parents, the verdict could be staggering. I was the odd man out, convinced we could win a defendants' verdict, if with disastrous effects on Ashley. A counteroffer was arrived at—funded almost totally by those insurance companies that were so anxious to avoid trial—and I communicated it to Attorney O'Toole. The following day, the plaintiffs accepted the counteroffer, two-thirds of which was placed in trust for Ashley, with the final third funding a trust for Seth. So after all this work, the case was resolved and done with, almost anticlimactically.

Needless to say, Rhonda Wilkins was ecstatic with delight at having to chip in so little to the settlement amount, and she gave me her ultimate compliment before hanging up in my ear. "You do fucking good work, Counselor. I just may give you another case someday." And equally needless to say, my client, Susan Sears, was elated that there would be no need to testify at trial—a proposition she had been dreading for over three years at that point.

I never heard anything more about Ashley or her adoptive parents, who partway through the litigation had sold their massive house and moved out to somewhere on the West Coast. The following year I again ran into the clinical director at Seth's sexual offender program and asked how he was doing, and the answer remained the same: wrong kid for the program. Three months or so after the settlement, I packed up boxes and boxes of documents and transcripts from the case to be shipped out to the law firm's off-site document storage and thought that was the end of my involvement with the case.

It wasn't.

*

Roughly five years after the *Doe* case settled, I received a call from the executive director of a small children's social service agency I had represented for years. This agency ran half a dozen halfway houses located in towns to the north of Boston, and one of them was having some friction with an abutting neighbor who had hired an attorney. I gave this attorney a call, and we agreed to meet on-site to try to resolve the issue.

The evening in question turned out to be unseasonably hot and sultry for late spring, when the light lasts well beyond nine o'clock. Opposing counsel was an entirely reasonable gentleman, and we soon had the small matter between the neighbors ironed out. The program director and I ended up sitting on the front stoop for a few minutes as the heat of day faded into a delicate evening breeze.

I asked the director about the nature of the population of the boys in the house, and learned that they were sexual offenders who had done well in one of the three or four offender programs in the commonwealth. I was just saying good-bye when a young man came out and asked the director for the key to the game closet. She went in to get it, leaving me with the boy. I nonchalantly said hi, but instead of replying, he cocked his head to one side, as if trying to place me. I certainly did not recognize him.

"Attorney Freiberg?" he asked.

"Yes, that's me," I replied, completely puzzled as to how he would know my name.

"You don't recognize me, do you?"

"I'm sorry, I don't. Should I?"

"Maybe not. My name is Seth. You were the attorney for the adoption agency that placed me and my sister for adoption, and there was the whole lawsuit thing."

All of it, all that we had been through, came back in a flash. "Oh my God, now I know exactly who you are," I blurted out. "You've grown and changed so much, I would never have recognized you."

"No problem. Hey, can we talk? I'd love to ask you a few questions. Are we allowed to talk about the case?"

I felt unmoored. But a settled case is a done deal, and given the circumstances, I couldn't see why or how there could be a problem. "I don't see why not. Where can we talk?"

"Um, this is not a good place, obviously."

"Are you guys allowed to leave the house to get an ice cream or something?" I asked. "My treat."

"As long as we're accompanied by an approved adult."

I checked inside with the program director, who immediately approved the idea when I told her that I had been involved in the litigation around Seth's adoption disruption. Seth, now six feet tall but still as blond as ever, showed me to the local sweet shop, which looked like it hadn't changed one bit since World War II. In fact, they still had the old, weathered hand-painted sign on the wall that had no doubt hung outside for many a decade: ICE CREAM: 5 CENTS. We each ordered a sundae, and then strolled across the street to a park bench that faced out over the pond near the town green. Neither of us spoke for quite a while, and I used the time to try to think through what I could and couldn't say to an opposing party after a case is settled. It was hard to think straight, though, because the dark chocolate sauce was so ridiculously good that it kept grabbing my attention from the matter at hand. I had to say something, though, so I just went with the chocolate sauce.

"This always happens to me," I opened the conversation. "Whenever I eat something I really like, I stop talking. My wife gives me all sorts of trouble about it, but I can't help it. It just . . . happens."

Seth laughed good-naturedly, "I know what you mean."

"You said you had a few questions," I said. "So shoot."

Without a moment's hesitation, Seth asked, "Do you know what happened to my sister?"

"Well, as you know, the lawsuit was settled, and some of the money was put aside in a trust for her and some for you as well. But that's all I know about her. I never had cause to hear anything further. Toward the end of the lawsuit, the family moved to the West Coast, but I never even knew which state. But I distinctly remember being impressed with how well she was doing when I saw her in her deposition. But that's old news; what, about five years ago now?"

"Yeah, about that. Do you think she misses me, or do you think she's angry with me?"

Now I started to become progressively more uneasy at the direction the conversation was taking. I was trying madly to think through whether there were limits to what I should say, even from a clinical point of view. Presumably Seth had had a lot of psychotherapy, and in all likelihood, his taking responsibility for what had happened between him and his sister was part of his treatment. I certainly didn't think I should risk blowing his clinical therapy out of the water with Putnam's hypothesis about the relative innocence of the intersibling sexuality. I hesitated just long enough for Seth to see right through me.

"Mr. Freiberg, I promise you—cross my heart and hope to die— that nothing you say to me today will ever be repeated. Who would I repeat it to? I literally don't know anybody who even knows I have a sister, let alone anyone who knows what happened, except you, and this is probably the only conversation I'll ever have with you. I give you my word of honor, no one will ever hear about this. *Please!*"

Seth's entreaty and his piercing stare cut through me. Then something inside my head just said, screw it. I wanted to talk to him about the case as much as he wanted to talk to me.

"Seth, your word of honor is good enough for me. And honestly, I have some questions myself. Let's see. As to whether your sister blamed you, the answer is a resounding no. The psychiatrist who examined you in his office—remember the office with the fireplace?" He nodded yes. "He told me that Ashley was very clear: she never felt forced to participate, and she sought you out as much as the other way around. What she reported was entirely consistent with what you had said, namely that what the two of you engaged in, you both did voluntarily. So as I understood things, she didn't at all blame you for what happened."

I could see the boy's shoulders relax. He turned back to his ice cream. Then, in a slow and even voice, he asked, "Was she sad that I was taken away?"

"Sad? Are you kidding? She was heartbroken. You were her only sibling, her best friend, and her last link to your family. She had the adoptive parents, of course, and they seemed to mean well and to intend to stick by her and do their best. But it was you she loved."

I thought he would smile or acknowledge this information some-how, but he immediately asked, "Do you think I can contact her someday?"

"I suppose, once she is an adult and out of the adoptive parents' home, you could try. I don't think I would suggest trying before that. And maybe you should have someone facilitate the reintroduction, like a social service agency. That might be a good idea, Seth. They could help you locate her, and they could feel out the circumstances to see if she too wanted to reestablish contact—but I don't doubt that she would. That might be the best way to go about it."

"How would they find her?"

"After her twenty-second birthday, after she presumably will have finished her schooling and moved out of her parents' house and into her own life, a social service agency, or an attorney who works in the adoption field, might be able to help you. If you don't have any better way, feel free to give me a call and I'll see if I can help find the right person to help you."

"Okay, thanks. That would be great. But from what you saw, do you think she is probably doing okay?"

"That would be my guess, yes. That psychiatrist found both of you very 'intact' as he put it at the time. He was enormously impressed with how resilient both of you were, especially given everything you'd been through. And after your deposition, and also after Ashley's, the whole room full of attorneys talked about each of you, and we all had the same impression. You both had held it together remarkably well, and through some rough times. So I would imagine she is doing just fine. How about you? How are you doing?"

He paused, and looked me right in the eyes. "Do you really want to know, or are you just saying that to be polite?"

"No, I do really want to know. There is a lot I would like to know. I had no way to learn anything after the lawsuit ended, and it ended so abruptly."

"Okay," Seth said. "Ask me anything."

"Okay. Let's start with what happened to you in the Juvenile Justice System. I knew the basic details at the time, but what was it really like being in the system?"

"It was awful. Dreadful. At first, I was locked up in Roslindale; that's a prison for kids. Do you know it?"

"I do."

"Then they moved me to the sex offender program. That was better, but it still was a lockup, with super strict rules. I was sort of a little kid. I didn't know the first thing about how to defend myself or how to deal with these guys. And some of these characters were very hard on me. They were older, bigger, and streetwise. A few of them were very aggressive sex offenders, and that's what was on their mind." He paused, looking down at the ground. "Anyway . . . a lot happened. But I survived it, you know how?" he asked rhetorically. "Because I didn't care. I didn't have anywhere to go. I didn't have anyone to go back to. I didn't have any real parents or even adoptive parents—no sister, no friends, no home, no nothing. I really didn't care how they used me."

I was left wildly fishing for some way to respond to this. "Didn't you have *anyone* on your side, like a sympathetic social worker or a good program director? Maybe a teacher? How about the lawyer who did the case for you?"

"No, that lawyer disappeared at the end of the case. And I never lucked into having a social worker or a shrink who I really got to know. I kept getting social workers who quit. Every three or four months, I'd get a new one, and each one knew less about my case than the one before. And as time went on, each of them showed less and less interest in learning much about me. I was just a quiet kid who didn't cause any problems in the program. Maybe I should have. Causing trouble got some kids more attention. But that's not my nature. And with each new social worker, my file kept getting thinner and thinner. I always thought that was sort of ironic. Remember how fat my old file was? Not anymore. My current worker meets with me for about fifteen minutes and has no clue about my case. Mostly she just compliments me for behaving. No one knows, I swear, no one knows what you know about my background. No one. They only know from the folder that I'm a registered sex offender who stays out of trouble in the program and who has no visitors."

I had to think about what to ask him next. It took a few moments. "So how long can you stay in this halfway house?"

"Only about five more months. I'm in the system until my eighteenth birthday; then I'm out on my own."

"So that's cool. Are you excited about that?"

"No, not really. Not at all, actually. I'm too scared. A guy like me, with no education and no job skills . . . What the hell am I going to do?"

"Well, at least you have the settlement money. It must be safe and sound, and more by now. You could get a start with that, no?"

"Yeah, there's that, I suppose, although I haven't heard about it in years. The lawyer took a third of it, but there's an account somewhere. But that's not what matters. What matters is that I don't have anyone to call when I get out. No one at all to call or go see. No one."

Again, I was desperately at a loss for what to say. Seth noted this, I could tell, and let out a long breath that nearly broke my heart. "I'm lonely, man. Lonely to the point of being weary. And that's here in the program where at least there are a few people around me I can talk to. Once I'm out of here, I'll be even more alone. Then what do I do? Who am I even going to talk to then? Some stranger on the sidewalk? That's what really scares me. I hate being alone. Loneliness for me isn't an idea. It's a feeling, an awful feeling. Am I making any sense?"

"Yeah, you're making a lot of sense. You're saying things that are nearly the same as what Dr. Putnam told me during your case. One day he said something just like you said."

"Great. I'm a goddamn expert on loneliness. Maybe I'll write a book about it."

"Maybe you should," I replied.

"No, *you* should," Seth shot back. "You know how to write. I don't. And if you do, talk about my case, would you? Tell people what happened to me. *Please*."

"Maybe I will someday. Who knows? Maybe I will. But I've got a question for you. When I feel hungry or thirsty, I start thinking about getting something to eat or drink. What do you do when you feel lonely?"

"What do I do?" He looked down at the ground again. "Mostly I go backward, back into myself. I try to refind the feelings that I had for my family when I was little, at home. But I can't really get back to them anymore, not since I lost Ashley. I know our home was nutty and what my family did was completely unacceptable, but I didn't know that then, or care. I was just a kid. What I search for now when I take walks back inside myself is what it felt like being part of my own big family, whether they were crazy or not. But now I just have a few vague memories. I can't get back to the feelings of family like I could when I was younger."

"But, Seth, you didn't really answer my question, and I really want you to. You said when you feel lonely, you mostly go backward to a time before you were alone. Do you ever think of going forward? Do you ever think about making new friends, new connections?"

He didn't hesitate. "I think about it, sure. But I can't really make friends while I'm in these programs. Kids come and go, and you're not supposed to talk about your background and personal stuff with other kids in the program. People who work here come and go. They burn out quickly and leave the job. Then in comes some complete stranger who doesn't know you and doesn't care. Maybe I'll be able to make friends, or find a girl when I leave here at the end of the year, but I don't think that's so obvious."

"Why do you say that?"

"Because when I turn eighteen in a few months and leave this program, what the hell am I going to do? I'm a registered sex offender. You're a lawyer; you know what that means. I'll have to report to the police wherever I live. You tell me: How do I get a job? From what I hear, employers check the registry. That's what it's there for. How do I rent an apartment? Landlords check the registry. That's what it's there for. Now you tell me: How do I make friends? Do I lie about my background? Do I just leave out where I've been for six years? And what will I tell a girl? Do girls date registered sex offenders? I don't think so. Or do I just not mention it, hoping they won't ask or learn? If I did keep it secret and they learned about it, they'd leave in a heartbeat, wouldn't you? But if I don't keep it secret, how do I explain what happened? Am I supposed to try to convince a girl that it was okay under the circumstances for me to have sex with my own sister? You tell me: What am I supposed to do?" There was such desperation in his voice, I wasn't at all sure how to respond or what to say next.

Seth was patient as I gathered my thoughts. But my mind was chaotic and not at all on topic. In a flash, what came to mind was the stark difference between my own eighteenth birthday and Seth's upcoming confrontation with adulthood. Mine was filled with excitement and anticipation. My dad took me on a little vacation to celebrate my high school graduation, and the University of California, Berkeley had by some miracle admitted me for September. I had had family. Seth had none. I had had education coming my way; Seth had none. I had had every reason to be elated and optimistic; Seth had none. I had had a whole range of connections to support my transition to adulthood; Seth had none. What to say?

The only option was to answer honestly. "I don't have any magical answers for you, Seth. I really don't. When I was your age, I had family and college and a future all mapped out for me. I know you don't have any of that. But you're a great guy. If I met you and were your age, I'd definitely want to make friends with you."

"Yeah, but you say that because you know I'm *not* a sex offender, because you understand what really went on between my sister and me. But no one else will understand that, *ever.*"

Once again I was frozen, trying to find something useful to say. "Well, what about that idea of reconnecting with Ashley when you're both adults. She'd understand."

"My shrinks have told me that she's probably gone forever to me because even if I could locate her, her shrinks and parents would probably advise her not to see me. And she may not want to. I'll bet you she tells people she's an only child. I wouldn't blame her." He paused and looked down at the ground. "It may be better for her if I don't ever show up again."

Now I was at a total loss for words. All I came up with was, "Look, that decision is years away. If you get your life up and ticking, who knows what the world will look like to you six or seven years from now. Have you ever asked an attorney or social worker about the ins and outs of getting your sex offender registration changed to a lower level?"

"Oh, sure, we talked about that. My best social worker—she got cancer and quit suddenly, wouldn't you know it—she told me two or three years ago that she called the lawyer for the Sex Offender Registry Board to see if there was an appeal process. She said the lawyer told her the board couldn't and wouldn't reconsider my registration status until at least ten years after my adjudication and that, in all likelihood, I would probably have to wait the full twenty years until my duty to register would end automatically. That's fifteen years from now." He went silent, back into his own thoughts for a moment. "You know what? She was really cool, that social worker, because it was after she got sick and had to quit her job that she followed through and took the time to call me at the program to tell me about all this. What a cool lady."

"It doesn't get a lot cooler. I hope to hell she's okay."

"She died actually, not that long after."

How to continue? I had no idea. What came out was, "So how's it going for you here at this program? Is there any way I can be of help? I've been their lawyer for years."

"It's fine here these days. I don't have any complaints. But when I turn eighteen, like I said, I'll have to leave, because my funding stops. But where do I go? What do I do? Do you have any ideas?"

I thought for a moment. "What about going to school? You're obviously smart. And you've got money in your trust."

"School? Based on what? I had essentially zero education in the two foster care homes, and then I had a year and a half-year of remedial work when I was in the adoptive home, and I was starting to catch up. But since I was arrested, I've had almost none. The offender program had a schoolroom on the campus, but it was a joke. Once I got in this halfway house, I wanted to go to the local high school, but with the sex offender registration, no dice. They have a teacher who comes into this program to teach two hours a day, but you can imagine the quality of the education. Kids of all ages are sitting there; some can't even read. So you tell me: How do I get out from behind the eight ball and get a real education? I read fine, but I have no historical knowledge or scientific understanding of how things work—nothing that takes a teacher and a classroom to learn."

I took out a business card and handed it to him. "Listen, you keep my card, and for God's sake, Seth, *you call me*. And call me with time to spare so I can help you generate ideas. Nobody eighteen years old should be left completely on his own. It isn't right."

"Okay," he murmured, looking down at the ground.

"Seth, I mean it. Call. I have resources and contacts, and who knows, maybe I can help you find a job and a place to live. You have your whole life in front of you. Don't give up. You've survived so much, and you've stayed so strong through all of it. You've done harder. Trust me: it *will* get better."

"But what hope is there?" Seth said, his voice choking up a bit.

"I'll tell you what, if you call me at my office, we will research if anything can be done to appeal to have your status changed at the registry. I'm sorry I can't tell you anything about the law on that issue today. I just don't know offhand how the registry works. But let's double check that your social worker got that right. And if we can make a try at it, I'd be glad to do it for you. And let me try to help you find a job and a place to live when you leave the program. I might fail, but I'll sure as hell give it a try. Will you call me?"

"Yeah," he replied, unconvincingly.

I wasn't going to let this go. "I'm serious, Seth. I care about how this turns out for you because I know all the details about how you fell into this trap, and I know it wasn't your fault. And don't tell anyone you're alone anymore, because I'll personally take that as an insult. You have at least one connection now—*with me*. And I promise you: I'll help you make five more connections. It's all about connections, Seth. Let's go make some."

To my complete and utter delight, as we both stood up from the bench, I saw a truly beautiful sight: a smile spread across his handsome face, only the second one I'd ever seen.

The short drive back to the group home was silent, but I sensed we both enjoyed the relaxed, quiet silence that comes over those who have said what they have to say. When I pulled up in front of the building, he looked at me and gave me yet another smile that I will never forget as long as I live as he told me "Thank you" in a deep and warm tone of voice. Then he opened the door and walked up the path toward the program's front door, without looking back.

There was no call the next week or the week after that. But I wasn't going to give up that easily, so I called the program director. She told me Seth was gone; he had run away from the program two days after I'd seen him, and had not been heard from since. I called his probation officer, who hadn't heard from him either. He told me that while that was normally a problem, since Seth was just about to age out of his probation status anyway, he didn't intend to do anything about it.

About a month later, I called the program again, but by then there was a new director who didn't even recognize Seth's name—or my name for that matter. I called the Division of Youth Services and found out who his case manager had been, but she was on maternity leave, and her replacement told me that she had never seen Seth's file. She promised to find the file and get back to me later in the week. And indeed, she dutifully did call back, but only to report that she had not been able to locate the file. Apparently it was lost. How ironic I thought: Seth had described how his file had shrunk over time, and now it was gone all together. Just like Seth's future. I thought about putting my private investigator on the matter, but I had to admit to myself the likely futility of this idea. And so I let myself get caught up in life, and let myself forget about Seth. Or so I thought.

*

The following winter, I had a court hearing in Salem, the next town over from where the group home where I'd run into Seth was located. After court, something made me drive over to the program, searching, I suppose, for some type of closure to the matter. I met the new director with whom I'd spoken. She was somewhat taken aback that the agency's attorney was at the door, unannounced.

"Don't worry; don't worry. I'm not here in any official capacity. I knew Seth, the resident I called you about a month ago. I knew him because I was one of the attorneys involved in a law case that grew out of his adoption disruption. I'm very concerned about him, frankly. I was hoping to give him a helping hand when he aged out of your program, but he never called. I was just wondering if you'd heard anything more about him since he ran from the program?"

"No. I've never even heard his name mentioned except by you on the phone when you called, and now again this afternoon. Actually, after you called, I asked several of the longer-term residents what they remembered about him, and they said they never had any real contact with him. They said they really didn't even notice when he left. They said he tended to keep to himself."

I thanked her, then turned and started down the walkway. I was halfway to my car when she called out to me from a window. "Hey, Counselor. You know what? There is a cigar box in a closet here that I think has his stuff in it. Do you want to see it? You're the only person who has ever asked after the boy. You can have it if you want. Otherwise, I'm going to throw it out."

I went back in and we opened the cigar box together in her office. The first thing I saw was my business card.

"Well, there you go," she said. "It's his box all right, and like I say, you're welcome to it."

Underneath the five or six random boy's treasures in the box was a photo. It was of the adoptive parents, Ashley, and Seth. But the photo had been mutilated: The parents' faces were both crossed out with blue ink. Ashley's face was crossed out with a black pen, presumably at a different time. And Seth's own face was crossed out with a third pen—a red ballpoint pen that was one of the items in the box. A cold chill ran up my spine and made me shiver, and inadvertently I made a funny little sound that somehow expressed the horror I felt at this discovery.

"What does all this mean?" she asked.

"What does it mean? It means, it's all about connections."

"What?"

"Oh, nothing, just an old saying. Hey, you take care. I have to get home. We have friends coming over to dinner."

*

My own words, *friends coming to dinner, friends coming to dinner, friends coming to dinner,* kept reverberating through my mind as I wound my way slowly through Friday afternoon traffic back to Boston. I couldn't get my mind off the lonely boy who was out there somewhere, presumably without friends, and quite possibly without dinner.

II

Fifteen Years in Solitary Confinement

> Sitting on the low-slung bed, staring at the [prison cell]
> wall, I felt the room full of aloneness. It was not just the
> absence of other human life, but the presence of alone-
> ness that seemed to fill the room, to shimmer between
> me and the wall, to weigh down the otherwise empty
> air until it seemed to press in and threaten to suffocate
> me.[10]

While the other law case stories shared with you in this book are a
product of my dual training in social psychology and the law, I only
came to know the story of the man who wrote the above words because
I got lost and took a wrong turn. One sunny, gentle summer morning
in 1968, I found myself walking across the University of California, Los
Angeles, campus, where I was a graduate student in my midtwenties. I
was trying to find a building in an area of the vast grounds that I wasn't
at all familiar with, and I took that fateful wrong turn around the corner of a building I had never seen before. There on its side lawn I came
upon a Tai Chi class going through their ultra slow motion movements

---

10. Sidney Rittenberg and Amanda Bettett, *The Man Who Stayed Behind* (Simon
    and Schuster, 1993), p. 414.

of graceful martial arts postures. I stopped to watch, mesmerized by the fluid, lissome dance and captivated by a particularly stunning blond practitioner in the back row. On a whim, I stepped in next to her and began to copy the unhurried but deliberate postures. This chance encounter was to change my life, if through an entirely improbable chain of events. A discussion with the blonde led to a coffee, the coffee led to a relationship, the relationship led to my taking up Tai Chi as a hobby, the hobby morphed into a study of Taoism, the study led me to write an article entitled "The Dialectic in China: Maoist and Taoist." The article was published in a Massachusetts Institute of Technology (MIT) academic journal, and the magazine was read by a visiting scholar at MIT: the hero, and narrator of much of this chapter, Sidney Rittenberg. By the time Rittenberg called me to discuss the article, he had learned from a colleague of his (who was a law client of mine), that I was a practicing attorney by trade. During the call, after a lengthy discussion about my little article, Rittenberg inquired if he could retain my legal services. One thing led to another, as you shall see, and, in the fullness of time, I found myself walking by his side through the streets of Beijing. All because of that beautiful blonde.

This chapter brings to you Rittenberg's remarkable story as he told it to me, half in Cambridge, half in Beijing. His experiences with Mao Zedong and postwar China provide unique insights to our twin topics of loneliness and connection, because Rittenberg experienced both the most extreme loneliness and the most extreme connectedness of any individual I have ever met. But I must ask your indulgence, for to relay to you the tale of how on two separate occasions Rittenberg became far more closely connected to Mao and his revolution than any other westerner ever did, only to be cast down each time into the heart-breaking loneliness of solitary confinement, the narrative must review in some considerable detail the tumultuous history of post–World War II China.

Loneliness comes in many forms and means different things to each of us. To Rittenberg, it meant two periods of solitary confinement in Chinese prisons from 1949 through 1955 and from 1968 through 1977—fifteen years out of the summertime of his life, spent entirely alone. "Alone alone alone alone alone. The walls beat my solitude into my head through aching eyes every hour of the day and night—great spots and bands of color floating and pulsating before my eyes, silence making my ears ring."[11] Can any of us even begin to comprehend what these words convey? Can we at all conceive of being so terrifyingly alone that we would prefer the presence of a grand inquisitor—and his torturous interrogations—over his absence?

*

The mutual acquaintance who had introduced us had briefly mentioned to me that Rittenberg had been one of the best-known personages in Chinese political circles around Mao, only to then be condemned to spend many years in the harshest conditions imaginable in political prison. Given this introduction, I expected to meet a hardened, embittered person for whom contact with an unknown attorney would be formal and cool. I couldn't possibly have been more wrong. Rittenberg—and let's call him Sidney, he would want that—by the time I met him in the early 1990s was still ruggedly handsome, despite being pretty nearly bald. He was blessed with the brightest pale blue eyes you can imagine: somehow, they seemed to have their own internal light source. But it wasn't how the man looked that was so notable, it was how he acted and interacted. When Sidney spoke to you, he had the habit of concentrating intently *just on you*. You could tell he was blocking out all other distractions. And perhaps his most striking trait was the aura of calm and quietude about him that seemed to settle over the room like a San Francisco fog.

Roughly three weeks later, after our third meeting about the legal matter at hand, I was thrilled—even honored—when Sidney invited me to dinner at his apartment the following Saturday. He fully warned me that he intended to further pick my brain about some of the topics I had covered in the article he had read, and I, in turn, had my own conversational goals in mind, for I hoped to learn more than the little bit I had heard about his firsthand experience in the historical events that changed forever one of the world's great nation states.

---

11. Ibid., 415.

It was a steamy, humid summer evening when I found my way to the house near MIT that Sidney and his wife were renting for the academic year. As always happened when I became involved in any way with faculty from one of Boston's colleges and universities, I felt a sharp pang of sadness for my forsaken academic career. It's an amazing city to teach in, arguably one of the best in the world, because whatever your area of study, your collegial group of like-minded scholars cuts across the fifty-four institutions by field of interest.

Anyway, Sidney's wife, Yulin, had prepared a wonderful meal for us from the cuisine of the Shanxi province of China, where she had been raised. The makeup of each dish was almost musical, so carefully were they composed. When there was heat, it was balanced with fresh; when there was crunch, it was offset against smooth; and when a dish had a dominant flavor, it was harmonized against background seasonings. At the table that evening were two of their children, both in their early twenties, and three academic friends of Sidney's from MIT. It was a classic Cambridge evening, completely distinguishable from a Boston evening, notwithstanding that the two cities are only separated by the modest waters of the Charles River. If the conversation at Boston dinner parties is typically centered on state and national politics, Cambridge evenings are more likely to involve discussions about art and literature and poetry, often leading to seriously animated debates. I listened intently as the three dinner guests, professors one and all, debated just such matters, but there was part of me that would have greatly preferred speaking with Sidney about his adventures in China.

All too soon the evening came to an end, or so I thought. The other guests and the two children were the first to thank our hosts and leave, and they were halfway down the front walkway to their cars when I began to thank Sidney for his having included me and Yulin for her extraordinary culinary efforts. To my complete delight, however, Sidney asked me if I didn't by chance want to sit on the back porch and chat for a while. I leapt at the opportunity.

*

As we sat together, the sounds of the crickets blended together to fill the small screened porch with their summer song. The breeze that evening was gentle, almost caressing, and the high humidity kept the temperature from falling.

"Some tea?" Sidney asked, quietly breaking a peaceful silence. "I brought it back from Beijing a month ago. It's supposed to have 'yin' qualities to balance the heat of summer." For some reason, he giggled after saying this; there was a disarming lightness to the man. He poured the drink from a visibly aged and greatly dented metal teapot.

"Thank you, yes," I replied. "And why do I think that teapot has some history to it?"

"Good eye, young man!" Sidney replied. "It was the first object I ever acquired in China. It was a gift from a man who before the war had carried it with him all the way north to Yan'an on the Long March. By the time the war was over, he was too old to accompany us, but he knew we were headed east to battle, and he thought the teapot should be involved in the revolution from start to finish. You can't imagine how remarkable it is that I still have it around, given everything that's happened. I cherish it."

Before we could fall back into silence, I grasped the opportunity that had presented itself.

"Sidney," I began. "Would you tell me more about the teapot, and about what happened to you in China? I'd love to hear about your time there, if you don't mind talking about it." I was fully expecting him to politely decline, but to my surprise and delight, I was once again completely wrong.

"I'd love to tell you the story. But I also want to speak more with you about your ideas for the second article on Taoism you referenced in the one I read. But I'll go first, if you like. Do you prefer the shorter or longer version?" he asked with a twinkle in his eye.

"I'd stay here all night to hear this story. I'll *definitely* take the detailed version. And I have a favor to ask as well, if you think it's appropriate. I have an idea about writing a book some day about the social psychology of loneliness—how loneliness is what we sense when we lack adequate connections to others. From what I've heard about your history in China, you hit both of these extremes. When Jim described you, he said you were as close and connected as possible with those who made the revolution happen, but at a later time you were totally isolated in solitary confinement. Would it be fair to ask you to highlight these issues for me? I think I could learn a hell of a lot for that book—if I ever get around to actually writing it."

Sidney nodded his assent and looked away from me, peering out over the back lawn and garden, silently sipping his tea in the stillness. Something about the serenity of this man made him unlike anyone else I had ever met. How could such a tranquil and gentle person possibly have survived so many years of harsh imprisonment? I was about to learn just that, and I hope you don't mind if I basically step out of the way and let Sidney's voice narrate his story to you, as he told it to me that summer evening long ago.

*

"I was drafted toward the end of World War II, and by some process I never grasped, the army determined that I should learn Japanese, which I had no interest in doing whatsoever. I was ordered to show up at an intensive language-learning program that had been set up during the war at Stanford University, so out to the West Coast I went. The first thing I did upon my arrival was plead with my superior officer to be allowed to switch to a Mandarin Chinese language course that was starting up at the same time. Such requests were routinely turned down in the army, but again for some unknown reason, mine was approved. I was thinking that perhaps something more adventurous would come of learning Chinese than learning Japanese. Little did I know.

"By the fall of 1945, I found myself in southwest China working as a language specialist in the military legal system. One of my first tasks was to travel around to interview witnesses and investigate specific law cases involving American military personnel. And that is how I learned about the death of Wood Fairy, the case that would change my life.

"Wood Fairy was the name of a little girl. She was the only child of a rickshaw puller, or at least she was until she was run over by a truck driven by a drunken US soldier. I did my best to arrange for decent compensation, but all the system allocated for this grossly negligent killing of a peasant child was twenty-six dollars. It upset me deeply that her father found no injustice in this pitiful stipend, and that he had no problem at all with the fact that a goodly part of it had to be paid over to neighborhood protection racketeers. It was just one case among hundreds that I handled, but for some reason, maybe because it was my first, it's always stayed with me.

"I cannot describe to you the level of poverty and corruption that was endemic throughout China at that time. I constantly saw unattended corpses lying along the roadsides. The ancient, narrow streets were clogged twenty-four hours a day with millions of peasants in their postwar migration to cities in a fruitless effort to find some way to make a living. Chiang Kai-shek, the political and military leader of China's Nationalist Party (or Kuomintang [KMT]), had his soldiers impose a brutal martial law, and there was nothing—no police, no courts, nothing—to protect common people against the Nationalist troops, who were only marginally easier on the population than the occupying Japanese had been during the war. Then there were the exploiters, layer upon layer of them, and the pervasive government graft, and the feudal warlords who controlled each locality of China. Young women were bought and sold for a dollar, young men were forcibly captured and conscripted into the army, and anyone could be summarily executed by a KMT soldier for the slightest offense or for no reason at all.

"The war ended shortly after I arrived, and the wartime truce between the Chinese Nationalist Party and the Chinese Communist Party became more strained day by day. There were a number of efforts by the United States and other allied powers to mediate between the two forces, but there was never a desire for a peaceful resolution on Chiang Kai-shek's part. During this period, I would practice my budding Mandarin with absolutely anyone who would speak with me, and in these conversations I began to hear more and more gossip about Mao. People spoke of him like he was Robin Hood. They were fascinated by the idea he spoke of, about changing the life of the common man. I felt like I was watching history unfold, like finding yourself in Paris just before the French Revolution. With all my being, I wanted to be a part of what was about to happen, and obviously that depended on getting my Mandarin skills rock solid. I could barely make out written

Chinese at the time, but you never saw a more eager student. I always had a paper under my arm, and I would unabashedly ask anyone and everyone to spend a few minutes with me going over an article. That was a great idea by the way: I learned hundreds of characters through these conversations. And as for my speaking skills, I would get in any conversation with anyone about anything at anytime; I was shameless. And I would do this all day, every day, no matter what else I had to do.

"I knew my Chinese language skills had advanced when at some point I could make out not just the words behind the characters in the newspapers, but also the politics behind the words. By the time a year had gone by, I could actually compare the various newspapers I read, and the one I found most alluring was published by the Communist Party. This wasn't completely by chance. As a college student, I had briefly been a member of the Communist Party USA in 1940. I had been attracted by the party's positions on free speech and race relations: matters we take for granted today. I resigned when I went in the army. It seemed the right thing to do, and frankly, the party itself hadn't been that big a thing to me, in part because the national leadership was stodgy and old and didn't have a single leader with an ounce of charisma.

"But the Chinese Party at the end of World War II could not possibly have been more different. It was young and vibrant, and its followers were romantically trapped in caves in the mountainous, northwest hinterlands, pinned in by hostile forces. And, of course, it was led by one of the most charismatic leaders on the planet.

"There was no doubt about it: I didn't miss the party, but I did miss the fellowship and camaraderie and the sense of connection I had had with other progressives I worked with. I found myself irresistibly drawn to search out Mao's party and his movement, despite the fact that doing so had its risks: the party was strictly illegal in those parts of China controlled by Chiang Kai-shek's regime, and it only operated underground. But it didn't take long before I located a few members and I began—very furtively, of course—to get together with them in my free time. That's when I first heard about the village town of Yan'an in the remote northwest of China, to where Mao had made his famous Long March before the war. I was astonished when several people encouraged me to go out to Yan'an to meet with Mao to learn about the future of China, but I dismissed the idea as essentially impossible.

"For one thing, I was still in the army, and I couldn't just take off and travel across the country. Worse still, at that time the American forces were preparing to leave China, and I was ordered in late 1945 to travel to India en route to returning to the States. But by this point, I *desperately* wanted to stay in the culture and country I was ever more adopting as I learned the language, and partly through diligence but mostly by good luck, I succeeded in getting my orders changed. I was to report to and serve at army headquarters in Shanghai. Just before I left on the journey south to the great port city, I obtained a letter of introduction from my new friends in the party that would introduce me to a contact in Shanghai. I tucked the letter away in my wallet and took off alone in an open army jeep on a journey of over fifteen hundred miles. I was all of twenty-three.

"The tiny, winding roads were mostly single lane, almost entirely made of dirt, and, truth be told, were little more than a series of ruts. They were covered with stones, many of which were large enough that they needed to be attentively avoided. My average speed can't have been more than twelve or fifteen miles per hour max, often less. But driving this slowly had its advantages: it made it impossible for me to ignore what I drove through. And what I saw wasn't pretty. Coastal China exhibited a level of abject poverty that, as an American kid, I had never even imagined, and inland was said to be even harder off. Shanghai was starving. Once again, I saw corpses along the sidewalk, prostitutes wandering the streets, and a general population virtually unable to feed itself. The economy was in ruins, and inflation was completely out of control. All of this fanned the fires of my desire to get involved in the movement for social change—even in a country that I barely knew anything about. I became ever more convinced that something big, something historical was very likely coming, or so it seemed to a twenty-three-year-old optimist. And I desperately wanted to be part of it. So risk-taker that I was, I couldn't wait to find the right circumstances to take that letter out of my wallet and make contact with the party in Shanghai, even though the risk was even greater in

Shanghai, given the massive KMT presence. But you know kids: they think they're immortal.

"As I became more interested in Chinese politics and culture, I doubled down on my efforts to improve my Mandarin. And the snowball continued to grow: The more I mastered the language, the more I was welcome to participate. And the more I participated, the more convinced I was that history was going to change right there, right then. So day by day, I became ever more determined to figure out a way to stay in China—whatever it took. Then came the evening that made all the difference and would prove to be the key to the locked door that would allow me to stay on after my discharge from the army. Almost by chance, I was invited to dinner at the house of Madame Sun Yat-sen, widow of the first president and founding father of the Republic of China, a man who was and still is experienced in China very much in the way George Washington is for us. That evening, my greatly improved Mandarin was much admired by my hostess and the other dinner guests, and it allowed me to make connections that would soon make all the difference.

"Now, I should mention that my growing links to China played off against the fact that I had no significant connections whatsoever pulling me back to the States. My father, who raised me, had passed away, and I was single. So I had no family network writing me letters and anxiously awaiting my return. I had no particular set of friends aching to reunite with me, no job waiting for me, nor any job ideas that particularly interested me. In contrast, every other GI I spoke with couldn't wait to get back to his family, his girl, his job, whatever. I have no idea what I would have done if my wild desire to stay in China had had to be balanced against a normal set of connections back in the States, but in any case, it didn't. I was as free as a bird, and I knew exactly where I wanted to fly, even if it wasn't going to be easy to arrange.

"Getting discharged wasn't the problem. After all, the war was over and the American armed forces were being greatly reduced. My hurdle was that GIs weren't allowed to stay in China after their discharge unless they could document that they had obtained a full-time job—and that was a virtual impossibility since there were hardly any jobs for the Chinese, let alone foreigners. It soon dawned on me that I had only one hope for obtaining employment and such a letter, and so I recontacted Madame Sun. And sure enough, she came through by arranging for me to be offered a position as an observer for the United Nations Relief and Rehabilitation Administration.

"It wasn't long before my orders from the UN sent me into the central plains of China—an area controlled by the communists. This area had been ceded to Mao's army after the Japanese surrender by the terms of the cease-fire that had been negotiated between the Communist Party and the Nationalist Party, all under the watchful eyes of United States General George Marshall.

"The contrast I encountered in the central plains was stark. Here, Mao's People's Army was in control, and the way these soldiers treated the common man could not possibly have been more divergent from the way I saw the Nationalist army treat civilians. With the People's Army, every single interaction with peasants and villagers was designed to elicit popular support. Where KMT soldiers seized whatever they wanted from anyone, Mao's army never took a grain of rice that wasn't paid for; where KMT soldiers made what use they would of attractive young girls, Mao's army treated everyone with respect. It would have been one thing to write about egalitarianism and fairness in theoretical works, but the Chinese population didn't read. What Mao understood was that the only way to promote meaningful ideology in China was to put it into practice in everyday life. And this is precisely what I saw the People's Army do. It was all about institutionalized humility and complete fairness *put into actual practice*. You could see this—everyone could see this—in the distribution of scarce food and other resources. Army generals and political cadres lived on exactly the same rations, and in exactly the same conditions, as did everyone else. If there was only enough for half a bowl of rice per person, it didn't matter who that person was, major general or peasant laborer. Everybody sat together at meals with absolutely no division by status or rank. Everyone waited in line with equal status, and everyone used the same latrines. I can't possibly exaggerate what a total contrast this presented with everything I had seen in the Nationalist-controlled areas, where troops ran roughshod over all commoners. And mind you that "commoners" comprised well over ninety-five percent of the population, for everyone in China was dirt poor, save for a tiny elite class that was wealthy beyond belief. I trust you can imagine how powerful this contrast was to a young idealistic kid in his twenties.

"At the time, I asked myself whether this egalitarianism was simply a clever strategy of winning hearts and minds, or whether it was actually part and parcel of the social reality of the movement. I remember well the first time I became confident that it was all very real. That was when I first met Zhou Enlai.

"I was in a hamlet called Fresh Flower Village. The US was making a last-ditch effort to bring the two sides to a peaceful settlement, and completely unknown to me, of course, there was a meeting scheduled at the village just as I arrived. General Marshall didn't attend the meeting, but one of his top aides was there to meet with both parties: a senior KMT general and the vice chairman of the Chinese Communist Party's Revolutionary Military Commission, Zhou Enlai.

"As I drove into the village, I saw another young American soldier standing by his jeep, so without thinking much about it, I parked alongside him. As we were two American boys of about the same age, we were chatting away within minutes, and I learned that he was an aide to the senior US officer attending the meeting. I introduced myself as a UN relief observer, and asked what the meeting was all about. His response was to laugh out loud and tell me that the meeting was just a farce. He said he had overheard a discussion that made it clear that the US Army knew full well that the KMT was soon to attack the communist lines, and that it had no intention of bargaining away anything at this meeting. Of course, he had no idea where my personal sentiments lay when he off-handedly mentioned this to me, and I certainly didn't clue him in. But best of all, when I mentioned that I had been trained in Mandarin, he offered to ask the officer he was escorting if I could sit in on the meeting—I think his idea was that I could provide a backup set of ears for whatever might be said in Chinese—and the officer agreed. For me, this was a dream come true.

"When we entered the building where the negotiations were to take place, there sat Zhou Enlai himself, the man I had heard so much about. The KMT general spoke first and laid out the Nationalist position stiffly and with visible disdain for the Communist delegation.

He didn't bat an eye at espousing what I knew to be a lie—assuming what the aide had told me was accurate. Then Zhou spoke and my life changed. I know that sounds melodramatic, but it's true. It wasn't so much the content of what he said; that was predictable. It was more the serene and honest tone of his voice and the respect he showed for everyone present. He was absolutely transfixing. This was a man with arresting charisma—and of course, a man who was to have enormous influence on the direction China would later take.

"Anyway, after the meeting was over, I came upon Zhou and his group—though only because of where their van was parked. I don't know how I got up the nerve, but in my mediocre Mandarin I introduced myself to Zhou. I still can't believe I did that, but I was still a kid—you know, nothing ventured, nothing gained. But it didn't stop there. The next thing I knew, I heard myself telling him that I wished there were more I could do to be useful. Those were my exact words. He looked me square in the eyes for quite a while, sizing me up, I suppose. And then he invited me to look him up if I got to Nanjing, which as you know was the capital city of China at that time.

"I left the building with my head abuzz. I would have *walked* to Nanjing if I'd had no other way to get there. I couldn't believe I was going to have a chance to meet again with a man of such extraordinary stature. There was no way I was going to pass up this opportunity, but how to get to Nanjing? My UN position was coming to an end, and while I had the right to stay in China thanks to Madame Sun's letter, now I had no way to earn a living. But a job wasn't the issue I cared about. By this point, I had become totally enthralled with the idea of getting personally involved in what I saw as the most idealistic and most improbable social movement since the French Revolution. Nothing else really mattered to me. I had exactly two hundred dollars to my name: ten twenty-dollar bills. Period. What the hell? I took half of them out of my pocket and bought a plane ticket to Nanjing.

"I don't really know what I was expecting. Once in Nanjing, I had no idea whatsoever how to find Zhou's offices, and many of the people I asked were visibly shocked that I could speak Mandarin and were certainly not about to reveal anything they knew to a Westerner. Everyone I asked was suspicious of my intentions, and scores of inquiries led nowhere. But finally, after three or four days of solid effort—and I'm talking about twelve-hour days—I finally managed to convince a very worried looking gentleman to lead me to Zhou's office. You can't imagine the relief on his face when Zhou's receptionist convinced him he had done the right thing.

"As I waited in the outer office of the humble building, I fully expected to be told to come back in a week for a response, or some such bureaucratic runaround. But no, that's not who Zhou was. He not only came out to greet me personally but actually invited me to dine with him and his wife that evening, along with some other party officials. Can you imagine? At dinner when he asked me about my circumstances, I replied that I had less than a hundred dollars to my name, had no way of earning a living in China, and would probably have little choice but to hitch a ride back to the States on one of the many US steamers heading that way. But Zhou wouldn't hear of it. He strongly encouraged me to stay long enough in China to go to Yan'an and meet Mao. I think what he had in mind was for me to see what the liberated areas looked like so that I would have that information to write and speak about when I returned to the States. If I could get to Yan'an, he promised me, I would be well received.

"And I did get to Yan'an all right, but via a very circuitous route. Northwest China, you see, was behind enemy lines, so I couldn't just go there directly, especially since I was now bereft of the UN identity papers I had had to return at the end of my work. But I had heard that the Communist Party was setting up an English language radio station in the city of Kalgan, which lay in a small neutral area, and I was able to get transport there in the back of a truck. I had no trouble locating the station, and when I offered my services as a native English speaker and made reference to my party contacts in Shanghai to convince people of my bona fides, it worked! I actually considered mentioning my dinner with Zhou and his wife but thought the better of it: Who would believe that? Anyway, within days I had a profession that would allow me to stay in China for the next three decades.

"At the station, I mostly corrected manuscripts that others had translated and trained English language broadcast personnel. And Terry, talk about forming connections and feeling solidarity with those around you; these were remarkable times for me. I found myself constantly more and more enmeshed with people who were actually living out all of the progressive ideals that were so dear to my young heart. And, of course, the magnitude of what they were attempting to pull off was utterly captivating. They were out to completely transform one of the largest, poorest, and most oppressive societies on the face of the Earth. This feeling I had of being so connected with the team at the radio station was like nothing I had ever experienced to that point. It was completely exhilarating. Intoxicating, really.

"It was just about at this time when the mounting tensions between the KMT and Mao's forces blossomed into a shooting war. This increased the element of danger to my work, but I was a kid, so this only heightened my feelings of solidarity with the movement. And then, suddenly, the KMT launched a hugely successful frontal attack on the region and broke through Mao's lines to the north. Just a few days after this, I was asked by party authorities at the radio station to meet with an army general, and I felt certain that he would tell me it was getting too dangerous for a foreigner and that I should head back across the KMT lines. But I was totally wrong. As it turned out, I had by then been fully accepted into the movement, and he *ordered* me to leave for Yan'an to resume my radio broadcast work out there. I couldn't believe my ears. How often in life do you get ordered to do exactly what you dream of doing?

"And so I set off on my second journey across China, but without a jeep this time. I walked most of the distance, but occasionally I found myself on horseback. Needless to say, it took me many months to get to Yan'an, and as you might guess, it was one of the great adventures of my life. The part of China I was crossing was to my eyes a rich and fertile land. I hailed from South Carolina, remember, and I knew rich soil when I saw it. But the history of traditional China—the China that Chiang Kai-shek intended to perpetuate—was a history in which very few had benefited from such extraordinary fertility. Most of the Chinese I met and spoke with on my trek could barely house themselves in stone buildings that wouldn't have looked any different a thousand years earlier. Modern medical care and education were unobtainable luxuries and were not even common concepts. And because it had been this way for thousands of years, the myriad of people I spoke with on my journey couldn't even begin to conceive that anything could ever change. They were completely prepolitical. Life for them was just about scraping out a living, and most of these people had never heard of, let alone taken a position on, the struggle between the Nationalists and the Communists.

"I saw poverty on my long march, to be sure, but rural scarcity is different from urban poverty: it's not as abject, not as lethal. And as my Mandarin improved, and my experience with China expanded, I was able to see more, or I guess I should say, I was able to see more deeply into things. My pilgrimage was a journey through time as much as a journey across the countryside. I was walking through places that looked no different from how they had looked for millennia and where everyday life had never changed. For me, it was also the moment of my full integration into China and its culture. Nothing symbolized this more for me than the night I arrived on horseback at an inn that still had a livery stable. Can you even picture that? When I unpacked the small satchel in which I carried my few possessions, I realized that I hadn't tied it securely, and the small bag in which I kept personal items must have fallen out on the trail that day. In it was my US passport, but I found that I really didn't care. As it turned out, I didn't replace that passport for well over thirty years.

"With no passport, there was only going forward; that was the sole option. But going forward had its challenges. You see, Mao had chosen the northwest corner of China precisely because he knew it was so inaccessible. I walked over rugged countryside, for week, after week, after week. But eventually I arrived in the village of Yan'an in the fall of 1946. And I will never forget the evening I arrived.

"It was a Saturday. And on Saturday nights, it turned out, everyone from all levels of Mao's army *went dancing*. After I had settled into the cabin where I would be staying, I noticed there was hardly anyone around. The little village was absolutely deserted, or so it seemed. Then, at some point, I realized that the music I could barely hear wasn't a radio, as I had first thought, but was live. I followed the sound, and it proved to be coming from a stone building on the edge of town. Being a curious kid, I opened the door and walked right in. The room was full of couples dancing just as they would anywhere, and when my eyes focused on details, I was absolutely stupefied by what I saw: stepping and spinning with a noticeable grace, was none other than Mao Zedong! He looked over, saw me, stopped dancing, and smiled broadly. As I was taken over and introduced to him, the room went silent, and then with a big smile, Mao welcomed me as 'our American comrade.' He no sooner said this than, to my total and complete amazement, the band struck up 'Turkey in the Straw.' I laughed out loud, and Mao joined in at the complete absurdity of it all. Then he signaled me to walk with him to where there were two open chairs along the wall. We sat for quite a while discussing the Spartan life I would be leading—which of course at age twenty-five sounded more romantic than daunting. Other legendary figures entered the dance hall that evening, including Mao's commander-in-chief, Zhu De, and an attractive woman twenty years younger than Mao, who, I later learned, was his third wife, Jiang Qing. Little did I know that many years later she would play a key role in sending me to prison. But then again, little did *she* know that a few years after that, she would end up in the same prison herself.

"Anyway, before I knew it, I was deeply involved in the daily routine and living side by side with the central cadres of the party. We had no choice but to live in actual caves just outside of the village because Yan'an proper had been almost entirely destroyed by Japanese bombing. About three days after I got settled in, I was picked up in a jeep and sat in the back with Mao. I was introduced to those I would be working with, and I was proud this happened in his presence; only later did I come to understand how out of step I was with my childish pride. The antihierarchical pattern of conversation and interaction that were at the very ideological heart of Mao's social movement—and army—meant that the most common foot soldier might find himself conversing with Mao—and not think anything of it. As time went on, and as I saw more of Mao and saw more deeply into the movement he was inspiring, I came to understand that alongside his humility and capacity to relate to even the most humble of his recruits, there was another side to him altogether. Mao had a majestic charisma, a degree of presence that was qualitatively different, even from Zhou and the other central figures of the revolution. There was a remove, a distance; being with him was like being in the presence of a king or a president. But presidents come and go, and dynasties eventually end. Mao seemed different to me. I kept saying to myself, 'I'm talking to a man whose name will be in history books a thousand years from now.'

"As the only native English speaker, my day was mostly spent polishing up the writing of those who translated Chinese texts into English, and working on the spoken English skills of those who did the broadcasts. I can't exaggerate how excited I was about making my humble contribution to the collective effort. I felt one hundred percent connected to everyone around me, and to the cause. It is a remarkable feeling—this connection thing you might write about someday, Terry.

"I had wanted to join the Chinese Communist Party from my days in Kalgan, and now I reopened the topic in Yan'an. It was a good while before a top official called me to a meeting to discuss the matter. He told me there would be an exhaustive background check and that I would need the direct approval of all five members of the Secretariat of the Central Committee, including Mao and Zhou. Eventually, they all agreed, and I became the one and only American admitted into the party.

"But as connected as I was to those around me, deep down in some ways I was still a disconnected 'individual' in the Western sense. I'm not sure you can get that out of you once you're an adult, any more than you can start believing in magic if you've grown up in a world of science. And it wasn't long before this contradiction came bubbling up to the surface. What brought it up were bombs: big, frightening, powerful bombs dropped by the KMT's B-29 bombers and aimed right at us. You see, during this period, Mao's forces were being overrun, and KMT troops had broken through the lines in several sectors. Even the caves of Yan'an were no longer safe, and we spent weeks and weeks retreating through the mountains in an effort to escape the bombardments. So it was fear that brought the Western man out in me, fear that brought the 'I' principle to the fore. On one level, my fears were reasonable: these were very real bombs, and they made enormously loud explosions. Everybody was afraid. But the disconnected man in me reacted so differently from my Chinese compatriots. Something about the character of their connection to one other, about the depth of their cohesion to their collectivity, allowed them to react so differently to the fear they felt. I never saw a single Chinese comrade—man, woman, or even child—run from the trail. Not one. They just kept in line, trekking along the path. But not me. I just couldn't get myself to remain in formation when the explosions began. Something Western in me made me run off by myself in a desperate effort to find a rock outcropping or a thick grove of trees for protection. And this was from deep, deep inside me: I wanted with all my heart to be like the others, but I couldn't stop myself from doing this. And trust me, I tried with all my heart and soul to stop, because everyone noticed, and what I was doing was aberrant and highly embarrassing. But I simply couldn't stop myself.

"So why am I telling you all these details? Because, if I'm not mistaken, they really shine a big, bright light on the issue of connection you asked me to highlight. Here is what I think my inability to stay on the path reveals: Chinese and Western worldviews are radically and fundamentally different on the individual–collectivity issue. I think I'd go so far as to say that the difference is so vast that the perennial Western inquiry about the dynamic between the individual and the collectivity doesn't even arise as a question in the East. I mean it. I've spent a lot of time in Chinese culture, and I've never once heard this issue discussed, let alone debated. In other words, I think philosophizing about the interplay between the individual and society is a purely Western inquiry. In the East, the connection with others and the immersion in the collectivity is so basic to social life and such an integral part of the worldview, and the emphasis on individualism is so limited, that your inquiry might never even arise. This is very important for you to realize, Terry, because while I don't doubt you will someday get around to writing your book, and while I understand the issue of the individual and the collectivity is not precisely the same inquiry as your interest in loneliness and connection, it may be close enough for me to warn you about something: sales of your book in Asia might be terribly modest—or even worse."

*

We both had a good laugh before Sidney stood up, stretched a bit, and suggested we take a break. He offered to refill the humble teapot that had seen so much history and then disappeared into the house. Left alone, I rose and walked out the screen door into the softness of the summer night to stretch my legs in a walk around the yard.

And as I walked, I mulled over what Sidney had said about the depth of the connection he felt in the 1940s to his fellow party militants. While I hadn't participated in any revolutions lately, I could still relate to what he described by thinking back about my involvement in the Free Speech Movement during my undergraduate days at UC Berkeley. The movement, which rocked the Berkeley campus in 1964, drew the attention of the national and international press and launched the worldwide student movement that soon followed. Our initial protest had been against the decision of the university's administration to shut down leafleting at the entrance gate, but it soon blossomed into a generalized intergenerational cultural confrontation, and over the next year morphed into protests against the Vietnam War. Sidney's description of the bonds he had developed with his fellow militants brought flooding back to my memory the powerful solidarity I had felt with the other students and professors in the marches, the rallies, and the ultimately successful campus strike. Sidney was right: concerted and prolonged involvement alongside compatriots in a social movement can forge connections that endure across great expanses of space and time. In the 1960s, I had opportunities to travel not only in Western Europe, but also in parts of Eastern Europe and across all of North Africa, and I remember well that elements of the movement that had begun at Berkeley could be found everywhere. The 1960s were remarkable in this sense. The student movement had produced a connection among young people that I could sense—and act on—everywhere I traveled. If you were wearing any symbols of identification with the movement— old jeans, a blue work shirt, a few beads, long hair, whatever—you could literally go up to another young person just about anywhere on the globe and plug in to the electricity of the bond that united the entire generation. While of course this experience of mine in the student movement of the 1960s paled in the face of Sidney's involvement in the Chinese Revolution, it served to drive home his point about the power of the connection he felt with his fellow militants.

I must have been in my tenth circle around the modest yard when Sidney's gentle voice came wafting out into the stillness of the humid air: "Do you want to go back to China?"

I did indeed.

*

"Anyway, where was I?" Sidney began after we had each sipped at our tea. "Ah, yes. By the spring of 1948, the People's Army had made significant headway against the KMT, and Mao and the other party and military leaders were now centered in mountains only about six or seven hours west of Beijing. My broadcast and language group was moved near these central headquarters, and the air raids and their effect on me were matters of the past. By this time, the intensity of my involvement in the movement was greatly magnified by the fact that victory was clearly just a matter of months away. We worked together, we strolled together in the evenings—and we still went to those Saturday night dances. It was an amazing time for me. Early one misty morning, I was taking a stroll and saw Mao walking alone. He crouched down and spoke easily with peasants who were squatting by a stream, smoking their thin-stemmed pipes. When he finished, he came past me and we chatted in a relaxed fashion about why I was up so early. He said he hadn't even been to bed yet. There was not a hint of what was just around the corner for me.

"It was January of 1949. I couldn't have felt more a part of the whole enterprise. I was told to pack up my few belongings—this teapot was among them—and to prepare for a special assignment in Beijing, which was to be the new capital. I couldn't possibly have been more excited! I had every reason to believe I would be used as a translator in talks that would surely ensue between Mao's new government and the United States, and I relished the idea. Mao, you know, wanted to forge a mutually beneficial working relationship with the US, and I found the idea of participating in that process absolutely exhilarating. But just before I hopped in the jeep that was to take me to Beijing, I heard puzzling news over the wire: Anna Louise Strong, a journalist I knew, had been arrested in Moscow as a State Department spy. This made no sense to me whatsoever. There was no way in the world this lifelong progressive was a spy. But my head was full of the dreams a young man dreams, and off I went.

"It turned out I was not to arrive in Beijing for many, many years. Within a few hours, I was taken to a small building and placed under arrest. It was a decade before I learned it was Stalin who had suggested my arrest, reportedly fearful that if a foreigner from the United States was too close to the Chinese leadership, he might play a role in diluting Soviet influence.

"My clothes were taken from me. I was searched from head to toe and given worn-out black cotton padded pants and a jacket. I was shoved into a tiny cell that was almost completely filled by a brick bed. The only light I was to see for years came from a tiny oil lamp that sat in a notch in the wall. I was in shock, total shock, as you can well imagine. I had been at the center of the revolutionary movement, I had worked alongside its leaders, and I was totally integrated with my peers. Then, just when victory was in sight, I was catapulted into the darkness of solitary confinement in a foul-smelling, cramped little cell. But that turned out to be only the beginning.

"I was almost immediately taken to my first round of interrogations, where I first heard the accusations leveled against me: I had accepted instructions from the United States aimed at sabotaging the Chinese revolution. I was told to confess or suffer the consequences. Of course, I had nothing to confess, so I was in a terrible pickle. It was immediately clear that no confession meant no rehabilitation meant no release. I knew that. But confessing also meant I would lose China and everything I had worked for. And confessing, in effect, could mean I was stateless, since I thought I might have already given up the States by joining the Chinese Communist Party—I wasn't sure. But it didn't matter, because I almost immediately settled on a two-pronged survival strategy: refusal of confession and denial of loneliness.

"After that first interrogation, I was returned to my cell, where life was simple. I had exactly two options: sit on the brick bed, or pace the four small steps it took to cross the room. Meager rations were pushed through a slot in the door three times a day. There was just an arm. I couldn't even see the person who brought the food, and he or she never spoke. That was my entire life.

"So back to your fascination with loneliness and connection, let me tell you what I meant by 'denial of loneliness.' First, I determined that my survival depended on taking the 'solitary' out of solitary confinement. That is, on some level, I needed to not be alone. I hit on the realization that by not revoking my party membership, the Chinese state had given me *exactly* what I needed to pull this off. All I needed to do was to convince myself that I was still connected to other party members, if hampered from seeing them temporarily by the party's need to make certain that a foreigner working so close to the central authorities presented no risk. Strange as this proposition might sound, remember, I had no family or links back to the States to even potentially stand in as the object of my strategic attachment: the single candidate was the very party that was imprisoning me.

"This being decided, I resolved to use this personal reinterpretation of my imprisonment to deal with my grand inquisitor. I quickly settled on the tactic of telling him in each session that I respected his efforts as a party functionary to probe and confirm my devotion to the party and the absence of any duplicity on my part. He seemed to ignore this remark, which I thought was clever on his part, but it was working wonders to help me persevere.

"The interrogations were intermittent. Sometimes they were on consecutive days, sometimes there were months when I saw no one, spoke with no one, and had no relief from my isolation and the all-enveloping darkness. The sessions were designed to be psychologically oppressive, and the interrogator was conversationally violent. But here's the strange part: there were times when I actually welcomed them, primarily because of the human contact, but also because hearing myself praise the interrogator turned out to be an important part of the process of keeping myself convinced about my connection to the party. On the other side, the logic of the inquisitor's interrogation was just what you would expect. I was told to confess my spying and intrigue, in which case the party would be lenient, or to continue to maintain my innocence, in which case there would be no end to my solitary confinement and the hearings would go on indefinitely.

"It wasn't long at all before I was convinced my plan was working. It was clearly helping me avoid the cascade of calamities that would otherwise have been the end of me: loneliness, despair, resignation, and depression. So in each interrogation session, and there must have been a hundred of them over the years—I wasn't counting, when the interrogator had run out of steam for the day and was done screaming at me for being a spy and a traitor to the revolution, I would end the session by reasserting my connection to the party and the remarkable changes it would bring to Chinese society.

"Ah, but grand inquisitors are not without their powers in contending with those who refuse to confess. And mine found his sweet revenge. At some point, I began being forced to take pills three times a day. To this day, I have no idea what they were, but they gave me horrific nightmares and greatly weakened my mental capacities. And without control of my mind, I worried about the viability of my strategy of elevating a mental construct of connectedness over the all too palpable reality of how alone I actually was. If my plan failed, I was sure I'd go mad. I told the guards, and the grand inquisitor, that the pills made me ill, but they couldn't have cared less. I was still compelled to take them. Days and weeks went by that I couldn't account for, and in the darkness of the room, the hopelessness and timelessness of my situation began to blend with the torment of my drug-induced dreams. Strange visions flowed through my mind; images from my memory played with one another. There were mingled visions of Mao and of a gorilla and of me dancing with Ginger Rogers and God knows what else. Weeks and then months went by like this. I had no way to keep track of time.

"And then, two years into my imprisonment, I was blindfolded, put on the back of a truck, and, after about half a day, delivered to another facility. My room was a touch larger, but as before, the windows were completely boarded up. The nightmares continued, but now that the pills were discontinued, I regained the mental strength that I needed to hold fast to my survival strategy. And in the second lockup, from time to time I was taken out into a small courtyard. What a treat! By then

I was too weak to do anything but lie on the ground, but it was such a blessed relief to see even a tiny bit of sky. I used to lie on my back and savor every cloud that floated by. And then one day, a bird flew through my little rectangle of sky and my heart and soul were lifted on high. I can sit here tonight and remember with astonishing clarity the sight of that bird and the metaphor it represented for me of sticking with my plan. The one-second view I had of that solitary bird made all the difference. I redoubled my determination to get through my imprisonment and back into life.

"In my new prison, the cell was two steps longer, but the food was three steps worse. I was so hungry and wasting away from the thin soup and small quantities of rice that I was given, that I readily ate the crickets that found their way into my cell.

"But by and by, my strength got too meager for me to even move around enough to catch the crickets. At this point, I was near the edge mentally, no doubt in part because of the long period of taking those damn pills, but mostly because of my isolation and aching lonesomeness. I just didn't have the strength anymore to do what I needed to do, and as a consequence of this, I lost control of myself for the only time in all those years. A guard yelled at me for no reason, and instead of congratulating him on his acts in support of the revolution, I gave him a push. Oh boy, what a mistake that was. For months and months after that, I had to wear crude handcuffs that hurt my wrists. Worse still, with the restraints on, I definitely couldn't catch any more crickets, so day by day I became yet weaker and more despondent. Apparently even the little bit of protein they had contributed to my diet had made a critical difference. And so, after all my efforts to keep it together— physically and psychologically—I found myself beginning to give up, ready to let myself descend into loneliness and despair and malnutrition the way a man overboard must at some point stop paddling about and just allow himself to sink below the surface of the sea.

"Ah, but I was not the only player in the game. For some unknown reason, the prison authorities were determined to prevent me from letting myself die, and that's what surely would soon have happened. One day, when I couldn't even stand up anymore to greet him—which was required protocol—the warden came in and told me that the party was making progress on my case. That day, the handcuffs were removed, and the following week, they took the boarding down off the windows. I remember well what it felt like to have the summer light come flooding in. It filled the cell's darkness the way water from a tap fills a glass, and it lifted my spirits just like that solitary bird had done so many months before. Within a few more months, my rations were improved, and so my strength started to return. And blessing of blessings, they allowed me to read. Sometimes I think that the newspapers they brought in were just as important to me as the additional food, because they connected me once again to the outside world. I remember grabbing the first paper the guard brought to see the date: it was midspring, 1950. I'd been completely alone in the second cell, and completely in the dark, for almost two years.

"One thing I've always remembered is that after not having had a conversation for years on end—I don't count the harangues and my responses in the interrogation room as conversations—I could barely put together enough words to converse. Following the easing of my conditions, the warden told me that if I wanted to go back to the States, that could be arranged. But like I told you, Terry, I had no connections to go back home; there was nobody to rejoin. So returning to the States just wasn't at all an attractive option. In contrast, if I remained firm with my conviction to stay in China, I could nurse the hope of being released and rehabilitated and reactivated in my work. And I was still a member of the party; they never threw me out for some reason. But you know what else I thought? I thought part of the revolution was mine, goddamn it, and I wanted my share of what I had helped make.

"In the spring of 1955, a man I had never seen before came to my cell and told me that the investigation of my case was complete. As of that day I was free to leave. He gave me the official characterization of what had happened: I had been wrongfully charged and improperly imprisoned, and he apologized in the name of the People's Republic. I was elated, of course, but for some reason I burst into tears. When he asked me how I was doing, I told him that physically, I would soon return to form, but that politically, I was not the same person who entered prison six years earlier. When he asked me what I meant, I told him—and anyone else who asked for the next couple of months—that

I had learned from the experience that my personal affairs should always take a backseat to my connection to the party. I remember this stranger giving just the tiniest of chuckles at my remark. It took me another twenty years to fully appreciate what those chuckles meant.

"I was out. I was finally out of prison. But it took time to put what had happened to me in perspective, and I didn't get everything right. In reestablishing my role in the party, I committed an error that was to cost me dearly: I conveniently forgot that my 'connection to the party' for all those years in prison had been nothing but a fantasy. Somehow, I allowed myself to be convinced that I had actually grown and bene-fited from the experience and that I had finally learned how to control my Western individualism. After all, my stay-connected-to-the-party scheme had been vindicated: it had saved my sanity, and quite proba-bly my life. Maybe it had, but that didn't make it anything other than a strategically useful fiction. But this was not at all the same thing as being a fundamentally remade man. Was I correct in thinking that the new me would stay walking on the path with the others as the bombs came raining down? Could imprisonment have actually changed the leopard's stripes? You'll have to judge for yourself as I tell you the rest of my story."

*

But there was to be no second half to the story Sidney was telling—or not for years to come. Yulin had approached so quietly that I hadn't even noticed her. But Sidney had.

"Sweetheart, perhaps you should think about coming to bed," Yulin said. "It's well past two o'clock in the morning, and you have a class to teach tomorrow."

"Of course. You're right, dear. I'll be right in."

"I'm so sorry," I said. "I feel guilty about keeping you up. I had no idea it was so late."

"No, no, it was my pleasure. It does me good to keep these memo-ries alive and vibrant. I suppose there's some kind of ongoing therapy in it for me. But I've only told you half the tale. Would you like to hear the rest another time?"

"I'd walk to Yan'an to hear it."

"Ha! You've been listening! Give me a call in about a week and we'll set something up."

*

I was so energized by Sidney's astonishing story that I didn't for a moment regret the two-hour-long drive I faced heading down the Massachusetts coast to the small seaside town where I kept my sailboat. At noon my close friend and I were to race her, and I looked forward to the cleansing effect the wind and waves would have on both the long week's work and the very thought of eating crickets. Sidney's story reverberated through me. As I drove, vivid images flipped through my mind. One frightened me deeply and literally made me shiver: the concept of spending *years* in a dark, dank cement cell with no natural light. I kept picturing Sidney walking the four little steps back and forth in the dim light of the one small oil lamp, day after day, month after month, year after year. I barely noticed the drive; some other, automated part of my brain took over to make the turns and stops.

I really didn't become fully aware of where I was until I arrived on the beach in front of the sailing club where I kept my little fifteen-foot boat. It was just after four o'clock in the morning when I parked and walked out to the beach. A nearly full moon lit the sky halfway to day and reflected off the stillness of the nighttime sea. Almost in a trance, I began to walk south along the beach, unable to stop imagining the scenes and settings from Sidney's tale.

In fact, my mind was a big movie screen of images. I pictured Sidney driving at fifteen miles per hour all the way south to Shanghai, passing through the abject urban and coastal poverty of postwar China. And over and again my mind ran the film of Sidney walking across the rural planes of central China as he made his way west to Yan'an. I could hear the mingled babble of the conversations he fell into with peasant farmers along his path, and I could picture him absorbing what he learned from them—about their way of life, about their timeless, hopeless subjugation to the ever-present poverty that rural China had always known. And I could visualize this boy from South Carolina, who knew rich soil when he felt it, squatting and crumbling the dark-brown loam between his fingers, adding up what all this meant when you put it all together.

On and on I walked, and image after image flowed through my white-night mind: Mao ballroom dancing, Sidney running from the path as bombs fell nearby, Mao's generals waiting in line with peasant soldiers to use the latrines. But something in me I couldn't identify was deeply disturbed, causing all the images, each and every one of them, to lead back to Sidney's cell. My meandering, beach-walking brain did what it willed, taking me back to the prisons I had seen, to the cells of clients who waited for a young lawyer to work miracles he could not achieve, cells where there was not a moment of relief from the hard and the cold; cells that didn't distinguish violent criminals from petty thieves; cells that didn't care about guilt or innocence. Saddest of all, *each and every one* of my clients was innocent—or so they claimed—even if not a hint of evidence in any client's favor ever came my way.

A large wave slapped down on the sand and sent a flash of sensation racing through me, sending me back to the sound of a prison cell door slamming shut, to the sour smell of imprisoned men, and to the repellent sound of their fabrications and empty pipe dreams. Then came that day—that moment—when I knew I could take no more of the cells and the smells, and from then on, I referred out every criminal case that was offered to me, passing them to other counsel who could somehow stomach, somehow live with all the hard surfaces and the even harder people that make up the world of jails and prisons. My mind traveled back to Sidney: How had he ever survived his? How had he ever stayed so gentle? How had he managed to elude loneliness and despair and despondency? I had absolutely no idea. I remembered his words, of course, what he had said during the evening about his strategy of imagining himself as remaining connected, holding on to the party the way a man overboard in the ocean holds on to a life buoy. But his words, his thoughts, were just that—words and thoughts, and the more they ran through my flustered mind, the less I understood how they had been enough to overcome the hard cold stone of his cell, and the life-crushing force of long-term imprisonment.

Finally, the first rays of the rising sun broke through my strange trance. I headed off in my little sailboat across Buzzards Bay toward Cape Cod, and the effects of wind and water soon cleared my senses of the residue of my memories. Sidney's words were still with me, to be sure, but the sensations they had generated in me from my brief foray into criminal law gradually quieted as I guided the little craft along the peaks of the ocean waves that built rapidly as the tide and the current battled one other.

Two hours later, I headed back across the bay to find my friend and sailing partner, for to race these little boats takes a crew of two. And as we sped along that afternoon—as always vying with one or two other boats to stay out of last place—I took note of the coordinated efforts we made at bow and helm, at the smiles and wisecracks and nonsense that make up friendship. I thought long and hard—probably to the detriment of our results—about the beauty of *not* finding oneself alone, about the serenity in finding oneself connected to others. As I sat at the helm, maneuvering the boat against other pairs of friends toward the finish line, I thought about what I had learned from Sidney's story—a story about sometimes being too connected and sometimes being too alone. It's important, my mind rambled on, to be able to be alone, to be at peace with oneself, and to maintain one's integrity, even in a crowd. But it's equally important to be connected to others, to nurture the attachments one has to family and friends, which protect against loneliness the way an umbrella protects against rain. The challenge, I said to myself, is to be able to do a good job of being alone and a good job of being together; two very different skills indeed.

The other challenge, of course, is to keep your eye on what you're doing. I didn't, and we lost the race. But you know what? When we got to the bar and had a beer with the other pairs of friends in the race who'd beaten us, it didn't make any difference at all.

*

When I called Sidney a week later, his schedule had changed dramatically, and there was no time for him to tell me the rest of his tale. The academic season soon ended, and he and Yulin returned to their home on the West Coast. The opportunity was lost, and I was heartbroken about it. I did, however, pick up a copy of his autobiography, which he had told me about, and a great deal of the story was available in its narrative. But as informative and as well written as the book was, I so missed Sidney's running commentary. And I especially missed his laughter.

*

Just over three years later, destiny intervened. A new case came into the office that would take me to China, and to an unforgettable afternoon during which Sidney would complete the tale as he guided me through the streets of Beijing.

For a long time, I had served as general counsel to a children's social welfare agency located in a coastal city in southern Massachusetts. The agency was able to provide a wide range of counseling and associated services to its clients principally because of the profitability of its large and successful adoption program. Throughout the nineteenth and first two-thirds of the twentieth century, the babies placed by the program had arrived in a steady flow from young women who found themselves inconveniently pregnant. But by the late 1970s, advancement in the efficacy and availability of birth control, and a concomitant reduction in the stigma attached to raising a child born out of wedlock, had almost completely eliminated the domestic source of babies. Then came China's infamous one-child policy, and suddenly Chinese orphanages were inundated with accidental second children—and especially with baby girls rejected by families anxious to try again for a male heir. Adoption agencies across the Western world were thrilled to step in; this new source of adoptable infants was a godsend to the ever-increasing number of couples with fertility issues. That's when the proverbial bomb went off.

The explosive device in question was a certified letter that arrived in the name of the CEO of each adoption agency that had been placing these Chinese children for adoption. In one brief paragraph, it announced that the Chinese state's policy on the matter had changed, and there would be no more international adoption allowed from

Chinese orphanages. Needless to say this caused panic in these agencies, since there was no other available source of babies to fill the empty cribs of the growing numbers of infertile young couples. Within minutes after opening the letter, Jim Sanders, the executive director of one of the children's social services agencies I represented, called me to inquire about the legality of the abrupt termination of the contract the agency had had with three Chinese orphanages. He mentioned that the scuttlebutt in the industry was that an underminister in Beijing had made the decision on purely ideological grounds. Apparently, this bureaucrat had decided it was scandalous to ship these socialist babies abroad to be turned into capitalist adults.

Sanders asked me if I could contact Sidney, whose life story he knew about only because I had loaned him my copy of Sidney's autobiography. He also mentioned that he had formed a consortium with seven other Massachusetts adoption agencies to look into whether there was any chance of appealing the policy change to the Chinese state. He said he was authorized to ask me if I would represent the consortium in its efforts to seek relief, and I readily agreed.

What a splendid excuse to call Sidney! Since their immigration to the States, Sidney and Yulin had launched a consulting operation that connected US business clients with appropriate government agencies or companies in China, making good use of Sidney's extraordinary set of contacts throughout the Chinese state. After we exchanged pleasantries, I asked Sidney how I might go about contacting someone to explore if there was any possibility of a reconsideration of the new state policy on international adoption. He responded that he had no idea whatsoever which ministry would have been involved, but that he would research the matter and get back to me.

When Sidney called back ten or twelve days later, he had good news: there was a likely solution to the problem. He had located the minister's superior, who (no surprise here) Sidney had known for thirty years. After only a week's investigation, this gentleman had returned Sidney's call to say that his review of the matter had determined that the change in policy engineered by his overenthusiastic underling was untenable. Apparently there was a virtual flood of abandoned baby girls unable to be placed with adoptive parents within China, and there was no other sensible solution beyond reopening opportunities for international adoption. This was great news indeed. Better news yet was Sidney's proposal that I arrange to meet him in Beijing the following month, when he would be there anyway. He would schedule a formal meeting with the state minister at which I, as the representative of a consortium of US adoption agencies, would formally request the policy reversal, which would then give Sidney's contact the opening he needed to raise the issue with his supervisee.

The following day, I reached Jim Sanders. He was thrilled to learn what I shared and told me he wanted to send the director of the agency's adoption department along with me to visit and appraise the three orphanages from which the agency's children came. Five weeks later, on a stunning early summer afternoon, I stepped off an airplane in Beijing, China.

The next morning, on a bright and sunny day, we visited a titanic orphanage facility that housed over seven hundred children. The industrial-sized, multistory, whitewashed cement building was composed of mammoth rooms, each holding children by age group. Two of the rooms contained hundreds of evenly spaced cribs for the babies. That's a lot of babies: you never heard such a racket. The adjacent, cavernous room was for the one-year-olds, the next one for toddlers, then one for three-year-olds, and so on. To my unknowledgeable eye, the agency seemed clean and professionally administered. But best of all, and this was clearly visible, the state policy of creating work for everybody paid off big time in this particular industry. There were scores and scores of employees milling about, which meant there were plenty of people to pick up the children and coddle them. It was quite a sight. I even joined in, holding one darling little ten-month-old for a good forty-five minutes as we were shown around. It wasn't at all easy to replace her in crib number 233 at the end of our visit. I can still picture the look in her beautiful dark eyes that so clearly said, "Are you *sure* you don't want to take me home?" I wasn't at all sure. The children made me think of puppies in a pet store—searching for love and connection.

A cab picked us up from the orphanage and took us to meet Sidney in front of the ministerial office where the official meeting with the state minister was to be held. The meeting itself took place in the classic

Chinese government format we all know from television coverage of Mao's meetings with visiting diplomats. We sat around the perimeter of the room in large, overstuffed armchairs, each adorned with an anti-macassar. Sidney, of course, served as translator, and after pleasantries were exchanged, on behalf of the consortium of adoption agencies, I formally presented the request that the recent change in the Chinese state's international adoption policy be reviewed. I had the distinct impression, given Sidney's background conversations with the minister, that the outcome had been entirely prearranged and that the matter would be favorably resolved. The meeting then turned to a constructive and valuable conversation about some potential logistical improvements in the international adoption process that would be put in place "if indeed the request met with a favorable outcome."

At the conclusion of the meeting, the minister invited us all to a restaurant for what turned out to be an unforgettable state luncheon. I will never, for example, forget the beauty of one of the many courses we were served. It made dazzling use of a particularly large circular platter that was placed in the middle of the round table. The platter presented fried whole miniature squabs, each one resting in its own thoroughly realistic-looking "nest." These nests were made from fine intertwined fried noodles, and each was dyed to take on the subtle irregularities that we all know from inspecting a fallen bird's nest. But even more amazing was the tray's central décor: rising up eighteen inches, sitting on its cut-off end, was two-thirds of a green melon that was perhaps nine or ten inches in diameter. The melon's green skin had provided a kitchen artist with a palette, and he had carved the entire melon into a scene of a rocky mountain escarp with streams and bridges and trees, and even in one place a tiny boat being paddled by minutely carved seated rowers. The white skin of the melon's meat showed through the carving, and the effect was to reproduce, with extraordinary finesse and subtlety, the sort of mountain scene typical in ancient Chinese scroll paintings. As an amateur cook by hobby and the son of a professional caterer, I was floored by the craftsmanship that went into making this stunning dish.

But I digress. As we left the restaurant, the minister excused himself, and the agency's adoption program director chose to return to the hotel for a rest. Sidney asked me if I would like to spend the afternoon having a tour of the city, which was the second easiest question I have ever been asked. I jumped at this opportunity of being guided through Beijing by someone who knew it so well, and of course, I also desperately wanted to hear the second half of the remarkable story of Sidney's life in China. Something about the tale having been halted halfway through had kept its early chapters incredibly fresh in my mind. I still, for example, maintained a vivid image of Sidney chasing down the ill-fated crickets that wandered into his prison cell.

So you won't be surprised to learn that not long at all after Sidney and I had begun our walking tour of Beijing, I unabashedly asked if at some point during the day he minded recounting the second part of his adventures in China. My request elicited his characteristic youthful sounding laugh—and an admission: "I was hoping you'd ask." Then he giggled once again and shot me his patented smile: it had the warmth of the summer sun to it.

I mentioned that since I had seen him in Cambridge, I had read his autobiography but that I was immensely curious to hear in person his description of his second stint of solitary confinement. I asked him if he would describe his survival strategy this second time around, and if it again was centered on maintaining connections by force of mind to avoid the pitfalls of loneliness.

"I can hardly believe our last conversation was already years ago. Time flies by," I commented.

"Not when you're in solitary confinement," Sidney chimed in with another laugh. He seemed almost anxious to switch into his storytelling tone of voice and continue the tale of his life in China, and as we wound our way through mile after mile of Beijing's ancient streets, Sidney completed the story, pausing in his narrative from time to time, to give me his illuminating explanations about the city's sites and its rapidly changing profile.

"I'm pretty sure that when we ended that evening in Cambridge," Sidney began, "I had just been released from my first imprisonment and reassured that I remained a member in good standing of the Communist Party. At that time, my English language skills were more in demand than ever, and I was anxious to return to work, as you might imagine. But as it turned out, the years of solitary confinement had had a very debilitating effect on my social interaction skills. You know, Terry, when you present yourself to others in the world who don't know you—say to a shopkeeper—you have to have a certain degree of presence, of self-assuredness, even in something as petty as ordering up what you want to purchase. My problem was that my coerced subservience to the guards and the inquisitors during my confinement had completely eroded my self-confidence and my ability to present myself to others. These skills of everyday life came back, to be sure, but not without a good deal of work. One thing I learned for sure: human beings are absolutely *not* designed to live isolated and alone without interaction, conversation, expression, and touch. I remember at the time analogizing my having lost my social skills to what happens to your car when you don't start it up for a few years. A lot of rust under the social hood!"

Again the lightness of his laughter rang out in the Beijing summer. "And, there was a second remnant of my imprisonment to break free of as well, and that took quite a bit longer to put behind me. I was cautious, very cautious—even borderline paranoid—about being followed and watched and rearrested on some trumped-up charge. The strange part was, that while I was fearful of making a misstep vis-à-vis the party, at the same time the only connection I had to *anything or anybody* was through it. I had no links left to the States at that point, none whatsoever. And my life in China at that point was without attachments as well. I had no wife, no kids, and for that matter, no friends. I only had acquaintances, and those I had aplenty. Remember, I was a public figure, and most people I encountered on the street recognized me from articles in the press about my history, my rehabilitation, and my service to the party. Many admired my resilience in prison, and it was fairly widely known that I was the only American member ever admitted to the party, at least at that point. Moreover, I was a party member whose membership dated back to Yan'an, and that had a certain cachet, I can assure you. So while I was definitely wary of how quickly things could change in revolutionary China, on balance, my connection to the party was intensified rather than reduced by the party having imprisoned me. Strange situation I was in, wasn't it?

"Anyway, before long I was fully ready to reengage, and right away I found employment at the Broadcast Administration. This vast state agency is in charge of all the state-owned mass media, both print and broadcast. My supervisor immediately pointed out to me that I was the *only* party member in the entire Foreign Broadcast Department and that I would be reading and working with highly classified documents and information. So just a month after my release, I could only interpret the fact that I was being trusted with state secrets to mean that I was being granted acceptance back into the inner circle of the party. Obviously, the effect of this was to put the prison experience behind me and out of mind all the more quickly.

"But while I eventually moved beyond what had been done to me, I don't want to minimize its effect on me. For the first few months after I was pardoned, I slept fitfully and woke suddenly, often in a cold sweat. During this period, I suffered nightmares almost nightly that carried me back into my cell and nearly suffocated me with the feelings and sensations of the crushing loneliness I had known. But as I reconnected with the world, these frightening flashbacks tapered off, the sensations of being so disconnected subsided, and within three or four months, the past had been put behind me, or so I thought.

"But let's talk about my work in the Broadcast Administration. I think you might find it interesting how I experienced the ambiguities and contradictions inherent in what I was doing. On one level, I arrived at the point of convincing myself that the manipulation of information delivered through the mass media was an entirely legitimate practice for instructing people about policy decisions taken by the authorities. But at the same time, on another level, there was always a faint little freedom-of-the-press voice deep down in the middle of my being that from time to time would inject itself into my work. Years later, that little voice inside me would break out and land me back in prison during the Cultural Revolution.

"But to return to 1955 for the moment, I was positively amazed by how China had changed while I was locked away. There simply was no comparison with how it had been just after the war. Now there was no visible poverty, no military presence, no pickpockets, no prostitutes, no beggars. And how clean Beijing was! The ubiquitous litter that had covered the wide boulevards and sidewalks was gone, and the streets were pristine. There was no question about it: Beijing in 1955 was a far, far better place than it had been in 1945. Mao, of course, was now chairman of the party that governed the country, and Zhou Enlai was premier and a top-level international diplomat. The two other men who had originally sponsored my application to join the party were now state ministers. In 1955, as I told you, anyone who had been in Yan'an was guaranteed a high-level career and was known and admired. As I walked down the street—and, obviously, I wasn't hard to spot—I was somewhat seduced by the attention paid to me, I have to admit.

"But that wasn't why I stayed. It wasn't about fame, or power, or influence; that's not me. It was about involvement, inclusion, and connection. By the time I emerged from prison, more or less everything in China had changed for the better. These early years of the new China were incredibly exhilarating times. I had never experienced such generalized unselfishness and sincere devotion to working for the common good. Even the Mandarin pronouns that were commonly used were noticeably different: you heard 'us,' 'we,' and 'ours,' much more than you heard 'me,' 'I,' or 'mine.' And on top of all this, during this period there was a considerable degree of democratic process taking place in every village, every office, and every school—all manner of things that had historically been dictated from on high were now discussed and debated at a local level. This was the golden period of the revolution, the zenith of popular involvement in decision-making. You want to study connection and solidarity for that book of yours? Focus on this time frame in China. *Everyone* in the country felt connected and integrated into the new China. You can't imagine the amount of good will that was part of everyday life. There were no strangers, no outsiders during this honeymoon period. If you saw a piece of trash in the street, you picked it up and put it in a trash can just as you would inside your own home. It was an absolutely intoxicating moment in history. The entire society operated like a sports team: it was all about the common cause. It was an amazing experience to be part of.

"But this was not to last. With the advantage of hindsight, I would say that the first sign of the changes to come appeared as early as 1956, when we were told that Mao, Liu Shaoqi, Deng Xiaoping, and others had launched a movement asking all persons to be on the lookout for counterrevolutionaries and secret agents. And here's the tough part of my story to relay to you: I was deeply involved in this process as a reviewer of the dossiers of others. We looked at 'bad' backgrounds, such as bourgeois origins, and at 'ideological deviancy.' I didn't see it at the time, but these were signs that a more autocratic, more centralized form of state was coming. Later in my life, when I had nearly a decade in solitary confinement to contemplate all this, I asked myself a thousand times how I could have been so blind.

"Actually, 'being blind' is an inadequate metaphor. No one chooses to be blind. To be honest with you, if *anyone* should have been aware of the direction things were heading, it should have been me because my work at the Broadcast Administration and my high-security clearance meant that I was one of the few people who had access to real news. Every day I read the *New York Times*, *Le Monde*, and *La Prensa*, as well as all the required internal party bulletins. But even with this advantage, I failed to question the meaning of the ever-increasing number of directives that I received, nor did I take note that each one progressively constricted what I could say and how I was to say it. This was unpardonable on my part, because as these directives became ever more restrictive and detailed, they became increasingly absurd. How could I have missed what was happening? How did I fail to even perceive what all this meant? Whether or not I could have done anything about it was a different matter altogether, obviously. The exception that proves the rule: I do remember one directive that was so extreme that it surprised even compliant me. It was directed at controlling the 'propaganda tone,' which at that point was an entirely new focus. The directive promulgated detailed directions as to whether a particular topic should be presented in an enthusiastic tone, or in a neutral or a cool tone. I remember thinking that this one was clearly excessive, but that didn't constitute questioning it, and it certainly didn't constitute disputing it. So the overall truth is, I simply *failed to perceive* the erosion of democratic input that all of this signaled. It happened step, by step, by step—and I was part of it."

*

"So skip ahead to the mid-1960s when the Cultural Revolution was just beginning. While Mao had on several occasions purposefully, and very unsuccessfully, attempted to manipulate and stimulate the Chinese economy from the top, the Cultural Revolution came from the base. In some ways, it paralleled the contemporaneous student movements in the West, or seemed to at the time. In this sense, it was a social movement that came *at* the state from young students and young men in the army. It first appeared in the guise of the famous *Little Red Book* that contained Mao's most well-known sayings. Soon after that, teenage student activists, wearing red armbands that said 'Red Guards,' became more and more active and ever bolder in their criticism of centralized power. I should have sensed the anarchy that lay just below the surface, but I never saw it at the time. I was married by then, having children with my lovely wife, Yulin—whom you met in Cambridge—and totally connected and involved in the movement and the events. It seemed as if the movement would bring democracy to China's socialism; finally there would be a democratic socialist state. Or so I thought.

"My fall from grace, while long in the making, began when I was solicited by a group of Red Guards to give a talk on the international situation. Foolishly, I agreed to do so. In reference to the situation in Vietnam, which I had visited in a semiofficial capacity, I articulated my personal views on what was then a very hot issue concerning the internal politics of the South Vietnamese Viet Cong. The Red Guards, despite a promise not to do so, published my little speech in their newspaper, and as it turned out, the point I had made was entirely contradictory with the official Chinese stance. Given the position of authority I held, it was ambiguous whether my words were or were not intended to be taken as a new position of the Chinese Communist Party on the war in Vietnam. Nothing happened immediately, but this transgression set in play the machinery that would lead to my downfall.

"The level of chaos brought on by the Cultural Revolution grew almost daily. It was essentially a civil war, although along very unclear lines. Then one day, the Red Guards, who had up to this point been afforded an almost unbridled degree of discretion, made a fatal faux pas when they attempted to import their movement into the army. Mao had strictly prohibited this, and for him this was the final act. He simply announced the end of the movement through a supreme directive: all factions were to reconcile, unite, and return to normal work. Period. It all ended that abruptly.

"But not for me. When the reconciliation made its way over to the Broadcast Administration, I was excluded from the newly appointed power structure and told to wait at home for a special assignment. Week after week I waited with no word. Then one day a friend stopped by to show me a photograph from an English language magazine. It was a picture I knew well. Originally the photograph had been printed in the official party newspaper, *The People's Daily*, and it showed me standing with Mao, Zhou Enlai, and Jiang Qing. In the new version, I had been airbrushed out. Not a good sign.

"Posters attacking me soon began to appear throughout Beijing. Next the disconnecting began—literally. My security pass at the Broadcast Administration was canceled and collected at my door by a functionary. Friends stopped coming by to visit me and Yulin. Then, one day, Yulin was told that her work was terminated as well. The next week, taunting Red Guards showed up in front of our house. Next, on Christmas Day 1967, a spokesman for the Broadcast Administration came to our house to tell me I was under house arrest, and that I would be subject to a series of interrogations. Soon after that, even more ominous news reached me: Mao's wife, Jiang Qing, was denouncing me as an American spy. In February 1968, I was arrested, and unbeknownst to me, after I was imprisoned, Yulin and the children were also taken into police custody. I didn't even know about that for years to come.

"Imagine the transition for me: At one moment, I was connected to countless others in an all-consuming social movement. On top of this, I had Yulin, and we had four beautiful little children—two of whom you had dinner with all that time ago. And then the next thing I knew, I found myself entirely alone and cut off from everybody and everything—not to mention being once again thrown into a small, dank cell to serve an indeterminate sentence of solitary confinement. From being as connected as possible, I went to as disconnected as possible. I was devastated.

"Being married and the father of the cutest little kids you ever saw made this second imprisonment very different. Very, very different, and very, very difficult. I went from rolling around on the floor with my kids playing all sorts of silly games to being completely removed from them for the indefinite future. I don't know how other prisoners with families handle this kind of loss and isolation, but I had to handle my separation from Yulin and the children in my own way because I knew that my mental stability depended on it. I concluded that my only hope was to actively avoid thinking about them. At all. Otherwise, the pain was just too great. And I knew the prison officials would use any suffering I evidenced against me. So as much as possible, I actively shut them out of my mind. That sounds terrible, I know. But I had no choice.

"The hardest moment each day was waking up. Somehow, my sleeping mind knew what I would face upon waking, and it seemed that as time went on, I sank deeper and deeper inside myself each night, so that opening my eyes was harder and harder to accomplish each day. It was like being underwater and paddling madly to the surface for a gasp of air. Each day that I awoke, I began from farther down beneath the waves. Often, I actually found myself gulping air when I first woke up.

"You asked about whether I used the same psychological approach I had during the first imprisonment to get through the second. The answer is no. It was clear to me that I couldn't use anything like the same technique that had sustained me in prison the first time around. The party itself was too divided, too devastated by the Cultural Revolution, and way too undemocratic to have any further allure for me. Besides, soon after I was arrested, I was shown a copy of my arrest order: it had been personally signed by Mao, Jiang Qing, Zhou Enlai, and all the other high officials whom I had known, worked closely with, and had so greatly admired. Clearly, I was no longer welcome to be part of it all, nor did I want to be.

"My survival strategy therefore had to be totally different. The first time it was all about staying connected to the East; this time it was about getting reconnected to the West. Something inside me stirred and awakened; then it sprouted and grew. Each day I could feel an expanding reassertion of my *droits de l'homme*, my *rights* to be treated fairly, my *rights* to due process. Increasingly I felt wronged—greatly wronged—at being imprisoned and deprived of my family. I had done nothing illegal or in bad faith. Not even close. Firing me from my position at the Broadcast Administration was arguably justified, given my faux pas in speaking publicly about Vietnamese politics, but there was no cause to imprison me. This time I was infuriated at the party for transgressing my *rights as an individual* without even a nod to due process. And outrage led to disillusionment, which led to detachment. And with the detachment from China came a regeneration of my attachment to America. I was ready now to take my family to where the rule of law and the respect for human rights made life predictable and safe. So I knew early on during my second imprisonment that this time, if I got out alive, I would return to the States with Yulin and the children. From the moment I made this decision, I saw myself as an American citizen again and spent a great deal of time thinking about what that meant to me. And this time around, *that* was the connection that helped me overcome the desolation and despair of being so isolated, and so profoundly lonely. Every day, this reborn connection to the States became ever more vivid and concrete in my mind as I lay there on my brick bed.

"I realize looking back that the language of my reawakened connection to the values of the West was more feeling than thought. I was too devastatingly hungry to think rationally, and my ravenous hunger caused me to have powerful dreams—dreams that could overtake my mind at any hour of the day. Wild visions popped up and ran through my mind: I remember holding personal conversations with Voltaire and Montesquieu and other great French intellectuals who conceived and authored *les droits de l'homme.* These took place in flawless French, no less, though in college I'd always been a C student in the language. Thomas Jefferson and I also met often to discuss such matters, and we talked a great deal about how we Americans owe a great debt to the French for the ideas that underlay our Bill of Rights. In my confused state of mind, these historical giants seemed almost like friends—and ever more so as month after month passed by. And the more I attached myself to the values and great statesmen of the West, the more I rejected my links to the East.

"While my internal life was completely different this second time around, my physical setting and daily life was essentially identical. I was once again held in a small solitary confinement cell and, for a second time, subjected to brutal interrogations. The cell was formed of ancient stones, irregularly piled into uneven walls. These stones made the room bone-chillingly cold; the walls seemed to delight in drawing heat out of me. Sound, however, somehow made its way through the solid walls, and I could hear other prisoners being physically tortured, although I never was.

"The process of trying to break me so that I would confess that I was involved in espionage involved eliminating all regularity and certainty of treatment and routine. Weeks of listening to the terrifying sounds of prisoners being tortured, for instance, would be followed by periods—including interludes of months on end—when I could hear absolutely nothing. Even the arm that placed my tin plate of meager rations through an opening low on the door, took great care to make no sound. Then, without warning, I would be grasped from the jaws of silence and thrown into progressively more aggressive and terrifying weeks of interrogation. In these sessions, I was screamed at, drilled with the same questions dozens and dozens of times, insulted, and belittled in every way imaginable. Whatever I said was thrown back in my face. There was no response, shy of confessing, that would bring relief. But like the first time, I was determined not to concede. I would have preferred death. And, of course, the more it became evident that I wasn't going to crack, the more my new grand inquisitor ratcheted up his shrieking attacks. Sometimes these were done from where he sat across the interrogation table, sometimes he came around the table and stood nose to nose with me, covering my face with his spittle as he shouted his insults and accusations.

"These interrogation sessions continued for three full years. Above and beyond being aimed at breaking me psychologically, the interrogations were designed to be physically taxing. I was often kept standing for hours on end and given no water. While I was never physically tortured, I was constantly threatened with it, and even threatened with the prospect of being executed. I would come out of these long, brutal sessions tired to the bone, craving sleep. But the guards were instructed to wake me throughout the night by screaming insults at me through the tray delivery hole in the door. I was treated as the lowest of the low; not a single vestige of privilege remained from the high position I had held—absolutely none.

"But, goddamn it, I was determined to survive. This time there was much to live for. The thinnest of soups and bits of bread revived my taste for crickets; that, apparently, is the effect of the total absence of protein in the diet. But there was a problem this time around. The urban setting of my new political prison meant that I had to settle for cockroaches; there were no nice clean rural crickets on the menu. Never mind. I ate the roaches with gusto and a fierce resolve to survive. I exercised as best I could in my tiny cell, but over time as I grew weaker, this became ever more difficult. I was increasingly dizzy, and then my vision began to blur.

"But let's face it, I was an experienced prisoner by this time, and that helped enormously. I knew from the beginning this was a marathon, not a sprint. And I also knew the country inside and out, and if I understood anything about postwar China, it was that it kept shifting all the time. I convinced myself that change would come, and that at some point all that had happened during the Cultural Revolution would be old news, and my role in it would become irrelevant. I just needed to survive.

"About a year after the interrogations ended, without any warning or discussion, I was moved to a bigger cell and allowed to have newspapers. Shortly after this, Henry Kissinger negotiated the terms of President Nixon's 1971 visit to China. As the political thaw between the two superpowers progressed, I became ever more hopeful, especially as my conditions kept being upgraded. I was moved to a still larger cell, and the new guards were clearly under orders to be less aggressive toward me. At the same time, my rations improved significantly, and I began to receive medical and dental care for the first time. The absence of the interrogations worried me in one sense, however: I feared I'd be forgotten and left to rot away forever in prison. As time went on, I became ever more certain that no reconsideration of my case would occur before there was a change of regime, and I turned out to be correct on that score. Zhou Enlai died in 1975, followed a year later by Mao. Certainly, I thought, that should generate change. And sure enough, in the months that followed I could see in the newspaper that with new hands at the helm, China was really beginning to transform and this engendered still more hope in me that at some point there would be no logic to keeping me imprisoned.

"Despite my reawakening as an American, I still had deep emotional ties to the China I had adopted and the revolution I had helped make. When Zhou died, I cried for weeks. I had treasured my relationship with him, in spite of his having assented to my imprisonment. He was like a father figure to me in some way I can't explain. News of Mao's death, however, brought no tears, not one. There were many ways in which I greatly admired him, and it was an amazing experience to have personally known a world historical figure. Think about it. In terms of historical stature, what Mao accomplished will be ranked with what Constantine the Great and Julius Caesar each did in their time, and he will be read and spoken about for as long as civilization continues. Richard Nixon, I don't think so. So you have to understand, despite his assent to what happened to me, I was and still am greatly indebted to Mao for how far he had let me advance toward the center of it all. But that being said, there were no tears.

"Then, one night in late 1976, something signaled to me that really big changes were coming. I will never forget the sound that reached my ears. It was a shrill and belligerent voice—a voice I thought I knew—the voice of a new prisoner being dragged in. The woman was causing an enormous scene in the hallway, and the more she yelled at and insulted the guards, the more certain I was that I recognized the voice: it was Jiang Qing herself. Mao's third wife, the living, breathing heart and soul of the Cultural Revolution was being thrown into political prison! Clearly, this heralded major change in the dynamics of Chinese internal politics. I could only think that things were looking brighter for me.

"But while I was right, it took until November 1977 for me to be released from prison. This time I had been nine and a half years alone in solitary confinement. Before I left, I was taken before the chief inquisitor who had been so hard on me in earlier years. He called me 'comrade' and told me my case had been a mistake. When they had told me this after my first imprisonment, I had cried; this time I did not. I was a different person now, and I had very different plans for my future.

"Yulin and the children had had a difficult, impoverished time throughout these ten years. They had lived in a one-room unit on extremely limited funds, and early on, Yulin had been forced to work in a labor camp in the harshest of conditions. She had only her family and, of course, our children. But she waited for me with loyalty and love. Now that's connection!

"So here I was, back on the streets of Beijing, the same streets we've been walking through all afternoon. What did I see? What did I hear? I learned that the party had become the center of corruption, and that people felt little, if any, heartfelt loyalty to it. And I could see with my own eyes that everyday life no longer involved the enthusiastic cooperative spirit that had been so palpable in the 1950s. Instead, what I saw now were people thinking only of themselves, people seeking opportunities to further their own private interests. You could see these changes in small matters, such as the reemergence of trash being allowed to blow along the street. But you could also see these changes in great matters, such as the infamous closing down of the Democracy Wall by Deng Xiaoping, one of the few vestiges of free speech that had remained from the honeymoon period. It was sad for me, enormously sad, to see that all the magical communal spirit of revolutionary China I had known in the mid-1950s was gone from everyday life. China was something else now, and it was time for us to return to the States, and in March of 1980, we did just that."

*

The story completed, we stopped in at an ancient teahouse Sidney favored, and he ordered for us in his flawless Mandarin. There he surprised me by turning the tables and becoming the inquirer.

"So my turn now, and I have a question for you. You were a social psychologist before you were a lawyer. Does the concept of attachment disorder encompass those who are overattached as well as those who are underattached? Sometimes I wonder if that's what happened to me in China—I mean, especially with how I let myself participate in ideological manipulation through my role in the mass media. Is there a psychiatric explanation for why I was so blind?"

I thought about his question, sipping the delicious tea that had been served to us before I responded. "No, Sidney, the psychiatric concept of attachment disorder is meant to describe disorders in very young children. It refers to the failure of young children from aberrant or pathological family backgrounds to be able to form normal attachments to their primary caregivers. And so far as I know, there's no other psychiatric concept that has any explanatory power for what you're talking about. There's dependent personality disorder, but that really has to do with people who exhibit a pervasive and excessive need to be taken care of that, in turn, generates overly submissive behavior and fear of separation and rejection.

"So, to be frank with you, I don't know of any psychiatric models that help explain what you described. Personally, I think it's better to go about it from a different direction. I think what's involved is just a question of the *balance* we all try to maintain between our individual beliefs and values on one hand, and the doctrines and dogmas of the groups we belong to on the other. Some groups allow their adherents a decent amount of sway as to their personal views, while others permit no deviation from the official line. And some groups, in extreme cases, demand complete internalization of the party line, to the point where there is no room allowed for even internal debate. I imagine that's what your grand inquisitor was doing—probing the discourse of your internal debate. There are some well-done case studies of 'true believers'— adherents to groups that publish a credo as an entrance requirement. The credo is meant to be internalized, not just memorized."

Sidney sat silently enjoying his tea, listening intently with that incredible power of focus that I've never seen matched, so I continued. "I certainly don't mean to compare Mao and the Chinese Revolution to Charles Manson and his Family or Jim Jones and his Guyana community. But on the single issue of understanding the process by which your Western freedom-of-the-press values were silenced—even inside your own head—there may be something to learn. In fanatical cults like these, studies document that members who are interviewed after they abandon the cults, report just what you do: they describe having fully abandoned their capacity to judge, let alone debate, even internally, the cult's values. That seems to be the ticket price for entry into a cult that is controlled by a charismatic leader."

Now he spoke up. "But why wouldn't I have sensed what was happening as it built up, step by step, and at least *thought* about where it was heading and what it meant for my personal values to continue to contribute to the process. What puzzles me and disappoints me is how I could be so naïve. Where was my internal dialogue?"

"I really don't think you can blame yourself for that. The total absorption into a cult's worldview—and again, I'm not saying a revolutionary social movement is in any *other* way equivalent to a cult— is a psychologically deep process. Very deep. The women involved in the Manson cult actually *failed to perceive* that their involvement in the bloody murders of pregnant Sharon Tate and her friends was at all problematic, and the parents at Jonestown apparently exhibited no reluctance, let alone opposition, to giving poisoned Kool-Aid to two hundred and eighty of their own children. True believers agree to abandon their individualism when they join a cult, and without that individualism, there is no reference point from which to contrast one's values with those espoused by the cult."

Sidney came back at me sharply for my choice of examples—I had pushed it too far, regardless of my caveats. "China wasn't Jonestown, Terry. That's not a fair comparison. There was every reason to be proud of what we were delivering to the Chinese people. We weren't poisoning our own children; we were transforming one of the cruelest and harshest societies on the face of the Earth into one where a vast percentage of the population could lead a reasonable life."

He fell silent after this outburst, seemingly far away for a few moments. Then, switching back to the thoughtful, soft tone of voice I had become accustomed to, he spoke again. "But having said that, what you say makes sense. It's not like I said to myself 'the altruistic ends of the revolution justify the ideologically manipulative means.' I would have preferred having done that, I suppose, but the fact is, I didn't say anything at all. I mean, there was no internal debate going on in my mind whatsoever. I was silent on the inside, just like on the outside. That's what disappoints me."

"But, Sidney, it's only when circumstances allow a balance between the integrity of the individual and the norms of the collectivity, that the individual can have the type of conversation with himself you're alluding to. When the balance tips too much toward the collectivity, the adherent—the true believer, the cult member, the social movement activist—actually *loses his capacity* to judge the collectivity's actions. Let me give you a banal example from a case I had a few years back. A client of mine had a son who was a perfectly normal kid and bright enough to get admitted to MIT. But when senior classmen from his fraternity had the brilliant idea of dropping full beer cans out of tenth story windows onto the sidewalk below, he joined right in. The father asked me to represent the kid as he dealt with the consequences, and it gave me a chance to talk to the young fraternity pledge about what in the world was going through his mind as those beer cans exploded near pedestrians, scaring the hell out of them and splattering them with beer. 'Nothing,' was his response, and the more I probed the issue with the kid, the more I came to believe him. And I think that's the silence you're talking about."

Sidney just nodded as we finished our tea. When we left the teahouse, I realized we were just blocks from my hotel.

"Sidney," I said as we began to walk, "one last question back at you. Do you think there'll ever be a socialist society that fully respects the rights of the individual—that gets the balance correct between the rights of the individual and the needs of the collectivity?"

He didn't hesitate for a moment. "I don't know, maybe not, but I'd join a movement in a heartbeat to try to make it happen. Give me a call if you hear of an opportunity, will you?" He looked over and smiled at me—a smile that lives on in my mind's eye.

We traversed the final block in silence and serenity. When we reached the front of the hotel, Sidney reached out to shake my hand good-bye, and all I ended up saying was, "Thank you. Thank you for sharing your story."

He simply replied, "You're so very welcome. Just promise me you'll write that book someday. And put my story in it, you hear me?" With that, and one last inimitable giggle, he turned and walked away down the street.

*

I ended up eating a late dinner alone at a rooftop restaurant not far from my hotel. It was a splendid summer evening, with a big, bright moon lighting up the cityscape. But I barely tasted what I ate, and I hardly took note of the glorious view.

If the evening in Cambridge some years back had set off my powerful averse reaction to prison cells, this time Sidney's story reawakened a sense of dread I experienced in the presence of police who serve a totalitarian state. And make no mistake about it: a police state is simply that—a police state—no matter how gloriously altruistic the intentions of those in power. The very idea that in each instance of Sidney's imprisonment the Chinese state did not even make a nod in the direction of due process sent a very cold shiver up my spine. To me, the fact that there was not even a bogus Soviet-style trial to produce a manufactured verdict was a gross insult to the historical era in which we live. We in the West put forth many harsh criticisms of our governing forms and political practices; that's what democracy is all about. But we should never for a moment forget what a blessing it is to not live in a police state.

I personally once had a misadventure with such a state, and Sidney's story had brought up feelings and memories in me that I thought were long since calmed. Of course, my brief encounter with totalitarian police can in no way be compared with Sidney's extreme experience, but I do think it explains why my reaction to the second half of his story was so visceral and psychologically powerful. Trust me: it doesn't take but a brief exposure to the police and prison personnel of an autocratic state to leave one with a memory that can come rushing back at you.

*

The year was 1976, and I was living in Paris on a National Science Foundation fellowship to undertake research that would lead to a book, *The French Press*. In the spring of 1977, the World Congress of Sociology was to be held in Varna, Bulgaria, and I was invited to travel with the French delegation to deliver a paper on the social psychology of political violence. At the time Bulgaria had what was arguably the most brutal police force and hardest-edged Stalinist regime of any Eastern European country, and, mind you, the competition was tough—think of the Stasi in East Germany.

On the return trip, the entire French delegation stopped in Sofia, Bulgaria's capital city. The itinerary involved spending the afternoon and evening exploring the city and then flying back to Paris at noon the next day. I was in my early thirties and dressed like an American academic of that era: jeans and a well-worn sweater, with considerably longer hair than I would dare sport today, four decades down the road. At the hotel, I passed a young Bulgarian hotel worker who was dusting a little table in the back area of the lobby. I shot him a smile, and in return—after furtively looking over his shoulder to make certain our conversation was unobserved—he asked me in high school French if I was with the French group. When I responded that I was, but that I was American, his mouth dropped open—literally. When he regained his composure at the wonder of it all, he took another look behind him to reconfirm that no one was watching, and then asked me if I wanted to meet some young Bulgarians later that night. Being both young and naïve, I agreed, and he described a street corner a few blocks from the hotel where I was to be at ten o'clock. I never thought twice about the matter. It sounded like an interesting proposition.

And it was. Sure enough a car with three guys and two girls more or less my age arrived on schedule, and somehow I squeezed into the backseat. Big hellos were said all around, translated by my new friend, Stanko. Stanko seemed a different man than the fearful fellow I had encountered in the hotel. In his own life, he was assertive and lively—and full of smiles. But it was his girlfriend, Milena, who really stood out. She was a knockout beauty, with flawless fair skin, huge pitch-black sparkling eyes, and long, straight black hair that she wore in pigtails. It was almost immediately apparent that the only linguistic bridge among us was the unsure span anchored on one bank by my college French, and on the other by Stanko's yet more modest abilities. No worries: it was all about young people having fun together, and in that era, the worldwide student movement made something common of all of us.

After about a fifteen-minute drive, we were in front of a six- or seven-story Soviet-style cement tenement building, lost in a row of identical structures. Up we went to the fifth floor, where the door opened at Stanko's knock. Inside were at least another dozen young people more or less our age, and the party was on—or almost. The music on the record player was shut down, and Stanko welcomed me on behalf of the group. It was pretty obvious from the looks on most faces that I was the first American they had ever met. And it was also obvious that my student-movement ways of dressing and acting spoke to them, even if I couldn't.

Now, as it turned out, there was a hidden agenda, an ulterior motive to the gathering that I certainly had not foreseen. Before long, and to a completely hushed room, Stanko asked me if I would translate the words of a Beatles album they had just obtained, *Help!* When I stopped laughing, I responded that I would try, and a general, if hushed, cheer went up from the multitudes. And so the evening began. Milena was in charge of the record player, and by placing the needle down and then quickly lifting it up, she tried her best to isolate each line. I would then translate it into French to Stanko, who in turn would translate the French into Bulgarian—usually to a room full of "ahs." One of the girls was actually taking notes on whatever wording arrived at the Bulgarian end of the bridge, which, I should think, was at least 50 percent inaccurate by then, given our combined ineptitudes. But a good time was had by all. After *Help!* we moved on to *The Night Before*, then *You've Got to Hide Your Love Away*. At this point, we took a well-earned break, and two bottles of some surprisingly strong alcoholic liquor were quietly passed around between the sixteen or seventeen of us who were seated on every square inch of the room.

Suddenly there was a hard and ominous knock on the door, and the room went stone quiet. Stanko got up and went over to the door. He opened it just a crack, but it was immediately shoved wide open, and in seconds the room was filled with plainclothes police, each one bigger than the next. While of course I couldn't understand a word of what was said, it was immediately clear that this was no laughing matter to do with the music being too loud or whatever. Stanko, with a look in his eyes that said, "Sorry, man, I've got no choice here," pointed to me.

An officer was in my face two seconds later with the one word I clearly did understand, "Passport." He took a glance at the photo, compared it to my face, and then slid it into his breast pocket. Gulp.

Within minutes, two massive officers, each tightly holding an arm, practically carried me out of the apartment, down the stairs, and into the back of their unmarked car. I never saw Stanko, Milena, or the others again, and for years I spent many a moment trying to imagine the outcome of the matter for them. But their fate was forever unknown to me.

As for me, I was taken to a police station, literally tossed into a cell, and left to my own devices. The cement walls and floor of the cell were cold and damp, and the cracked, seatless toilet bowl was so filthy it seemed to have a life of its own. The only light was a dim glow that somehow found its way down the hallway and snuck in between the bars. And that was that.

My watch had been taken from me as I entered the facility, so time was tough to judge, but more or less three hours later, around two o'clock in the morning I would guess, a guard making the rounds shot me a moment of kindness: he held up one finger, touched the face of his watch, and said, "English." And sure enough, roughly an hour later, an English-speaking officer appeared. He, like all of these officers, was in plainclothes. While initially my confidence in the man was somewhat shaken when he first greeted me with, "Good-bye," it turned out that it was not this man's lack of English that was my biggest problem, it was his lack of empathy.

"Come," he ordered, and I prepared to follow him.

Two new officers, each roughly twice my size, took my arms and half lifted me out of the cell and into a small interrogation room that looked like it was straight out of a Hollywood set. There were exactly four objects in the darkened space: a metal table, a chair on either side of it, and a gooseneck desk lamp. I was pushed down into one of the chairs by one of the heavies, and the English-speaking officer took the other chair, spinning it around to face backward before straddling it and sitting down. The other two officers stood along the wall with their arms crossed, trying hard to look as threatening as possible. Over and again I was asked who I was, where I lived, why I was with the French delegation, why we were in Sofia, and what hotel I was at. At one point, the officer went through my passport, asking me to explain every entry and exit stamp that appeared on each page and why I had visited each country. Of course, he saw the visa I had to live in France for the year, and there were many questions about why I was there, what I was doing, and even what I was *really* doing in Paris.

Then, after at least two hours of questioning, with progressive adjustments of the lamp putting me in ever-brighter light, came the real inquiries. Where did I meet Stanko? How long had I known him? How did I communicate with him? How did I know the others? What was the purpose of our meeting? Why were we meeting late at night? What were we talking about? Over and over again for about another two hours, I explained that it was just a chance meeting, and that the purpose of the meeting was just to translate the words to some songs. Each time I repeated the same answer, he shook his head no, and I couldn't blame him because I don't think I came even close to getting across the two-step translation logic.

Every thirty or forty minutes, the officer would suddenly rise and leave the room. I, of course, remained seated and motionless under the watchful gaze of the remaining two bulldogs who stood over me. My guess was that Stanko and others were in other rooms being asked the same questions, but I had no way of confirming that. Then the officer would return, settle into his chair, and pick his teeth with a toothpick for a minute or two before asking the same questions once again. But whatever was asked, throughout the night, I stuck with my strategy of responding politely and without a hint of exasperation. I kept thinking about asking to be allowed to call the American embassy, but each time I came to the same conclusion: it seemed a better idea not to "lawyer up" and get confrontational. At what was probably about six o'clock in the morning, the two exhausted-looking officers who had stood alongside the little table all night returned me to my cell without a word and slammed the door shut behind me. I had asked in the hallway for the return of my passport, but that drew no response whatsoever.

About an hour later, another officer came around the corner to my cell. His English was better than that of his predecessor, but his attitude was harsher still. He did everything he could do to convince me how serious a matter this was, and that they needed to know the *real* reason I met with Stanko and the others.

When I started to repeat the music translation story yet again, he stopped me cold, and punched the palm of his left hand with his right fist, exclaiming, "We need real answer. You want stay here? You want miss your flight? You think about that." And with that he turned on his heel and was gone, and I was alone again.

As drained as I was, I tried to concentrate on whether I should change my mind about asking to call the embassy. I think what finally convinced me not to switch tactics was the comment of the second interrogator about "miss your flight." As I saw it, this meant they knew exactly when my flight was, and therefore when their deadline was for returning me to my hotel. My best guess was that for me to miss that flight would have rung a lot of bells, and given that this good-sized police operation had uncovered nothing more than a Beatles translation session, my guess was that it was in the interest of the police to bring a quiet end to the matter. So I determined to stick it out without escalating the matter from my side; if it didn't end in time for my flight, I could always ask then about the call to the embassy.

And sure enough, in the end I was driven to the hotel and pushed out of the car hard enough that I tripped and fell to the pavement. There was not a word of explanation. I just barely had enough time to shower, brush my teeth, and grab my bag from my room and meet the bus that was taking the delegation to the airport. I still vividly remember the feeling of relief that shot through me when the plane's wheels lifted off the ground and Bulgaria was left behind. No one in the delegation had even noticed that I'd been gone, and I didn't much feel like announcing to the core of the French sociological professoriate that I had been so naïve as to have accepted the invitation to meet on a dark street corner the night before.

Even though this brush with a totalitarian state was of minor magnitude and quickly resolved, to me it was a powerful and frightening experience. But I thought I had long since processed the experience and more or less forgotten it. Apparently deeper fears than I realized were at play, helping to explain my visceral reaction to Sidney's story. My revivified images from that one crazy night made me appreciate all the more what Sidney had been able to endure for all those years, and it engendered in me an unlimited admiration for his having survived so intact, and so gentle. How had he lived to tell the tale—and with such dignity?

*

As fascinating as my trip to China was—and from Beijing we went on to visit two other orphanages, one in Hangzhou and one in Shanghai—I was thrilled to return home to Boston a week later and find the family and friends and office mates whose love and warmth and collegiality connect me to my life. But I have to say, there has always remained a tiny hole in my heart when I think back about that baby girl I held for three-quarters of an hour in the Beijing orphanage, because I cannot forget the look in her eyes as she waited and longed for someone to snatch her up, take her home, and fill her childhood with love.

III

The Truck Driver's Library

I think we all know that when you are exhausted, really exhausted, sleep can sneak up and grab you from behind, however determined you may be to stave it off. It's not a fair fight: the brain, after all, is an organ before it is a mind. Paul Cardarelli had struggled desperately to stay awake, using every trick he could think of. But in the end, sleep overtook him, and the next thing he knew, he was climbing out the passenger window of the massive moving van he had been driving. Once he had successfully extracted himself from the wrecked truck, bruised but uninjured, Cardarelli stood still in the crisp, bright moonlight of an early fall evening in 1992, completely unable to piece together how the massive vehicle had come to be alongside the *eastbound* side of the Massachusetts Turnpike when he had been heading *west*.

Within days of the accident, I had been retained by Cardarelli's employer to represent him in the matter. I immediately contracted the services of a traffic accident reconstruction expert, James Stevenson, PhD, to solve the mystery of the crash, since there were no witnesses to the accident itself—not a single one. Stevenson studied the remnants of the truck in minute detail and paid equally close attention to what was left of an eastbound car that had been traveling on the other side of the divided highway. He took meticulous notes of everything he observed at the accident site, particularly scrutinizing the lack of skid marks and the precise details of the damage done to the central fencing that runs down the middle of the Pike.

Working with estimations of the speeds the two vehicles had been traveling, the precise specifications of their mass and weight distribution, and technical details of the fence's steel cable reinforcement, within two weeks Stevenson deduced what had happened. He called me with the good news that he would be able to describe this to the jury "to a reasonable degree of scientific certainty." Bingo. Those are the seven magic words a judge needs to hear.

Stevenson explained that Cardarelli had obviously dozed off—hence the absence of any skid marks—and that the big rig had veered to the left, leaving tire tread marks in the ground to the side of the road. Once the two forward-most left tires were off the pavement, the truck had turned still further onto the downhill slope of the divider portion of the highway. This had the effect of pulling the truck into an even sharper angle as it careened, driverless, down the hill and into the divider fence. Stevenson calculated from the damage to the fence that by the time the cab struck the median, it was facing fully 38 degrees to the south of the nearly due east–west orientation of the Pike. This angle was so acute that the effect of the unbreakable two-inch thick steel cable that runs along the middle of the fence was to literally catapult the huge truck up into the air and over the partition. Stevenson ascertained that the momentum of Cardarelli's fully loaded Countrywide Moving Company van was so great that the massive vehicle was actually completely airborne for over sixty feet. Imagine that. He corroborated this with the location of the abrasions on the pavement at the place where the truck had slammed back down on the roadway after its flight.

Amazingly, with all the traffic the Pike brings into Boston from its western suburbs, only one vehicle was struck before the van cleaved off the southern side of the Pike, flipped over 270 degrees, and skidded to a stop on its driver's side—gratuitously uprooting a group of young willow trees that had been planted only days before. The unlucky

Toyota Avalon was being driven at approximately sixty-five miles per hour in the fast lane, Stevenson calculated, when the hurtling truck, which was going about the same speed in almost the opposite direction, passed directly over it. The problem for the Toyota, however, was that the truck was only thirty-eight inches off the ground—the height of the steel cable running along the divider fence. This meant that while the truck vaulted over the body of the Toyota, anything that stuck up above the car body was cleanly sliced off.

This included the driver of the Toyota, a twenty-six-year-old woman named Erin Waters, who was decapitated "as cleanly as if she had been guillotined," announced Stevenson, citing the police report. In total contrast, the drivers' parents, Barbara and Harold Waters, had been slumped down asleep in the backseat, below the critical height, and hence had not been touched by the flying truck. They, in fact, had barely been tossed about at all as the uncontrolled car somehow found its way across two lanes of traffic to the right before coming to a stop on a grassy area alongside the highway.

I was not quite a decade out of law school when the accident happened, and so I was thoroughly pleased to receive the case to defend from the moving company's insurer and equally excited about meeting and working with Dr. Stevenson. He had a sterling reputation and was often used by the insurance defense group of my law firm. When he had asked me if I wanted to join him in viewing the Toyota, I eagerly took him up on the invitation, and two days later we met at the police tow lot to where it had been taken.

Stevenson examined the car as closely as a mortician examines a corpse in a murder case. Running his fingers over the cleanly shaved metal where the windshield had once been attached to the car's frame, he explained to me that the greater the speed of impact, the greater the shearing effect on the metal and the less the bending effect. Stevenson had been able to use this differential to calculate that the closing speed of the two vehicles was just about twice the speed limit, as one would expect. One hundred and thirty miles per hour, he explained, is just under two hundred feet per second. This great speed, he continued, coupled with the truck's approach angle, meant that he would be able to testify that it was physiologically impossible for the deceased driver to have perceived the truck coming over the divider prior to the moment she was decapitated. Moreover, he had calculated that not more than a tenth of a second could possibly have lapsed from the earliest possible moment her car was touched by the truck she never saw until her instantaneous death. Because this amount of time is below what would have been required for the perception of pain from the decapitation to be processed by the driver's brain, Dr. Stevenson was prepared to testify that the driver could not possibly have experienced any pain or suffering. It was a tragic death, to be sure, but it was a painless, immediate death. While this conclusion may sound heartless and even macabre, it could prove quite significant in calculating damages in a civil lawsuit for wrongful death.

*

Just under a month after the accident, Paul Cardarelli came to my law office for our initial meeting about the accident. He came for one reason only: his supervisor at Countrywide Moving Company had directed him to. Wisely, Countrywide had the internal risk management practice of having a driver make contact with defense counsel as soon as possible after an accident. Why begin defending a lawsuit before it is even filed? Preservation of evidence. It isn't rare for plaintiffs to file months, sometimes years, after an accident, and by then it can be far too late to locate the evidence and witnesses that defense counsel needs to prepare for trial.

Cardarelli had taken the interim time off from work to heal the bruises and contusions he had suffered and to also begin the process of recovering from the shock of killing the Toyota's driver. But a month clearly had not been enough. It was apparent at first glance that this pleasant-looking, six-foot-three, broad-shouldered man with a full head of salt-and-pepper hair was haunted by what had happened.

Given that defendants in Cardarelli's position are often worried about the exposure of their personal assets above and beyond what their employer might be liable for, I was in the habit of beginning a first meeting by relieving them of that concern. Normally, this brings a huge, often audible, sigh of relief, but when I made this pronouncement to Cardarelli, he showed no interest whatsoever in what I had said. His stooped posture and subdued voice remained unchanged.

To break the silence that followed, I asked whether he had ever been involved in litigation before. He slowly shook his head, no.

"Paul," I said in my most comforting tone of voice. "I know how you feel about what happened. I'm so sorry."

"How would you know?" he responded. "Have you ever killed someone?"

My head shot back suddenly, reflexively. "Well . . . no," I replied, stumbling over my words. "But I've represented many clients who have been involved in accidents, some of whom have killed others, so I have *some* idea of what you're experiencing."

"But this wasn't an accident," Cardarelli responded in his monotone.

"Why do you say that? I assume you didn't swerve over the median into oncoming traffic on purpose, did you?"

"No, of course not," he shot back. "But I broke a safety rule that was designed precisely to avoid what happened."

"What was that?" I asked.

"I drove in excess of the ten-hour limit set by the federal government. I was just about at eleven hours when I fell asleep at the wheel. That makes it my fault, doesn't it?"

"We already know it was your fault, Paul. Your truck crossed into her lane; end of inquiry. The only difference that your violating the regulation makes is that it might allow the plaintiff to recover punitive damages. But that's just money. It doesn't change the fact that this was an accident. By the way, can I assume your driving times are logged in, in compliance with the regulations?"

"Yes," he said, still with a perfectly flat affect. "My records are accurate. So they will clearly show my violation. Could I lose insurance coverage because of my violation?"

"Let me make something clear. I represent *you*, not the insurance company that hired me to represent you. If they decided to contest coverage on that or any other basis, they're going to have to hire separate counsel to investigate the coverage question. Actually, if this ever happened, my job would then include representing your interests *against* the insurer in the collateral action about the coverage issue, just as I represent your interests in this accident defense. Do you understand this?"

"Yes, I follow. What do you think the odds are the insurer will contest coverage on this basis?"

"I think they are next to nil. Let's face it: they need your cooperation in the defense, and to start the case by refusing to honor your claim wouldn't exactly encourage you to be a cooperative witness, now would it? In fact, why don't we just get beyond this issue right now. Let's put in a call together to the claim agent and ask her about this."

"Okay, if you think that makes sense."

I hesitated for a moment, tapping my fingers on the desk. "Let's see," I began. "How do I describe Rhonda Wilkins to you? Well, to start with, she's a trial attorney by training, and sharp as a tack. She's actually a great ally on a case; she generates important ideas. But there's another . . . side to her, I guess I'd call it, that I need to warn you about. She's also quite a character . . . a unique one, let's say. You're going to hear a woman who talks like an army drill sergeant. Can you handle that?"

"Don't worry about it," Cardarelli replied without a hint of a smile. "I've run into some rough characters in the trucking business."

"Okay, you've been forewarned. But, let me ask you two questions before we give her a call. Do your logs show numerous days with more than ten hours' driving, and do you turn the logs into the company?"

"Yes, on both questions."

"Okay. Have you ever been disciplined by a supervisor for this or told to stop driving beyond the ten-hour limit?"

"Two different supervisors have mentioned it to me in the past, but both essentially said it while winking, if you know what I mean. The company doesn't enforce the rule, and the reason why is obvious: to stop the trucks for the required eight-hour rest period when they're an hour from their destination would cost the company a small fortune over a year's time. This is a big-dollar issue."

"Okay. I see. Do you know much about how other drivers handle this issue, and what they do?"

"Well, I don't know the statistical breakdown, of course. But I do know that some with families and young children don't want to work the extra hours; for them, the ten-hour federal limit is an argument to use *against* their supervisors. But I think most do what I do, which is sometimes stop, sometimes not, depending on a number of things. I would say that the unwritten policy is that if you're within an hour of your destination when you hit the ten-hour limit, you should finish the trip unless it's unsafe."

"'Should' or 'can'?"

Cardarelli took a deep breath and deliberated for a good while before answering. It was the first of many times I was to be impressed with his thoughtfulness.

"Unclear. But I think it was deliberately left unclear."

I dialed up Wilkins, whom I hadn't spoken to since the Doe case had been resolved. She remained the poster child for a New Jersey born and bred insurance claim agent. Her accent was thick, her eyeglasses were thick, and she was fairly thick too—physically, not mentally. She stood about five foot two, unless you counted the improbable tangle of black hair that stood up on end from her scalp. Wilkins brought toughness along with a huge intellect to her job: she absolutely refused to settle a lawsuit if she thought a plaintiff was exaggerating their injuries or loss, and she'd have you take the case all the way to a jury verdict. I *loved* working for her for just this reason. It was getting to be a rarity to actually get to try a case, and I enormously enjoyed the chess match of attempting to win over a jury from opposing counsel. In two different cases that had gone all the way to a verdict, Wilkins had shown up and sat through five-day-long jury trials, mostly to make sure I was tough enough in cross-examining the two greedy plaintiffs. I actually liked it when she did this because she was a wickedly perceptive reader of jurors. Her intuitions and input had proved enormously helpful in both instances.

We weren't two minutes into the call when Cardarelli answered one of Wilkins's questions in the depressed, barely audible monotone he'd been using with me. Without a moment's hesitation, Wilkins let him have it: "Speak the fuck up, goddamn it. If I can't hear you, how do you expect to keep jurors awake when you testify?" Cardarelli perked right up at the scolding.

"Rhonda," I broke in, smiling at Cardarelli. He didn't react. "The only curve ball I see is that we have per se negligence here: Paul was in his eleventh hour of driving, and there's an applicable federal regulation at the time of the accident that puts the ceiling at ten hours per day."

"Paul," she said without a moment's delay. "Is it common practice in the company for drivers to do more than ten hours?"

"Yes, ma'am."

"And if the company finds out, what do they do about it?"

"I was just telling the attorney that, while the supervisors know that technically they are supposed to warn you, that's not at all what they really do. They all but wink at you when they mention it. The informal rule of thumb is to finish the trip if you'll be an hour or less over the ten-hour limit."

"Have you ever received any discipline for driving more than the ten hours, like a disciplinary write-up or something, or heard of another driver getting one?"

"Me, no," Cardarelli replied, obviously fascinated by Wilkins's quickness. "I know of only one guy who got written up, but he always claimed the actual agenda behind the warning was the company's ongoing effort to build up the step discipline paperwork in his file so they could can him for cross-dressing."

Rhonda paused, something I don't think I'd ever heard her do. "Excuse me. What the *fuck* did you just say? A cross-dressing truck driver? You must be shitting me."

"I shit you not, ma'am. If I could make that up, I'd be writing novels, not reading them."

Wilkins laughed out loud at this. "Terry," she said, "I'm not getting off track here letting some bullshit coverage question be generated by that rule violation—not with the way the actual driving was being done in the company, day in, day out. And besides, if I take this down the hall to the complete asshole who handles coverage questions, he'd strut around the office for a month with a little hard-on. He's a mountain-out-of-a-molehill kind of wimp, you know what I mean? I'm not going down that road. From here on in, we are a team of three. There's no coverage question here. Now let's fucking concentrate on the fact that this is a death case. Do we all agree?"

"Done," I said, glancing over at Cardarelli, who nodded back at me.

But there wasn't time for further comment. Wilkins was out to immediately get down to business. "Terry, have you thought about stipulating to liability from the start of this case? Damages should be the only issue for the jury. You agree?"

"Absolutely. And by all odds, that should keep both the ten-hour issue and the accident details away from the jury. If I get any kind of a reasonable trial judge, nothing about the accident will come into evidence, save one brief summary description about what happened in the plaintiffs' opening. But you're absolutely right: there's no question as to liab—"

"Pain and suffering?" Wilkins interrupted.

"None. The expert says it was an instantaneous death. He'll actually testify that from a physiological perspective there wasn't enough time for her to possibly perceive pain. The big case here, Rhonda, is the parents' loss of consortium cases. They lost the love and company of their child. Sad business, and juries know that. Listen, once I meet them, I'll let you know what I think about them as plaintiffs and about what the settlement possibilities look like. The parents will have solid cases: they were very much in the zone of danger."

"I got ya," Wilkins answered. "So let's sit tight and see what back-of-the-yellow-pages ambulance-chasing motherfucker contingency lawyer they chose. Then we'll plot our strategy. We're going to put two million dollars in reserve for this, and that's going to fuck up my numbers for the month. So move this case right a-fucking-long, okay?"

"Yep."

"And Terry, do not spend a shitload of money on defense, goddamn it. And Paul," she continued, modulating in a heartbeat to a much more civil tone, "it was nice to meet you, if by phone. Listen to me. Are you all right about the accident? It must be hard for you, with the young woman having died and all, yes?"

"It *is* hard, yes," he answered, his voice cracking just a touch.

"Well, why don't you seek out some counseling. The company will pay for it. It's your right, just like if you'd broken your arm and needed to have your bones set. Do you understand that?"

"Yes, sure."

"Promise me you'll think about it?" Wilkins added with a warmth of tone I hadn't known she possessed.

Cardarelli paused before answering. "Sure, I promise."

"All right. You take care of yourself. Talk to Terry about it. He used to be a shrink of some kind. Good luck, okay?"

"Thanks, Ms. Wilkins."

"Goddamn it, Paul, Ms. Wilkins is my mother; and you don't want to have to deal with her, trust me. She's rough around the edges. You call me Rhonda."

They shared a laugh, and Cardarelli shot me the first smile I'd seen from him—and an electrifying smile it was: it flashed through my mind that the challenge of the case was to get this handsome smile operational. "Hey, Paul," Wilkins continued, "can you spare Terry for five? I need to talk to him about a completely different case."

Cardarelli agreed. He stood up, stretched, and wandered over toward the bookcases that lined one full wall of my office.

I switched off the speakerphone for the second part of the call. Wilkins carried on considerably longer than the five minutes she had asked for, and as she droned on, I was really only half listening, as my attention was progressively drawn to watching Cardarelli inspect the spines of my books. In this era, I kept a good part of my personal library in my office, and Cardarelli was looking over my collection in that peculiar manner typical of those among us who love books. One section of shelves contained novels and literature, and it was there that he stopped, carefully perusing each volume, title by title. Occasionally, he pulled a book out to take a look at the cover, and he opened a few for an even closer look. I suppose the main reason I was watching so intently was that as a trial lawyer I had been taught early on to try to learn what really makes your client tick. You need to sell a complete person to the jury, not just a litigant, so whatever you can learn about a client's personal life can play into their case in an important way. Glancing at Cardarelli, I remember thinking that I was looking at either a very well-read truck driver or at a phony who for some reason was trying to impress me by displaying a disingenuous interest in literature. I definitely intended to learn which was the case.

"Sorry she went on so long," I apologized after hanging up. "That's the end of the coverage issue, I assure you. Rhonda doesn't revisit decisions she's made. But I've got a question for you. You seem interested in my books, if I'm not mistaken."

"Yes, yes," he affirmed. "I love to read. That's the best thing about my job: plenty of time to read each night and at all those thousands of meals I've eaten alone."

"So what do you think about my reading choices?" I asked, putting Cardarelli to the test.

"You have some interesting collections here, no doubt about it. I can tell you're a fan of Latin American magical realism. I never run into anyone who even knows about these authors. And I like that you not only have the principal works of Gabriel García Márquez, but most of his lesser books as well. And you have Mario Vargas Llosa well represented on the shelf, and two favorites of mine by the Brazilian novelist Jorge Amado."

Absolutely floored by his comments, I stammered in response, "So you like magical realist literature?"

"Oh, yes. Big time. I love the way they mingle the workaday reality of everyday life with just a touch of wonder, just a hint of magic. It's like a good chef putting just a pinch of spice in a dish. Do you know Laura Esquivel's *Like Water for Chocolate*, or the film that was made from it? Or John Nichols's *The Milagro Beanfield War*?"

"I know them both, and I agree; they're utterly charming," I replied, noting that Cardarelli had reversed the tables on me, investigating whether or not *I* was serious about reading.

After a few moments of silence, Cardarelli picked up the conversation in an almost dreamy voice dramatically different from his earlier tone. "Sometimes I think that modern life is presented as so linear, so predictable, that we miss the fact that there are moments to it that science just can't explain. Did you ever think that we live in an era in which magic has been reduced to sideshow trickery, whereas earlier generations experienced the world as considerably more mysterious?"

"Well, I suppose that's what science has done to us, hasn't it?" I said, now thoroughly absorbed in a topic a hundred times more interesting than the details of Cardarelli's roadway accident. "I mean, you're absolutely correct. If a guy levitates in front of us, we literally cannot possibly believe it. Our science-driven worldview would demand that we go looking for the hidden wires, don't you agree?"

"Exactly. We *cannot* believe in magic. Not in the world of science." He paused for a moment, thinking about something, and I waited, content to be silent. "You know," Cardarelli continued, "Now that I think about it, Vargas Llosa wrote a wonderful story about a traffic accident not unlike mine. I hadn't thought about it until right now. And it even involved a truck. It's in a collection called *Aunt Julia and the Scriptwriter.* Do you know the story? I don't think I saw that book on your shelf." He launched into a précis of the tale without waiting for me to answer. "The driver clips a little girl who was walking alongside the narrow road. He stops, only to find he has killed her. He weeps over her body so despondently that he doesn't even defend himself as he is mugged, robbed, and left in the dirt by the local peasants who couldn't have cared less about the child."

I knew the story well, and I sorely missed it from my shelf. I had loaned the book out, never to be returned. I was astounded at the detail he was able to recall, and I agreed with him about the relevance of the fictional story for his real-world case. I kept my silence, respecting his almost trancelike need to repeat the story.

"I remember now that the truck driver recovers from the physical injuries of his beating, but not from the psychological trauma of having killed the little girl. He becomes a recluse. He loses his job because he won't drive anymore. He becomes completely unable to even ride as a passenger in a car. All he does, day after day, is to maniacally reenact the accident with some little children's toys he got hold of. Over and over again he replays the fateful moment that changed his life. Eventually his wife leaves him, and he has no life left, nothing at all. Then, I can't remember exactly how, he figures out he needs some counseling—like Rhonda was suggesting for me. So he walks across the entire city to see an aged woman psychologist whose method of therapy has a mystical, magical component to it. Remember? She figures him out right away, and to his complete surprise, she encourages him to keep reenacting the accident with the toys, just as he had been doing. He had expected her to tell him to stop and to reengage with the world, but no, she supports his repetitive, seemingly hapless behavior."

"You're amaz—" I tried to interject.

Cardarelli continued unabated. "At the end of the brief session, the psychologist tells him he only needs to come back once more and that he'll know when. He has no idea what she means. Months pass, and he essentially never leaves his ever-degrading home, still reenacting the events of the accident, over and over and over again. Then, one day he has an epiphany of some kind about the accident that he must describe to the therapist without delay, so he rushes from his home, jumps in a cab, and is whisked to her office. Throughout the ride, he focuses only on the details of his insight, afraid to lose his vision, the way one loses one's grasp on a dream upon awakening. Finally, he arrives at her office and bursts into another client's session to describe his revelation. He's only begun when she raises up her hands to silence him. She says there is no point saying more, because his spell is broken. That is why he was able to take the taxi across town. And she had it just right. The nightmares were over; he could return to life."

I was astonished by Cardarelli's monologue. It was an incredibly accurate and insightful summary of one of Vargas Llosa's best stories, and I took it as Cardarelli's way of saying he would seek out counseling to help deal with his own highway accident. But my mind was spinning, because of all the hundreds of attorneys and clients who had paraded through my office over the years, *not one* had ever looked at the spines of my books in detail. On the contrary, more than a few attorneys had joked about my incessant reading and my habit of keeping every book I read. Who would have thought that the one and only person to really understand what books meant to me would be a long-distance truck driver? Not me, I'm ashamed to say.

Cardarelli had fallen silent now, seemingly in a daze.

"Paul," I broke in to his reveries, "I need to interview you in-depth about your personal background. I do this with every trial client. Why? Because a key element of my trial strategy is to present a full person to the jury, not just a litigant. You follow?"

"Yes, sure. That makes sense."

"So let's start with where you went to school, what you studied, and how you got into long-distance truck driving. The more I know about you, the better."

A wry smile came over Cardarelli's face as he turned to look at me square in the eyes. "Why do I have a feeling that because you now know I like to read, you probably think I'm a middle-class kid who for some reason or other ended up with a humble job?" Not taking the bait, I didn't react. He paused and looked away. "Actually, that's not my background at all. I'm a working-class kid from a tough neighborhood of Detroit. My dad worked at Ford's central plant; he had a job on the production line that was right out of Charlie Chaplin's *Modern Times*."

Cardarelli rose from his chair and walked to the window as he spoke, but I had the impression he never saw the view over Boston Harbor and the airport beyond. His mind was far away in the past, and his breathing changed as he found the memories. "My father spent his life in two spaces: he was either at the Ford plant or scowling in front of the TV, drinking beer. He had a favorite team in every sport known to mankind, and the outcome of every game was a big deal to him. He tried to get me to join him in this addiction to sports, but even as a kid, I saw it as a waste of time. I had nothing in common with the man. Nothing at all.

"My mother was a cleaning lady. She worked so many hours tidying up other people's houses that she had no energy left to clean ours; the place was a perennial mess. I don't know, maybe she did that to piss off my father. She seemed to loathe him. They rarely spoke to one another, and I certainly had no interest in initiating a conversation with either of them. So because I was an only child, this meant it was essentially a conversation-free household. Just the ever-present din of the television."

"How about school, friends, hobbies?"

"To be honest with you, I wasn't particularly good at making friends. An occasional pal, sure, but nobody I would call a 'friend.' I never agreed to go play at another boy's home, since I certainly wasn't going to invite anyone to come into the marital war zone of my parents' house. So to be frank with you, I spent most of my childhood alone and most of it in silence."

"So were you a lonely kid?" I probed.

"I don't know. All children are lonely in some ways, aren't they?" Cardarelli mused. "But I don't remember experiencing being alone as being *lonesome*. I was actually happiest when I was alone. God, I remember waiting anxiously for 3:12 to appear on the classroom clock: that was the moment each day when I could get away from the other kids and their cliques. My problem was, I liked being home even less than I liked being the odd kid out at school. So I would arrive home just in time for dinner—which meant poorly cooked food eaten in silence with the TV blaring away. My father abhorred silence; maybe that's why I crave it."

Cardarelli gave a little shiver and didn't speak for at least half a minute, lost somewhere in his past. "To sit and read, that was what I really loved to do. When I was involved in a book, I was like a cat curled up next to a fireplace. I'd have purred if I'd known how. But I couldn't read at home: it only brought ridicule from my father. If he saw me with a book—caught me, I almost said, should have said—he belittled me about it."

"Wow. That must have been hard on a little kid."

"It was crushing, actually." He sighed deeply before taking up his narrative again. "Anyway, in reaction to all of this, I left home. Not physically, of course, I couldn't. But in my mind I was elsewhere: half-way around the world, or in another century, even on the moon—it depended on what I was reading. With all my heart and soul I was determined to escape the doldrums of this kind of life, of working-class Detroit. And I knew how to do it, or I thought I did. My plan was to excel in high school, and read, read, read my way into a scholarship at Harvard, or Yale, or some other great college. I remember lying on my back in bed at night with my hands under my head, picturing myself walking to class across Harvard Yard, having flown out of the wrong end of the wrong city on wings of words."

"Why not? What happened?"

"What happened? You have a PhD after your name. You know perfectly well what happened. I was a kid. How was I to know that straight As from a mediocre public high school in a working-class neighborhood meant little or nothing to admissions committees? In the essay part of the applications I sent in, I explained that above and beyond excelling at school, I had read hundreds of great works of literature and history to self-educate myself. I even appended the list, all neatly organized by categories. How was I to know that *that* meant little or nothing? I literally had no idea that the kids who get into universities go to prep schools or lived in the best neighborhoods of the best towns, and that these towns had public high schools with far, far greater science and library facilities and much better teachers than mine.

"Anyway, the last two months of high school were by far the worst two months of my life—until this accident happened. When I received the final rejection letter—it was from Yale—it was like a gate slammed shut in my face. I still desperately needed to escape the living hell of my parents' house, but now there was nowhere to go to. Then, completely by chance, I came upon truck driving.

"It happened a week after I graduated, and a day after an explosive argument with my father. I decided to hitchhike to California. And just like that, I left home and never went back. Never. Can you even imagine that? Never went back, and never wrote. I'd read Jack Kerouac's *On the Road*; I think that's where the idea came from. Anyway, after a few rides, followed by a four-hour-long wait by the side of the road somewhere in Wisconsin, I landed a ride from a guy in an eighteen-wheeler. Alan Ryder was his name." This memory elicited a slight smile. "At lunch that day at a truck stop, he told me the company was always looking for new drivers, and that if I wanted to make a few trips with him, he'd show me how to drive a big rig and then introduce me to his supervisor. So back and forth across the country I went for five months, helping Alan with the loads in exchange for meals, driving lessons, and the lore of the road. After that, I took some tests, received my own trucker's license, and landed a job just like Alan had promised. Suddenly, I had all the time alone I could dream of and no one to stop me from reading. And here we are, over thirty years later. Man, it's gone by fast."

The silence Cardarelli so loved enveloped us; it was as if he were sharing it with me. Eventually I spoke. "Anybody special in your life during all those years?"

"Not really. Given my interest in reading, which only increased as time went on, I became progressively more estranged from the people I associated with. I just couldn't stomach engaging in meaningless banter and vacuous conversations with my fellow truckers and the waitresses in the truck stops. Sometimes I'd try, but I was just sitting there pretending to listen, longing to get back to my room where there were philosophers and explorers and adventurers and even emperors waiting for me."

I had to smile at this image. "Do you read as much these days as you did in the past?"

"Of course. Reading is what I *do*, what I love. The downside of this, of course, is that it means that most of my friends are dead, some for decades, some for centuries, some even longer."

Cardarelli stopped speaking at this point, seemingly torn between having confided so much about himself and being proud of what he had revealed. Then out of the blue he added, "A jury would think I'm nuts, always alone with my books, wouldn't they? You're not going to tell them all this, are you?"

"When the time's right, Paul, you and I will work out together what we'll tell the jury. I promise you that. But everything you're telling me helps me understand who you are, and that's key."

"But Attorney Frei—"

"Terry."

"Okay, Terry. But I want to say something. I want you to understand something. It's not like I *wanted* to be so isolated in life. I always wanted to meet the right woman, make the right friends. But I couldn't figure out how to do it. The people in my life would have thought that Gabriel García Márquez was someone's gardener. It's like I've made myself into some kind of an anomaly: I'm not like the people I know, and I don't know how to meet the people I'm like. And I'm paying the price these days for being so alone, I can tell you. Nobody to help me deal with what happened."

As the meeting drew to a close, I told Cardarelli that when he was served with lawsuit papers, as he almost certainly would be, he should immediately send them along to me so that I could file an answer on his behalf. But Cardarelli wasn't going to let me off so easy. He shocked me with his next question.

"So Attorney Frei—I mean, Terry, what about you? Maybe I don't have a right to ask—just tell me if I am out of line here—but when did you fall in love with reading?"

No one else had ever asked me this question before. No one, ever. And no one has since. And while part of me wanted to say something about my privacy, or that while I had a need to ask him about his life, the reverse wasn't true—none of this posturing made any sense.

"Well, are you sure you're interested?" I stammered.

"I'm very interested. You're the first person I have ever spoken to about my reading. So, yes. Your turn to do the talking now."

There was no getting out of it now. What the hell.

"Well, in junior high school I had a close friend. Two actually. Two brothers, and they were my two best friends, although the two of them had absolutely nothing in common with each other, nothing whatsoever. The younger brother was two years younger than we were, and he was a bit of a wild guy, with whom my friendship involved adventure and daring and crazy wonderful teenage moments. The older brother was the complete opposite. He was a contemplative intellectual even as a kid, and oh, how he loved to read. Because I first connected with the younger brother—and remained close friends for many years to come—the older brother, called Bucky, paid little attention to our mischievous and childish amusements. The change came one night when Bucky was at home reading, as always, and his brother and I passed by. Bucky was laughing out loud at Laurence Sterne's *The Life and Opinions of Tristram Shandy, Gentleman*. He read me a few passages, and for some reason suggested that I pick up a copy and read it as well, so we could share the humor of it all. Not only did I take him up on that, but we went on to read all nine volumes of it, and we talked about them in great detail. I was hooked on reading after that. We both ended up at UC Berkeley for our undergraduate work, and the friendship grew from there—the friendship with Bucky, to be sure—but especially the friendship with the authors and characters who live through all those pages. And now . . . now I'm glad to meet you, Paul

Cardarelli. It's rare that I run into someone who shares a true passion for the written word."

"Well, I'll be damned. Thanks for sharing. I don't know the Tristram Shandy books, but I'm off to learn." With that, he stood and, without another word, left the office.

*

It took the parents of the decedent just over six months to retain counsel and have a lawsuit filed on their behalf. As expected, the suit claimed wrongful death damages against both Countrywide and Cardarelli as an individual. Counsel for the parents and their daughter's estate was Eric Findley, and he did what I thought was quite a competent job on the lawsuit paperwork.

Within a month, I filed an answer on behalf of both defendants. Two months after that, I was served with typical discovery documents: interrogatories (written questions to be answered under oath) and a request for production of documents. To answer the interrogatory questions, Cardarelli needed to return to my office both to provide the answers and to sign the responsive document. In the late morning, on one of those fall days during which I couldn't resist kicking at the leaves strewn along the sidewalk, no different from when I was a small boy, I met with my client for a second time.

Cardarelli looked and sounded far more vigorous and dynamic than the first time I met with him. Obviously, the passage of time since the accident was having its effect. We spent the first hour working up responses to the twenty interrogatory questions. Question by question, Cardarelli would provide the answer, which I would then translate into legalese and type into my computer. During the second hour, we reviewed the list of documents the plaintiffs had asked Cardarelli to produce and planned the logistics of how and where we could locate them. It was just about noon when we finished, and I invited Cardarelli to a local seafood restaurant where we could eat outside. He readily agreed.

The restaurant was a tourist's dream. It was part of historic Quincy Market, and venerable Faneuil Hall was right across the street. Even though it was only a few hundred yards from my office building, there was time on the way over for a chilly autumn breeze to swirl the leaves up in an eddy, reminding us both of the imminent arrival of winter. After we ordered, the new, more animated Cardarelli surprised me by initiating the conversation about the case.

"I've been worrying about how you're going to make the jury like me by telling them what a lone ranger I am. I mean, I appreciate in the abstract your strategy of presenting the whole person and not just a lawsuit defendant to the jury, but I'm *not* a whole person. Whole people have a family. I don't. Whole people have friends. I don't. My solitude makes me sound fairly weird—like a deviant. How're you going to get around that?"

"To be frank," I answered, "I haven't the foggiest idea. *Yet.* That's why I need to get to know you better. Sometimes I figure out what I need to say sooner; sometimes, I figure it out later. But I always figure it out. If I didn't, do you think Wilkins would keep sending me cases? You met her, if on the phone. For now, trust me. All that matters is that you keep teaching me who you really are. We'll figure out trial strategy later. *Together.*"

"Okay, okay," he replied. "As long as you live up to the 'together' part." Then, in a tone of voice I hadn't heard before, accompanied by a small, almost sheepish smile, Cardarelli let still more slip out about his solitary life. "To tell you the truth, I'm rather enjoying having an excuse to talk about my background. I guess that's because I never, ever get to talk to *anyone* about this stuff. Hell, I barely ever talk to anyone about anything." Then, he added wryly, "Does this count as one of the therapy sessions you and Rhonda Wilkins were referring to?"

I took the bait, hook, line, and sinker. "Absolutely not. What we are doing here is not clinical counseling, and in fact grief counseling is something I know absolutely nothing about."

Cardarelli broke into his handsome, broad smile over the exaggerated tone of my delivery.

But I was serious. "You do know that, correct?"

"Yes, yes. Relax, Terry. I do know that. I was just putting you on. And I'll think about getting some clinical counseling. I really will. But I'm doing much better with it all." He paused, and then said, "Now, back to my case. Is there anything more you want to know about my background?

"Well, we covered a lot, for sure. But there are a couple areas where clarification—amplifications really—would be helpful to me. Tell me more about how you fell in love with reading."

"This might be a long answer, but it's my story—my Bucky story," he joked, shooting me a smile.

Cardarelli's steady baritone voice was self-assured as he relayed his answer to my question. He was completely unlike how he had spoken in our first meeting, and I definitely had the impression he was recovering from his trauma. "My high school teachers were universally mediocre and in no way interested in my intellectual curiosity—nor anybody else's. In the Detroit schools I went to, minimal work was assigned, and it was always well below grade level. In fact, public school in any working-class Detroit neighborhood of the era was not even about teaching or learning. It was about disciplining and maintaining order. So my education had little to do with school. But I was a straight-A student. I did everything they asked of me; they just didn't ask much.

"No. My inspiration came from somewhere else—straight from the Detroit Public Library on Woodward Avenue. Actually, it was all thanks to one very special person: Louise McCarthy. She was the reference librarian, and she took me under her wing like a lost baby bird. I first met Mrs. McCarthy when I was nine or ten. Strangely enough, it was thanks to my father that I met her.

"I had taken out a copy of Cervantes's *Don Quixote*, which I was reading in my room, and I was so deeply involved, walking alongside the noble warrior who was seated on his rundown old nag, Rocinante, that I never heard my father calling me for dinner from downstairs. Anyway, he was livid when he burst into my room, and he grabbed the book away to see what I was reading. He almost immediately came upon the famous etching of the great optimist tilting his lance at the windmill, and he just stood there sputtering, shaking his head back and forth. And then he turned toward me, and with spittle flying out of his mouth, he bellowed at me, 'Goddamn you and these *fucking* fiction books. Working people like us don't have time for fairy tales.' Those were his exact words. I can hear them like he said them five minutes ago. He made me swear I would take the book back to the library the next day, and then he did the unthinkable: he took out the library card that was in the paper pocket glued to the inside of the back cover, ripped it up in front of me, and dropped the pieces on the floor." Cardarelli's entire demeanor and voice changed as he recounted this memory from his childhood—to the point where he had to stop for a moment, seemingly to catch his breath. "I was just a little kid. That was the *only card* of any kind that I had, and it meant everything to me."

Cardarelli paused before continuing quietly. "I never forgave him for that." He looked over at me. "Never. It changed our relationship forever. Actually, to be honest, I would say it ended our relationship. Just telling you the story brings up in me the suffocating feeling I had in my chest that day. God, I hated that man."

Cardarelli took a break to compose himself, buttering a piece of the sourdough bread that so enamored this restaurant to me. He exhaled deeply before beginning again. "Anyway, when I returned the book the next day, as he had ordered me to do, I broke down and started crying in front of Mrs. McCarthy. I was absolutely bawling, with streams of tears running down my cheeks. She pried out of me what had happened, and after she had dried me up with half a dozen tissues, she talked to me in the softest, gentlest voice that anyone had ever used with me. 'I'll tell you what, young man: we're going to make you another card right now, and I'll keep it right here in my drawer for you. When you want to take out a book, you just come to me. And maybe you better keep your reading to yourself—or better yet, why don't you share it right here with me. Would you like to talk with me about the books you read?'

"I was stupefied," Cardarelli continued, the memories now coming in a flood. "This was the first adult in my life who seemed to understand what reading meant to me, and the warmth in her voice was something I had never experienced before. Sometimes I think maybe she was excited to have an apprentice reader to train. Who knows? Anyway, she guided me in the early years through the kind of children's literature that opens a child's mind to the wonders of good fiction: Terhune's *Lad: A Dog*, Stevenson's *Kidnapped*, Defoe's *Robinson Crusoe*, Baum's Oz books, and books like that. Then, when I was a young teenager, she introduced me to history books that began to open up to me the wonders of the ancient world. I learned about King Ashurbanipal of Assyria and his great library of cuneiform tablets. There was a book about Cyrus the Great, who founded the Persian Empire and freed the Jews from captivity in Babylon, and another about Alexander the Great and the vast empire he created, and one about Emperor Titus of Rome and his burning of the second temple in Jerusalem, and on, and on, and on. And Mrs. McCarthy brought all this history to life for me when we met and talked about each book. Week after week, year after year, I spent my afternoons in the library, carrying on my clandestine studies. Often Mrs. McCarthy would reread or review a book during the same week I was reading it. Then we would meet in her office and talk in detail—and not only about what the author had written, but also about how the author's views were shaped by his times and his circumstances within his society. In the summers, I spent even more time with her. This apprenticeship went on twelve months a year, year after year. My parents never knew about it. Never. They were darkness; she was light. I worshipped her.

"Even after I started working, our relationship continued, essentially unchanged, until Mrs. McCarthy retired. Of course, I could only meet with her when I was in the area, but it was still the same story: she would probe me about what I had read and how I reacted to what the author had to say. By the time I was about twenty-eight or twenty-nine, she was becoming increasingly frail as she approached the end of her career, but mentally she remained as sharp as ever. I remember so well her little retirement party in the staff room of the library. There were only five or six other people there. One was her new boss, who showed up for a perfunctory five minutes and then left. And then there were three much younger colleagues who gave me the strong impression they were there mostly for a piece of cake. I was the only borrower in attendance, and one of only two people in the room who actually cared about Mrs. McCarthy. The other was the older man who for decades had been in charge of the library's card catalog files. I remember being enormously impressed by him and his work; he showed me how to make use of the marginal notes he had written in pencil on the cards. They provided invaluable cross-references to other works, and I used them when I was thinking about what I wanted to read next. Anyway, at the end of the little festivity, he came up to me and asked a question, which I remember like it was yesterday: 'You learned a lot from Mrs. McCarthy, didn't you?' When I nodded yes, he immediately followed up with, 'So what did you learn?' For some reason, I still remember the depth of his smile at my reply: 'How big the world is.' He shook my hand with such warmth and left the room. I never saw him again.

"The next time I was in the city—maybe a month later—I went by Mrs. McCarthy's rooming house, but she didn't answer the door. The lady who lived next door heard my knocking and came out. She told me that Mrs. McCarthy had been having some health issues and was in a rehabilitation senior center. She suggested I give her a few weeks to recover. I went by a month later when I was back in the city, but there was no answer again. I knocked on the next door over, and found the neighbor lady once again. She told me that Mrs. McCarthy had not recovered all that well, and had been taken to a retirement home some-where. But she didn't know where, and I had no way to learn. I never saw her again, and it sort of broke my heart. No, actually, it didn't sort of break my heart, it definitely broke my heart. That woman meant so much to me." Cardarelli took a deep breath and let it out slowly. "You know, looking back from the perspective of middle age, I can see what she did for me. You know something amazing?"

"What's that?"

"She was the only person I ever spoke with about what I was read-ing. *Ever.*"

I was stunned at this revelation. "What's it been like since, with all this reading, all this learning, just by and for yourself?"

"What can I say? We each build a life for ourself, a persona, out of the pieces and parts of the world we learn about as we grow. My parents offered me nothing, certainly nothing that I wanted to incor-porate. Mrs. McCarthy gave me the life of the mind. Truck driving gave me a profession that pays a decent living—and plenty of time to read. This was all that I've had, I guess, but I've known others with less."

*

For the next month or so, I was completely absorbed in a federal district court jury trial, so it was a good six weeks before I next even thought about the Cardarelli case. And one of the first matters I turned to in the case was thinking through how to take the depositions of the decedent plaintiff's parents. Clearly the questions needed to be gently and sympathetically phrased, in deposition and especially at trial. The jury, understandably, would see the parents as completely innocent victims, and I had seen juries severely punish the client of overaggressive and insensitive attorneys. The toughest area to inquire about was the nature of the parent-child relationship in the Waters family. As Cardarelli's own background made clear, some parents are closer to their children than others or are more reliant on them emotionally or financially—or both. The trick is to ferret out adequate information to evaluate the parents' loss of consortium claims, but to do so without seeming to invade the privacy of the family. No easy task. The depositions would also serve the critically important procedural purpose of "locking in" the parents' testimony about such matters to avoid any surprises at the time of trial. Finally, and just as important, it was only after I knew what the parents were like as witnesses—and as people— that I could evaluate what a settlement offer should look like.

Just about a year after the accident occurred, the day arrived when the two parents came to my office to be deposed, one after the other. What follows are selected excerpts, first of the deposition of the decedent's father, then that of her mother. Mr. Waters, I might mention, was a soft-spoken, pleasant looking, white-haired gentleman in his midsixties. He immediately gave me the impression that he would make a very credible and effective witness, indeed.

FREIBERG: Sir, can you please state your name and address for the record?

WITNESS: My name is Harold L. Waters, and I live at 232 Oakmont Street in Fairhaven, Massachusetts.

FREIBERG: And whom do you live there with, Mr. Waters?

WITNESS: I live there with my wife, Barbara. Before the accident, my daughter, Erin, also lived at home with us.

FREIBERG: And how long have you lived at 232 Oakmont Street?

WITNESS: Oh, my. About thirty years. Maybe thirty-one or even thirty-two. I'm not certain. My wife will know.

FREIBERG: Can you please tell me about your education?

WITNESS: I finished high school during the Great Depression. No one in my family had ever been to college, so there was no question of my going on for more education, nor, to be honest, was I very good with books. So my schooling ended at that point, at least my formal education. I learned a lot in life, I would say, but school was not my strength.

FREIBERG: All right. Let's talk about your career. Are you working now?

WITNESS: No, I retired when the plant where I worked was closed in the early 1980s. I haven't worked since then; my kind of work doesn't even exist anymore in this country, I don't think.

FREIBERG: And what kind of work was that?

WITNESS: I was always a metal worker, from the beginning. My first real job was at a small, family-owned wrought iron company that made fire escapes, banisters, grillwork, and the like. I was there for seven or eight years, and then I landed a job at Severan Metal Works in New Bedford where I worked for nearly forty years.

FREIBERG: Mr. Waters, I would like to ask you some questions about your family. Besides Erin, did you have any other children?

WITNESS: No, Erin was our only child. We tried to have another child, but my wife ran into some health issues, and that was that.

FREIBERG: Is your marriage to Barbara Waters your first marriage?

WITNESS: Yep, first and only. Same for her.

FREIBERG: Sir, you have brought an action against my clients for loss of consortium of your daughter, that is, for the loss of being able to be with your child and enjoy her company. Because of this, I hope you understand, I have to ask you a few questions about your relationship with your daughter. All of us know that parent-child relationships can vary from one family to the next, so I need to learn about some of the details of your relationship with your daughter, is that okay? [Witness nods assent.] I would like to organize my questions about this topic chronologically from when Erin was very young and working forward from there. Let's start when she was a baby. Were you what they call these days a coprimary parent, that is, did you get involved in feeding, bathing, diapering, putting Erin to bed, and so on?

WITNESS: Oh, goodness no, not really. My wife was home with the baby and did all that mothering stuff. I was your typical steelworker—sort of not involved with all that baby stuff, if you know what I mean.

FREIBERG: Sure. Now let's talk about when Erin was about five years old or so. Were you more involved with her during this period of her life?

WITNESS: No. To be honest with you, I really didn't know what to do with a little girl. Maybe if she'd been a tomboy type I could have done more, but she was the opposite. She was always a little lady who wanted to play tea party and girl games. Nothing

I could relate to very well. I left all that to my wife, who loved every second of it. She and Erin were inseparable.

FREIBERG: How about when Erin was about ten years old or so? Any changes?

WITNESS: No, not really. Same story. Oh, I went to my fair share of dance recitals and things like that over those years. Erin was always into ballet. Not a star or anything, but she had fun. But, as I say, it was mostly my wife who brought up Erin, not me.

FREIBERG: And when Erin was about fifteen. Any changes?

WITNESS: When Erin was a teenager, she didn't even have much to do with my wife, let alone with me. It was all about her girl-friends, and she mostly just moped around the house com-plaining that some boy or other did or didn't like her. Stuff like that. The ballet dancing had stopped by then, and her hobbies at school were not the type parents go see, like dance or sports. So I didn't have that much to do with her activities, to be frank with you.

FREIBERG: And when Erin was a young adult of about twenty, did you have more to do with her in that period of her life?

WITNESS: After high school, Erin was determined to go on to col-lege. Like I said, no one in my or my wife's family had ever done that. Of course, I didn't have the money for a fancy college, but Erin got herself into one of the Massachusetts state college systems where the tuition is reasonable. She was able to take, I don't know, about two courses at a time in the evening stud-ies program because she worked full time during the day. She worked as a receptionist at an accounting firm.

FREIBERG: Did you see her much during this period?

WITNESS: No, not all that much. She was so busy, always either working or studying. She lived with us, so I saw her a little bit most days of course, but she really had her own life. By the time she was twenty, she was pretty well grown up. After work she was usually either at her classes or studying somewhere, and when she was home, she was mostly in her own room reading and studying. But one thing for sure: she had time almost every day to speak to us, mostly to my wife. Those two couldn't get through a day without checking in with each other—usually more than once. But with me it was mostly, "Hello, Dad, how are you doing?" I'd say, "Fine." Maybe she'd ask a question about the Red Sox or the Celtics, 'cause she knew I loved sports. You know, looking back, I should have tried to create more conversations, but it just wasn't that easy to find things to talk about together.

FREIBERG: What about when she was twenty-five? Any changes?

WITNESS: No, there were no changes. From the time Erin began working and going to college in the evenings, it never changed from year to year. You see, if you can only take two courses at a time, it takes a long time to graduate. So nothing changed up till the day of the accident. It was always work during the day and school or studying at night. And a lot of studying on the weekends.

FREIBERG: What did Erin study at school?

WITNESS: I don't really know. That's a good one for my wife; she'll know. General studies I think, you know, undergraduate general education. I always saw books around, and to a guy like me they seemed to be about all sorts of topics. I can tell you this: she really cared about whatever it was she was reading about at any given time. She tried to talk to me several times about what she had just read, and she was always so excited about it. But I sort of put her off. I just had no reference points, so I always felt lost. Not her fault. Now I know. I should have just shut-up and tried to be interested and to listen better. That's one of the things I regret the most. I didn't give her the time she deserved, you know, the attention she deserved.

FREIBERG: What do you mean by that?

WITNESS: You know how people say sometimes you don't know how important something is to you until you lose it? Well, that's what happened to me. [Witness begins choking up and becomes difficult to understand.] All her life I sort of ignored Erin, because in my heart of hearts she wasn't a [unintelligible].

COURT REPORTER: I'm sorry, I couldn't understand what you said.

WITNESS: [Sobbing heavily.] A son. Because she wasn't a son. I wanted a boy to play ball with, to drink a beer with, to talk sports with. [Witness crying.] And I got this girl who didn't do any of this. She made tea parties with little tiny cups when she was young, and when she grew up all she talked about was books, books, books—and what teachers had said . . . and I couldn't do any of this with her. [Witness choking up; having difficulty speaking.] I guess I should say, "I didn't," not that "I couldn't." I *could* have, and I know now that I *should* have. [Witness pauses to catch his breath.] I have been searching inside myself a lot since Erin died about what she meant to me. I'm not going to sit here and lie about her being my best friend and my constant companion, because she wasn't. She was my daughter. Period. I don't give a damn, really, if some other story would increase the money this lawsuit brings in, because it wouldn't be true, and I don't really care about the money. I just want to have Countrywide and its drivers face up to the ten-hour rule they broke. I just want the company to lay down an ironclad rule with its drivers: don't drive *at all* past the safety limit. To me it's obvious that if one of these big rig drivers falls asleep at the wheel, someone is going to get killed. [Witness crying to the point where he cannot speak.]

FREIBERG: Mr. Waters, would you like to take a break?

WITNESS: No, no. Just give me a few seconds.

FREIBERG: Fine. I have just a few more questions for you.

WITNESS: Sure, I understand. You're just doing your job.

FREIBERG: Did Erin have a fiancé or a steady boyfriend at the time of the accident?

WITNESS: No. She never met the right guy. I think she was hoping to meet some interesting fellow at school, but it never happened. She was a pretty girl, with bright green eyes and the softest light-brown colored hair you ever saw. She dated in high school in a normal way, of course. But once she was both working and taking classes, she discouraged the two or three guys from the high school and the neighborhood who she knew. She was determined to marry a college guy. I think that is the only kind of guy she could have fully respected. But there just wasn't time for that to happen. Ask my wife about this stuff. The two of them spoke with each other a lot—and about just this sort of thing. But that's all I know about her dating.

FREIBERG: If I understand correctly, Mr. Waters, you were asleep in the backseat of your car when the collision occurred, and the first thing you remember about the accident was when you found yourself in the hospital room bed, is that correct?

WITNESS: Yes. The last thing I remember is my wife asking Erin if it was okay if we dozed off, and she said sure, she was fine to drive. The next thing I remember is what I thought was somebody's kid looking in my eyes with a flashlight, but the kid turned out to be a young lady doctor, and it wasn't a flashlight, it was one of those doctor's lights.

FREIBERG: Can you please tell me about your injuries in the accident?

WITNESS: I wasn't hurt at all, not even very bruised, really. By being slouched down asleep like we were, it meant that we were protected by the car frame. And we had our seat belts on as well. So I am not claiming Countrywide owes me for any injury to me. I was lucky. Same thing for my wife.

FREIBERG: Okay. Let's talk about what you are claiming damages for. First, you are bringing a claim in your own capacity for the loss of consortium of your daughter. What do you intend to say to the jury about what consortium you lost?

WITNESS: Well, as I told you earlier, I didn't pal around with my daughter. But she was at the table for holiday meals like any child would be, and she was full of life compared to my wife and me; we're sort of old and dried up. Erin was full of stories, sometimes about what happened at work, but mostly about something a teacher said or about something she'd read. She brought youth and energy and light into the house, and now the whole place is dark and glum. My wife mopes around and doesn't really clean very well anymore and almost never cooks anything decent. The house used to be sparkling clean. And she used to care a lot about cooking. She would watch those recipe shows on TV and try something new. Sometimes what she made was good, sometimes not so good, but at least it was different. Now she has no spark, no energy for anything like that. So my life has been greatly reduced: no daughter, no spark in my wife. Just a gray, dusty, dark-feeling home and spaghetti, spaghetti, spaghetti. And we're not even Italian.

FREIBERG: What do you mean, "no spark" in your wife?

WITNESS: She's depressed, she's tired, she's unclean, she doesn't care, she doesn't speak much, she doesn't smile, she hardly does *anything* anymore. It's like she's there but she's not there. She's empty, that's what it is. She's empty. Ask her, look at her. You'll hear; you'll see for yourself.

FREIBERG: Would there be anything else you would tell the jury about what you, personally, lost in the accident?

WITNESS: Yeah, one other little thing. I lost the future. My family's future. Erin was a pretty girl, and my dream was that she'd find the right guy and get married and we'd have grandchildren to play with, to come to Thanksgiving, to watch open Christmas presents, and to remember my name. When I'm dead, who's going to remember my name now? Why would I bother now to put it on a gravestone? Waste of money. Who's going to come read it now? That's what I lost. The future. My future. My father's future.

FREIBERG: And a final line of questions, sir. You and your wife are also bringing this suit in your capacity as administrators of the estate of Erin Waters, correct?

WITNESS: Yes, that's what I understand.

FREIBERG: What would you tell the jury that the estate would do with any money they award to the estate because of the death of your daughter?

FINDLEY: Objection.

FREIBERG: Is that an objection as to form of the question?

FINDLEY: Not really. It is an objection to the line of inquiry. But I'll reserve it. You may answer the question, Mr. Waters.

FREIBERG: Would you like the court reporter to read back the question, sir?

WITNESS: No, I understand it. But I don't have any answer. My wife and I live simple lives, and we have our retirement savings and social security. We're too old to change our lifestyle, and besides I'm too sick with my diabetes, and my wife is too broken in spirit to change much. I don't even think we're strong enough to take a big trip, you know, to go to Europe or something. So I don't really have an answer for you. Like I said earlier, for me it's more to make Countrywide learn a lesson than to get the money. Maybe we'll give the money to a charity, I don't know. But mostly I want Countrywide to tell me they promise to make their drivers respect the ten-hour rule. That's what I really want.

FREIBERG: I have no further questions.

FINDLEY: Thank you. I just have one question for the deponent. When you testified on direct that you don't really care about the money, that you just want Countrywide to face up to the ten-hour maximum per day driving rule, what you meant to say was that while you didn't care so much about receiving the money personally, Countrywide needed to be forced to pay a good deal of money to learn its lesson, isn't that correct?

FREIBERG: Objection as to form.

FINDLEY: Noted. Mr. Waters, you may answer my question.

WITNESS: Actually, I said what I meant. I really don't give a damn about the money. I know you do because you get a third of it. What I care about is the lesson, is a promise in writing from Countrywide that it will strictly enforce the government's rule. I know from this case that driving logs are kept. What I want is for Countrywide to say *in writing* that it will actually and

regularly review these logs, and that the company will discipline drivers who exceed the limit. That's what I care about.

*

Between the morning deposition of Mr. Waters, and the afternoon
deposition of his wife, I put in a call to Wilkins to report the outcome
with Mr. Waters, as she had requested. Our best guess was that wherever Attorney Findley and his clients were having lunch, by all odds
there was a stern discussion going on between them. There was no
way Findley was pleased with Mr. Waters's testimony about the money
issue. Plaintiff tort lawyers want their clients to tell the jury "big-dollar
verdicts send big messages." And, of course, there is some truth to this.
We both thought there was a good chance he would try to convince
Mrs. Waters to take a stronger stand on the social value of a large,
punitive verdict that would really teach Countrywide a lesson it would
never forget.

Needless to say, Wilkins saw right through to the danger that
lurked behind the superficial "good news" of Mr. Waters's testimony.
That's what I liked about working with her: she looked beneath the
surface. We both thought that the father's lack of concern with monetary damages and his emphasis on future highway safety could easily
impress the hell out of the jury and prompt them to amply reward his
absence of greed. I'd had three or four trials that went the other way,
where the same logic came into play at the other end of the spectrum.
In those cases, the visible greed of the tort plaintiffs had cost them—
big time. Here we had just the opposite, and that could prove to be a
major problem.

"Rhonda," I insisted, "we definitely need to settle this case. The
father is a frightening witness: he is sincere in what he says about caring mostly about safety reform, and he seems honest about recogniz-
ing that he wasted a lot of opportunities to get to know his daughter
better. But what is even scarier is how clearly he articulates the tragedy
of getting cut off from the future. And on top of all that, he is absolutely
pitiable in his description of what life at home is like postaccident.
Rhonda, I can't try a case against a plaintiff who is sincere, honest,

credible, and pitiable. The jury will hand me my head and hand him a bag of gold. I would if I were a juror. There would be absolutely no way to cross-examine what I heard today. No way. *No* way. The jury would love this honorable, bereft man, and the sky could be the limit for the verdict. We absolutely need to settle this case."

"Oh, fuck yes," Wilkins replied without hesitation. "I totally agree. But I have to say, I really like the idea that in negotiating the settlement, you could offer up a letter from Countrywide that shows that the company is taking real measures to do whatever it takes to assure compliance with the ten-hour rule. That makes sense for everybody. I don't want to go through another case of Countrywide's like this again in the future, I can tell you that. And I'll check in with our risk management team, but I'd bet good money they've already been all over Countrywide on this issue. Bargaining with that letter is monopoly money to me, Counselor, so make good use of it. What do I tell my supervisor about how much money we'll need to settle? The preliminary reserve is still at two million, and I know my supervisor would love to reduce that number if he could."

"I'd keep the reserve where it is for now. We're going to need some significant money here. The father was the first to say that he and his wife suffered no physical injuries; the suit is only about the loss of their daughter. Some juries figure out, and some don't, that if they give money to the estate of a childless decedent with living parents, that money is just going to go to the parents. But in Massachusetts we aren't allowed to point this out to the jury. All we can do is hope the jury figures out that awarding big damages to both Erin's estate and to her parents for loss of consortium is duplicative. But you never know, it can just as easily play out the other way, with the jury awarding compensatory damages to the parents, and really significant punitive damages to the estate. Unless the mother is a disaster for some reason, this case *cannot* go to trial. It would be the wrong thing to do for any number of reasons."

"Anything interesting in the testimony?"

"No, not really. Except you should have seen plaintiff's counsel when the father said it wasn't really about the money. He'd been looking out the window at the harbor view, and when he heard the father say that, he whipped his head around so violently, the next thing you know he may sue the father for whiplash."

She laughed out loud at the image. "Oh, that's fucking beautiful. That cynical remark has just earned you an award, Counselor: Honorary New Jersey Citizen for a Day. There's hope for you yet, Boston. Look, I'll keep the two million reserve intact for now. Call me again after Mom's deposition." With that, she hung up.

Again, what follows are those excerpts from Barbara Waters's deposition that contain the heart and soul of her testimony. Mrs. Waters was in her early sixties, with medium-length white hair and a pair of jade green eyes to match Erin's. She looked dazed and slightly disheveled; it was clear she had tried to spruce up for the day, without fully succeeding. There was a sadness to her that weighed her down and slowed her every movement.

FREIBERG: Can you please state your name and address for the record?

WITNESS: My name is Barbara H. Waters. My address is 232 Oakmont Street, Fairhaven, Massachusetts.

FREIBERG: Can you please summarize your education for me?

WITNESS: I graduated from high school, Framingham High. I didn't even think about going to college. It just wasn't an option in my family. I did take several evening courses later in life, mainly to try to learn to read better so that I could keep up with what my daughter was doing.

FREIBERG: Can you please tell me about your work history after you left high school?

WITNESS: I went to public high school. In those days there was a big chicken processing plant on the outskirts of town. It's gone, of course. There's a mall there now. Anyway, I had a friend who worked in the processing plant, and she got me a job interview.

I got the job, and worked there on the packing line for about ten years or so until my husband and I moved to New Bedford. Once we were down there, I worked part time in a supermarket in the butchery department.

FREIBERG: Did you retire at some point?

WITNESS: I left when my husband retired from Severan Metal Works. Our daughter, Erin, was grown by then and working full-time herself. My husband and I wanted to retire at the same time so that we could do things together.

FREIBERG: And did you do things together?

WITNESS: Sure. We bought a Winnebago—a trailer home. That was our big splurge. We decided to visit every state in the country, and we had some good times with it. We did other things too, like join a seniors' dancing club.

FREIBERG: Did you get to all the states?

WITNESS: No. At the time of the accident we had seen many of the states east of the Rockies, but nothing to the west of that.

FREIBERG: Do you still have the Winnebago?

WITNESS: Well, sort of. But it's at the lot, for sale.

FREIBERG: Why did you decide to sell it?

WITNESS: Too tired. I just don't have the energy or desire to travel anymore, not even close to enough energy to do that.

FREIBERG: Do you still take the seniors' dance classes?

WITNESS: No, not enough get-up-and-go for that anymore either. Maybe someday.

FREIBERG: You brought up the accident, and we need to talk about it for a few questions. I hope that you understand that I feel bad having to bring the topic up, but that's what happens in a lawsuit. I have to learn what happened to you in the accident, given the suit you filed against my—

WITNESS: Yes, I understand. I knew that would be the bad part of the lawsuit.

FREIBERG: Did you think there would be a good part?

WITNESS: Yes, that's why we did it. We want Countrywide to learn a lesson and never again allow a truck driver to drive so long that he falls asleep at the wheel. That's why we sued them.

FREIBERG: And how was bringing the lawsuit going to teach Countrywide a lesson?

WITNESS: Well, like any lawsuit. If they pay money because of something they did wrong, they'll think twice about doing it again.

FREIBERG: I understand. Now let me take you back to the evening of the accident. Can you please tell me what you remember concerning the accident? Not what you learned later from others, but what you actually remember seeing or hearing yourself.

WITNESS: It was very strange. Not at all like the car accident I had as a teenager. In that one, I suddenly saw that the car in front of me was stopped; I slammed on the brakes, and I can still hear the screeching of my tires and the sound of the crash. I can even remember the smell of the burning rubber from the skidding. In those days, there weren't any seat belts, so I was thrown against the steering wheel. I can still remember that feeling too, of course. But in this accident, I was asleep in the backseat, with my seat belt on. I had loosened it so that I could lean over on Harold's lap, sort of sideways. [Witness indicates by leaning over in her chair.] I never saw or heard anything. The very first thing I remember is the spinning light of a police car. I remember lights before I remember words. The words I first remember were from an ambulance driver who was explaining that there had been an accident, that he was putting a neck collar on me, and that I was not to move at all. He said I would be placed on a stretcher and taken by ambulance to a hospital for a checkup. And he said I wasn't bleeding. I remember that. And for some reason he repeated it twice. I tried to talk, I knew I wanted to ask some questions, but I just couldn't make my voice work. Isn't that strange? And then ever so gently he put his finger on my lips, which must have been moving, and told me not to speak. He said I should save all my energy in case I had been hurt and needed it. Then I guess I passed out.

FREIBERG: And what is the next thing you remember?

WITNESS: I remember waking up, and it was morning; the room was full of light. And I was alone. Where was Harold? Then I realized that I was in a hospital room, and I remembered the spinning lights. I suddenly knew there had been a car accident. Where were Harold and Erin? So I called out several times, "Is anyone here? Is anyone here?"

FREIBERG: And what happened next?

WITNESS: A nurse came running in, I remember that she was running. She seemed so young. She asked me not to move and said she would be right back with a doctor. That took a while, but then a young doctor came in, and he had me move one part at a time to see how I was doing. First, fingers. Then wrists. Then, arms. Then toes, then feet, then legs. Then he asked me to raise my head. Each time he asked me if I felt any pain, but I didn't. It was amazing. I wasn't hurt at all, so far as I could tell. And he said they had taken x-rays or that new thing—NRI [*sic*] or something. He said they couldn't find any broken bones or even any bad bruises. I remember his wording exactly, he said, "I think you came out of this unscathed," because I didn't know what the word meant. I asked him, and he smiled. Such nice teeth. I immediately thought about Erin and if he was married. Isn't that crazy? I was ready to do matchmaking in the hospital bed. And then my mind, for the first time after the accident, snapped to attention. "Oh my God," I said. "How are Erin and my husband?" Why did it take so long for me to think about them?

FREIBERG: How did he respond to your question?

WITNESS: He said he was also the attending doctor for my husband who was in the next room, and, just like me, Harold had not been injured. But he said he was not involved with Erin but would send someone in who did know.

FREIBERG: Did someone come in?

WITNESS: Yes, about fifteen minutes or so later, a woman came in. She said she was a social worker at the hospital. She was in her fifties or so, and I could tell she had a lot of experience. And she told me what had . . . what had . . . [Witness begins sobbing.]

FINDLEY: Can we take a break at this point?

FREIBERG: Yes, of course. Let's take a fifteen-minute break.

*

FREIBERG: We were at the point where a social worker came into your hospital room to tell you about what happened to your daughter in the accident. I know how hard this must be for you to talk about, but can you tell me what she said and how you responded?

WITNESS: Yes. She told me exactly what had happened to Erin. She said that Erin had been killed instantly because she had been . . . been, been . . . decapitated. [Witness sobbing and having trouble responding.] At the time, I didn't know what decapitated meant, and I was too embarrassed to ask. But she said that Erin's death had been instantaneous, so the only little piece of good news was that she didn't suffer any pain whatsoever.

FREIBERG: Did she tell you anything else?

WITNESS: Yes. She also told me that when people are in a really bad accident and someone they love is killed, it is a very good idea for them to receive treatment from a specialized grief counselor. And then she did something that I will never, ever forget.

FREIBERG: What was that?

WITNESS: She asked me if she could sit on the edge of my bed and hold my hand while we were silent together and I thought about what she had told me. She said that after we did this, we could talk as much as I liked, or not at all, about what had happened. She asked me if this idea was okay with me.

FREIBERG: And what did you say?

WITNESS: I told her I thought it was a fine idea. So for quite a while I lay there holding her hand, and I remember how good it felt just to touch and to be touched. It was like a boat being anchored. It sort of kept me from floating away on my ideas. But one thing was strange. I couldn't bring myself to think about Erin. I knew I was supposed to, but my mind wouldn't do it. I tried, but my mind kept switching to Harold and how he was. I felt so safe with her. I told her this the next morning before Harold and I left the hospital.

FREIBERG: And did it take a while for you to admit to yourself that Erin was gone forever?

WITNESS: Well, I have to say, no, it didn't. You see, later that day—the day after the accident—Harold and I were both able to go home. A taxi took us home. Our car was destroyed, of course.

FREIBERG: What was it like to see your husband again?

WITNESS: It was comforting, very comforting. He just kept asking me if I was okay and not hurt. He must have asked me fifteen or twenty times. He kept repeating the same question. He would even interrupt me to ask it yet again. He did this in the cab and throughout the evening when we got home. I asked him if the social worker lady had told him about Erin, and about how we might go through different stages of reacting to what had happened.

FREIBERG: And what did he answer?

WITNESS: He said he didn't need a social worker or a book to tell him how to respond. He said he knew that she was dead, and that we were "damn lucky," as he put it, to be alive. And then he held my hand. He hadn't done that for years and years.

FREIBERG: And what was that like?

WITNESS: It was good, of course, to have my husband to go through all this with—it still is. In some ways we take care of each other better. But he is a man who doesn't talk much about his feelings, and he doesn't often ask about mine. I used to have my daughter to talk to about such things of course, but now she's gone.

FREIBERG: About how often did you talk with your daughter before the accident?

WITNESS: Many times, every day. We shared everything: all our thoughts, all our feelings.

FREIBERG: Did she tell you about the people she met, say, about guys who she might be thinking about?

WITNESS: Goodness, yes. Every detail, every single detail, every thought about every guy.

FREIBERG: Did you talk with her about your life in the same kind of detail?

WITNESS: Oh, yes. Poor girl listened like she was the parent when it was my turn to talk about problems. I'd go on about her father or about yet another ailment the years were bringing my way.

FREIBERG: Is there anybody else you talk to about such matters?

WITNESS: No. Not really. Erin was both my daughter and my best girlfriend.

FREIBERG: How else is life different for you now that Erin is gone?

WITNESS: [Witness chokes up again; takes a few moments to respond.] I was a normal, loving mother. I had an ectopic pregnancy when Erin was about two—I think I said that right—and after that I never conceived again. So this child was everything to me, just everything. My husband loved her too, like a normal father, but he really wanted a son to go fishing and play ball with, so he sort of left Erin to me. She was my doll baby, my tea party girl. I bought her a tea party set when she was just a little girl, [witness chokes up again] maybe three or four, and we had a thousand tea parties. One would end, and the next one would begin. They were very special. In fact, it wasn't at all rare for a queen, sometimes several, to come to a tea party, and then Erin had to curtsy and be extremely formal. [Witness begins sobbing uncontrollably.]

FREIBERG: Why don't we take a break?

*

FREIBERG: What was Erin's day care situation like when you were working?

WITNESS: Erin was in day care while I worked in the chicken processing plant. I remember when I would pick her up at the end of the day she would come running to me as fast as she could and jump up into my arms. Those were the best hugs ever—with her arms around my neck and her legs around my chest.

FREIBERG: What activities did you do with Erin when she was an older child?

WITNESS: I took her to her ballet lessons, and I did her homework with her. Homework was a wonderful time together.

FREIBERG: Tell me about Erin's friendships in high school.

WITNESS: Well, let's see. Erin had one really nice girlfriend who lived just two houses down from us when she was a freshman in high school. Those were such happy times for her. But then that family picked up and moved to California just after the school year ended, and Erin was the saddest kid you ever saw when their car pulled away with her friend waving madly through the back window. Both of them were in tears. I remember that so clearly. That summer, I spent all the time I could with her when I wasn't working . . . But I couldn't replace the friend. She never made such a close friend again—not like that.

FREIBERG: And what did you and Erin do together toward the end of high school?

WITNESS: During the last several years of high school, Erin spent a lot of time alone in her room—studying. I couldn't help her anymore. She was way ahead of what I'd learned in school. So mostly I just took her cups of hot chocolate or tea, and tried to listen and pay attention when she would explain to me what she was learning. I always told her constantly how proud I was of her, and how much I loved her.

FREIBERG: Did she join study groups or school groups, or get involved in other activities with other kids?

WITNESS: No, not like I wanted her to. She used to tell me, "Don't worry, Mom. I'll make friends in college, with people with brains." Those were her words. I remember that line of hers so well . . . She must have said it to me twenty times over the years.

FREIBERG: Did Erin talk about what she wanted to do for work when she was done with her education?

WITNESS: Well, as I told you, Erin was all about going to college. She wanted to major in literature, and she wanted to become a licensed high school English teacher. More than anything else, she wanted to do for others what a wonderful ninth-grade teacher had done for her: she dreamed of exciting students about reading and learning. She loved to read, you know. She always had a book under her arm, no matter where she went. I don't think that girl ever spent a moment bored or just standing around doing nothing. When she was standing in line, or riding on a bus, or waiting for her appointment at the dentist, she would pull out her book and start reading. I have almost no mental picture of her without her having a book tucked under her arm, just in case there was a moment to read.

FREIBERG: What did Erin do once she graduated from high school?

WITNESS: Well, she applied to colleges of course, those that we could afford. The guidance counselor at the high school worked with her on this, and I have always wondered if he sort of doused cold water on Erin's big dreams. It seemed to me that she should have applied to one or two of the great universities and tried to get a scholarship, but he said that our high school had never placed a student like that. So one thing led to another, and she ended up taking evening courses at the Dartmouth campus of the University of Massachusetts. And during the entire time she was there, she worked as a receptionist at an accounting firm. But she had plans about moving up. Her goal was to get all As and save up her salary to have enough money to spend her junior and senior years at the best college she could get into. She lived at home, you know, so she was saving just about every penny she earned. I was so proud of the strength she showed in being so determined, and she definitely was getting the A grades just like she said she would. Erin had all sorts of college application booklets in her room when the accident happened, and she was ready to pull off her big plan. And she would have; I feel so certain of that. But, then, poof—everything went black. Like when the electricity goes off.

FREIBERG: You testified earlier that you spoke with Erin every day. What type of topics did you talk about once Erin was working and going to college classes at night?

WITNESS: Anything, everything. And I learned that the very best topic I could talk to Erin about was to ask her to tell me about what she was reading. She would light up with excitement like a Christmas tree, and tell me all about the latest book . . . More and more I was learning to see the world through her eyes. And of course, just talking with my darling girl was so wonderful—it didn't really matter much to me what exactly we were talking about. Some things I understood, many I didn't, but I just about always nodded yes and smiled back at her. Her words and her enthusiasm would surround me like her arms and legs used to in those jump-up hugs I told you about.

FREIBERG: Have you told me everything that is different in your life now that Erin is gone?

WITNESS: I don't know how to answer that question.

FREIBERG: Do you want me to rephrase the question?

WITNESS: No, no, I understand the question. I just don't know how to answer it . . . How do I put emptiness in words? I wish I had some close girlfriends, but I just don't. I did once have a really good friend, but she moved with her husband to Florida when he retired. I'm embarrassed to say this, but sometimes these days I don't even mind getting a sales call on the phone. At least it's someone to talk to. Isn't that strange? Daytime seems like nighttime now, and nighttime is like being in the mountains after dark, barefoot and without a coat.

*

I didn't even bother to call Wilkins after the deposition. Nothing had changed; on the contrary, it was clearer than ever to me that the case absolutely needed to be settled. I don't know if I had ever met two nicer people, and clearly their lives had been utterly destroyed by the loss of their only child. And Erin herself sounded like a wonderful young woman. Clarence Darrow couldn't get Countrywide out of the pit these two witnesses would dig. This case needed to be resolved short of trial, whatever the cost.

In due course, I received a notice for Cardarelli to submit to his deposition, so it was time to formally prepare him for the ordeal. When I mailed him a copy of the notice of deposition, I included full copies of the transcripts of the parents' depositions, as he had requested. Putting those documents in the envelope felt like I was packing up hand grenades in a box. I couldn't even imagine how devastating it would be for Cardarelli to pore over the parents' words—and I had an image in my head of him reading the transcripts over and over again. This was a man who loved to read, after all.

A few weeks later, the Sunday before my next meeting with Cardarelli, was a day I shall never forget. My wife and I, and our only child, Justin, lived on a narrow, one-way residential street in a modest neighborhood—the only exception to the modesty being our pride in knowing that President Kennedy had been born on the street. Justin was about eight or so, and quick like lightning. It was a sunny late fall day, and my neighbor and I were working together to pick up about twenty million leaves that had fallen on our respective yards from the enormous sycamore trees that lined both sides of the street. Our boys— who were the same age and in theory were supposed to be helping— were instead running around and kicking a ball through the massive leaf piles. And then it happened: the moment when my entire life came down to two seconds. The ball burst through the leaf piles and shot out into the street. Instantly, my son ran out to retrieve it—a knee-jerk reaction. He never saw the car, and the driver never saw the little guy darting out from between two parked vehicles. Bang! Justin apparently ran into the side of the moving car and was somehow bounced backward onto the strip of grass between the curb and the sidewalk. I will never, ever forget the moment when I looked down into the face of my beautiful child, my heart racing so fast it felt like it would explode out of my chest, and realized that somehow, miraculously, he was safe. He was alive. And he was even unharmed, but for what turned out to be a bruised knee. I vividly remember picking him up to carry him home, and then, for some crazy reason, I took a running dive into the center of the biggest leaf pile with him, to celebrate how lucky we had been. Even in the midst of this big, rolling, leafy hug, the thought shuddered through me that my life had careened dangerously close to being just like that of the Waters.

*

The following morning I met yet a different version of Cardarelli. He was brisk and all business at our meeting to prepare for his deposition. If there had been any warmth whatsoever developed between us based on our mutual fondness of reading, or by his sharing of the personal details of his past, he signaled early on that it would play no role in this meeting. There was a remove to him, a distance that had not been there before. So I immediately got down to the task at hand, and began the preparation for his testimony with the generalized discussion I had used a hundred times before.

I mentioned that when witnesses to traumatizing events testify at deposition or at trial, they often report being flooded by an extremely powerful recall of the sensations and emotions they experienced during the actual events. The feelings that are generated can be so intense and disturbing that they can significantly affect testimony. So as I advised him, it's important to not be surprised—or ashamed—if these intense emotions arise. Opposing counsel, and trial judges for that matter, will always allow a recess for a witness to take a breather to recover. And taking a break when this happens is just about always a good idea.

His response was maximally simple and direct. "I understand. What next?"

Somewhat put off, to be sure, but determined to get across the points I needed to convey, I explained to my client about how to answer multiple-part questions, how to deal with aggressive questions, how to seek clarification to unclear questions, and so on. And finally, though I figured I'd catch all hell for it, I couldn't responsibly ignore bringing up the topic I knew he hated talking about: I once again probed as to whether he had sought out some counseling.

If I interpreted his facial expression correctly, he thought seriously about coming back sharply at me for pressing him yet again on this issue. But apparently he thought the better of it, and he responded with considerable restraint: "Don't worry, if I had experienced any flash-backs, any nightmares or nighttime cold sweats—any of the PTSD symptoms—I would have gone to seek counseling. Rest assured, I'm aware of how powerful these symptoms can be, and I would not have ignored them. Trust me. What next?"

His response effectively closed off the topic: he obviously had looked up and was aware of the typical symptoms of PTSD. What flashed through my mind once again as I searched for a follow-up question was my image of Cardarelli perseverating over the parents' deposition transcripts, reading them over, and over, and over again. But how to ask about that diplomatically?

"Any questions about the parents or their testimony from what you read in the transcripts I sent you?"

"Just one," he replied. "These people, they seem so nice. What were they like in person?"

I could think of no way to temper what was perfectly apparent in what he had read. "I was impressed with them, Paul, as people, as parents, and as plaintiffs. And I was really frank about that in a phone call with Wilkins. I told her that this was a case that we absolutely needed to settle, whatever the monetary amount. She agreed, and she told me the insurer is prepared to offer up whatever it will take to get this case resolved—the full policy limit if that's what is needed. As you could see from the transcripts, the most important thing we need to settle this case is for Countrywide to take the ten-hour rule seriously. And I think there were clear signs in the father's deposition testimony that he intends to control the settlement discussions and not to simply acquiesce to their counsel's financial pipe dreams. I just don't have any doubt that this case will settle. By all odds, your deposition tomorrow will be the last day to have to deal with this lawsuit."

"That would be great," Cardarelli said. "That would be a big relief to me. I don't think I could confront the parents at trial. But I have a question for you: How angry were they at me? Be honest with me."

How to answer this? Do you get beyond anger when someone does something stupid that ends up killing your only child? Just because the psychological model for the stages of grief processing says you move from denial to anger to sadness to resignation, does that imply that as you move from stage to stage in your recovery, you completely move on from the earlier stages? Denial, yes: clearly once you convince the deeper parts of your mind that someone you were so connected to is gone forever, there is no going back. I follow that. But anger? I wasn't so sure, despite how I responded to Cardarelli.

"I think they are mostly beyond being angry. I think they are mostly just sad. To be honest with you, to the extent that they're still angry, I think their anger is directed toward Countrywide for allowing its drivers to breach the ten-hour rule. And on that point, I actually have good news for you. I spoke two days ago with Countrywide's in-house counsel, and she told me that it will not be a problem at all to document to the parents that Countrywide made this change within a month after the accident. I'm sure you know this, but let's make that a question: Did you receive some kind of written notice from the company of a new protocol about imposing sanctions for violation of the Hours of Service Regulations?"

"Yes, I did. I certainly did. We all did. And the supervisors have been told to enforce the regulation. Can I tell the parents this at my deposition?"

"Absolutely. Why not? If their counsel doesn't ask the right question on direct, I'll do it on cross."

"Okay. But I want to know something, and I want you to be straight with me. I only saw the transcripts, but you saw the parents. How are they doing?"

Nuts. Not at all the question I wanted him to ask. "Honestly?"

"Yes, be honest with me, please. I mean it. I insist on it."

There was no other way to say it. "I think they are about as sad as sad gets."

"There's nothing left for them, is there?"

"No, but—"

"No buts," Cardarelli cut me off. "Do you have a picture of this woman, of Erin?"

"I do," I confirmed reluctantly. I picked up my expandable file that held several dozen manila folders of case documents. One was labeled "Photographs." Most of the photos were of the accident scene and the vehicles. But there was one eight-by-eleven photograph of Erin's face that had been produced by plaintiffs' counsel. It looked like a formal photo, maybe from a high school graduation; you could tell it was taken by a professional photographer. The girl was quite beautiful, with exactly the green eyes and soft-looking, long light-brown hair her father had described. But what grabbed you most about the photo was the generosity and warmth of the smile Erin shot out at the viewer. There was not a hint of that teenage hesitancy to fully smile for a snapshot, and her teeth were so perfect, I felt like I was looking at a toothpaste ad.

Cardarelli took it in one hand, but was soon holding it in both. He didn't say a word for fully a minute—maybe longer. "Beautiful girl. Beautiful. And she always carried a book under her arm. Damn."

"Paul—"

"I've got to go," he interrupted, standing and heading for the door.

"We're done with the preparation part of this meeting, right?"

"Yes, but—"

"See you at the deposition."

With that, he was out the door and gone. I didn't see him, or for that matter talk to him again, prior to his deposition a month later. I called twice, but he didn't answer, and he didn't have an answering machine. I even sent a letter asking him to call. He didn't. To be honest, it's not like I spent a lot of time concerned about how Cardarelli was doing; when a case had a quiet spell, the space left open was immediately filled to the brim with pieces and parts from the dozens of other cases that were all taking place at once. My law practice was a jumble of calls and meetings. You could have a two o'clock meeting with a client whose entire life had just been thrown into a nosedive, and a three o'clock meeting with someone who had just unexpectedly inherited serious money. But from time to time during the lag between our preparation and his deposition, I did think about Cardarelli fixating on those transcripts, and that worried me for some reason.

On the morning of his deposition, Cardarelli arrived at opposing counsel's office no more than ten minutes before the procedure was due to start. I took him aside into a corner of the reception area and asked how he was doing, and if he had any questions. He seemed calm and collected and reassured me that he was ready to answer questions about his background and about the accident. He just wanted to get it all over with. And he expressly apologized, even with a certain warmth in his voice, for having been abrupt with me at our last meeting.

"I know you're out for my best interests, and I don't doubt your skills for a second. Forgive me. I didn't mean anything by my flippant remarks. I was just stressed out by those deposition transcripts. Anyway, let's just go in and get this over and done with." With that, we left the room to join opposing counsel and the court stenographer in the small firm's single conference room.

When we turned the corner into the room, I was completely taken aback to see that both the decedent's parents were seated at the long conference room table, one on each side of their attorney. Cardarelli froze. Clearly I had to talk to him about this unexpected turn of events, and since nothing cleverer came to mind, I blurted out that I had stupidly forgotten to use the men's room. Plaintiffs' counsel had no choice but to describe to me where it was located, and as I left the conference room, I signaled to Cardarelli to join me in strategic retreat. While it is entirely permissible under the Massachusetts Rules of Civil Procedure for parties to a lawsuit to attend depositions, this was the one and only time in my entire career that opposing counsel had failed to forewarn me. I was livid.

Once the emptiness of the bathroom stalls was confirmed, I explained to Cardarelli that it is accepted protocol for one counsel to alert opposing counsel if his clients intend to appear at a deposition. The point of this, obviously, is that it allows thought and preparation to be given to however this might affect the testimony. I asked Cardarelli if he had any issues with the parents being present, and I offered that, if he did, we could postpone the deposition on some pretext or other. To my complete surprise—and with zero hesitation—Cardarelli, having recovered from his initial shock, announced that he was actually pleased they were present. As he phrased it, "Now that I've had a moment to think about it, I just don't have a problem with this. Not at all. Let them see who I really am, how deeply sorry and broken I am by all this. Don't worry. This is for the better. I can handle it."

As we walked back to the conference room, I realized that, unlike Cardarelli, I remained quite concerned that the parents were present, but I couldn't articulate to myself why I felt that way. I was still infuriated at the amateurish move of plaintiffs' counsel in not giving me a heads-up, especially given that this was a wrongful death case. On the other hand, I had listened to what Cardarelli had had to say about the matter, and I had long since learned to respect his insightfulness and discernment. And on top of that, it was obvious that these gentle, sweet-natured people would be appropriate. Who knows, I thought, perhaps the calm resolve and understanding nature of the parents would help Cardarelli work through his issues with what had happened.

Again, what follows are the most salient excerpts from the deposition transcript. The questions, of course, were asked by opposing counsel, Attorney Eric Findley.

*

FINDLEY: Mr. Cardarelli, I have looked very carefully through your personnel record, which Countrywide produced, and I did not see any disciplinary letters. On the contrary, I saw three different letters written over the years by three different supervisors, and they were quite complimentary about your job performance. Do I have all this correct?

WITNESS: Yes, sir. I was never disciplined. I have always tried to be a reliable, trustworthy employee, and that is what the reviews said about my job performance.

FINDLEY: Were there trainings on an ongoing basis at Countrywide?

WITNESS: Not about driving, as such. There were trainings to keep us up to speed on changes in the technology, changes in record keeping requirements, changes in highway systems available to us, and so on. But once you are capable of driving a big rig, the assumption is that you would be able to continue to do so.

FINDLEY: Was there training with respect to maximum hours that you were allowed to drive in a given period?

WITNESS: Yes, sir. We all knew about the Hours of Service Regulations, and these were discussed quite often. They were somewhat controversial, with some drivers maintaining that they did not reasonably reflect differing circumstances, such as napping in a truck's sleeper berth at a truck stop, or slow driving because of adverse weather conditions, and so on. Also, there was training as to how to keep the logbook.

FINDLEY: And what was the daily limit that was in force at the time of the accident?

WITNESS: At the time, there was a ten-hour limit, after which a driver was required to rest for eight hours. In addition, you could not drive over sixty hours in a seven-day period.

FINDLEY: And do you know, sir, who made this limit?"

WITNESS: Yes, of course. It's federal law, and therefore applicable throughout the country.

FINDLEY: Are you a law-abiding citizen, sir?

WITNESS: I am, yes.

FINDLEY: But you broke this federal law?

FREIBERG: Objection. You can answer the question, Paul.

WITNESS: I did, yes.

FINDLEY: Why would you do that?

WITNESS: Because that was the culture in the trucking industry, just like people in cars go through yellow lights in some cities. The rule of thumb at the company was that if you were within an hour of where you were heading, you could finish up the trip.

FINDLEY: Excuse me, Mr. Cardarelli, but that's an answer as to why other people broke the law and what the rule of thumb at the company was. My question to you, sir, is why *you* broke the law.

FREIBERG: I renew my objection. You can answer the question, Paul.

WITNESS: Why I broke the law?

FINDLEY: Yes, why did you, Paul Cardarelli, break the law?

WITNESS: [Witness pauses before answering.] Because I wasn't insightful enough to foresee the danger in breaking it.

FINDLEY: Thank you. Were there other times prior to the accident when you had exceeded the Hours of Service Regulation limit of ten hours per day?

WITNESS: Yes, sir.

FINDLEY: Was it, in fact, a regular practice for you to exceed this limit?

WITNESS: No, sir, I wouldn't say so. Usually, I was well under the limit, but from time to time I did exceed it.

FINDLEY: Mr. Cardarelli, do you have knowledge about whether other Countrywide drivers ever exceeded the Hours of Service Regulations?

WITNESS: Yes, sir, I do. Drivers often spoke about this issue. And many of these drivers agreed with management in pressuring for changes in part 395.

FINDLEY: And what is part 395?

WITNESS: Part 395 is the way the trucking industry refers to part 395 of the Federal Motor Carrier Safety Regulations. You can find the controlling regulations in section 44 of the Code of Federal Regulations, part 395.

FINDLEY: Thank you, but I know how to look up federal regulations.

WITNESS: Sorry. When you asked what part 395 is, I assumed you didn't.

FINDLEY: Now, sir, can you describe to me what you understand to be the cause of the accident?

WITNESS: Yes, sir. I fell asleep at the wheel, the truck veered to the left, and the front left tires caught the downslope leading to the median. This must have turned the wheels still further to the left, and the truck then ran into the steel cable running down the guardrail fence. Apparently, the angle at which the truck caught the cable had the effect of catapulting it across the divider into oncoming traffic.

FINDLEY: What is the first thing you remember from that night— not what you have learned since—but your own first memory after the accident?

WITNESS: That's actually a difficult question. My very first memory is not of something I saw, but something I felt. I think it was the feeling of the truck slamming onto the ground after its flight. My first visual memory is of unhooking my seat belt and climbing out of the truck's passenger side window.

FINDLEY: Were you injured in the accident?

WITNESS: No, sir, hardly at all, just a few bruises. I had my seat belt on.

FINDLEY: And what did you see when you had exited the cab of the truck?

WITNESS: Traffic was stopped and people were getting out of their cars. At first I didn't see any damaged cars, but then I noticed that up ahead of the truck there were other cars stopped, and one car was sort of sideways on the edge of the road. It was the only damaged car that I could see.

FINDLEY: How was it damaged?

WITNESS: At first I thought it was a convertible, but then I realized that it had been a sedan, but that its entire top had been sheared off by the collision.

FINDLEY: Did you go over to that car?

WITNESS: Yes, sir, I did.

FINDLEY: And what did you see when you got close to that car?

WITNESS: I saw there were three people in that car; none were moving.

FINDLEY: Can you please describe what these persons looked like?

WITNESS: [Witness chokes up and has difficulty speaking.] The two people sitting next to you were in the backseat. At first they weren't moving, like I said, but then, bit by bit, they began to stir, and by the time the police and ambulance arrived, they were conscious and able to speak somewhat with the paramedics. I wasn't close enough at that point to hear what they said, because by then a police trooper was interviewing me about the accident.

FINDLEY: Did you look in the front seat of the vehicle, and if so, what did you see?

WITNESS: [Witness choking up and quietly crying as he speaks.] I looked just long enough to realize that there had been a terrible injury. There was a great deal of blood on and around the driver, and I could see that she had been killed in the accident.

FINDLEY: What did you see about the driver that made you so certain she had been killed?

WITNESS: [Witness unable to speak.]

FREIBERG: I think we need a break at this point.

FINDLEY: Fine, except that I would prefer the witness to answer the question before that.

FREIBERG: That's not going to happen. Come with me, Mr. Cardarelli. I need to use the washroom again.

*

Again I made certain we were alone in the men's room. Cardarelli was dipping his face over and over in cold water with his cupped hands—and in deep fall in Boston, the water runs cold—very cold. Only after his sobbing subsided did his breathing begin to return to normal. When he dried off with a fistful of paper towels, we had a conversation I will never forget.

"Paul, I can object to the question he wants you to answer and instruct you not to answer. I can't predict Attorney Findley's reaction, but technically, he would have the right to proceed to court to seek an order compelling you to answer the question, in which case we would reconvene for a second day of deposition. We have a decent argument that the question is inappropriate in a case where liability is not being contested and only damages are at stake. On the other hand, it is far more likely that the court would rule that the question is appropriate, at least for purposes of deposition testimony. So you tell me what you want to do about this."

"Why does this attorney want to inflict the horror of what I saw on the parents? I don't understand."

"I don't either. I could draw him aside before we resume and have an off-the-record conversation about that with him, if you like. Nothing to lose in that."

"Look, I just want it all to end today. Try to talk the attorney out of the question. If he insists, I will answer it briefly. The parents know she was decapitated; that's in the mother's deposition transcript. Just don't let him come back at me with more questions about this, looking for details about what I saw, because I will not hurt these lovely people any more than I absolutely have to. And I will never tell him what I'm sure the parents don't know, what even *you* don't know, because the state troopers were too sensitive to put it in the police report."

I had absolutely no idea what he was referring to. "What's that? What are you talking about?"

"The girl's head was in the backseat on the laps of her parents."

"Holy shit!" I blurted out. I paused to think about what we could do. "Wow. Does anybody else know this?"

"I don't think so. The state trooper, of course, if he remembers. But it's not in his accident report."

"Do the parents know? Would they remember?" I asked.

"I don't think so. I think the shock of the accident stunned them beyond when they were put in their ambulances. I think their depositions confirm this. Perhaps they might recall it if prompted, but I strongly doubt it. But I sure as hell am not going to be the person who reminds them. I just won't."

"All right, fine. Then don't. Let's agree right now that you will never tell another person what you told me, no matter what happens. Never. Neither will I. There is no need for this to get out."

"I don't care if they threaten me with jail. I'm not telling this to these sweet, good people. Not today. Not ever. Period."

"Okay. I'll try to get counsel to retract the question, but he won't. I'll let you answer this one question he has asked on this topic, and no more. Okay? Let's go."

*

FINDLEY: The question before the witness was, What did you see about the driver that made you so certain she had been killed?

WITNESS: [Witness choking up and almost unable to speak.] I could see that the driver had been decapitated in the accident.

FINDLEY: Sir, rather than summarize what you saw, I need you to describe each and every detail of what you observed about the condition of the driver's body.

FREIBERG: At this point, I am going to object on the basis that this line of questioning is inappropriate because it is unlikely to lead to the discovery of admissible evidence in a lawsuit where liability is not being contested. Accordingly, I am instructing the witness not to answer this question, or any other question about the decedent's condition after the accident. Counsel is welcome to file a motion to compel and we can have this discussion in front of the court, but for today this line of questioning is over. Counsel, do you have additional questions about other matters?

FINDLEY: Let the record reflect that I am suspending, not terminating, this deposition, so that I may file with the court a motion to compel as well as a motion for sanctions and costs, since the rules of the superior court do not allow a defending counsel to order his client not to respond—except in very extreme circumstances. I will see you in court, Counsel.

FREIBERG: And let the record also reflect that questions about the decedent's body beyond the testimony that Mr. Cardarelli has already given clearly constitute "extreme circumstances." And let it further reflect that the rules plainly state that counsel shall not summarily suspend a deposition when there is dispute about the propriety of a given question but shall continue the examination on all other questions not in dispute such that the trial court, in ruling on the disputed matter, may, if it elects, terminate the deposition. Do be aware, Counsel, that if you stop short in your questioning today, the defendants intend to petition the court to order that the deposition has been terminated on all matters. Your call.

FINDLEY: This deposition is hereby suspended.

FREIBERG: Come on, Paul, that's it for today.

Cardarelli got up to leave, or so I thought. But as I headed toward the door of the conference room, Cardarelli, who was behind me, veered to his right and went around the long conference table to where the parents were still seated, next to their counsel. He went up first to Barbara Waters and put his hand out. She didn't hesitate for a moment to take it in both of her hands.

"I'm so sorry for your loss, and for causing this accident," Cardarelli said in his sonorous baritone voice.

"I know you are, dear," replied Mrs. Waters, looking right into Cardarelli's eyes.

Mr. Waters appeared a bit more taken aback when Cardarelli next offered his hand to him, but he stood up and shook hands and accepted his condolences and apology. Cardarelli then turned toward me and followed me out of the room at a dignified pace. Over my shoulder, I caught an icy stare from Attorney Findley, whose calculated strategy in having the parents attend the deposition unannounced had just been turned against him by the genuine good nature of all three of the parties to the lawsuit.

*

Sometimes in life we say good-bye to people, and only when we look back from the future do we appreciate that it really was good-bye. The first I heard about the terrible and tragic repercussions of the deposition was three days later. I was in a meeting with a client when my assistant attorney knocked on the door and then entered to whisper to me there was an urgent call for me from the police.

Lieutenant Michael Harms introduced himself as the lead detective on a case involving the apparent suicide of a victim named Paul Cardarelli. He said he was calling me because he had found my business card in Mr. Cardarelli's pocket.

It took me the better part of a minute to catch my breath. When I could finally speak again, I confirmed that I was indeed Mr. Cardarelli's attorney in an ongoing civil lawsuit. The officer then told me that normal practice for the police was to call a family member to make positive identification, but he hadn't been able to locate any. I responded that I knew Mr. Cardarelli's background from serving as his counsel and that there weren't any family members to find. He asked me if I would come out to identify the body.

It took me over an hour to wind my way through Boston's gnarled late-afternoon traffic and arrive at Cardarelli's apartment. It was located in a residential neighborhood in the down-and-out city of Lynn, to the north of Boston. I had driven there in a complete daze, trying to understand why this had happened and wondering if there was something I had or hadn't done that contributed to the outcome. But there were no insights in my foggy ruminations, try as I might to focus on what had happened.

There were three police cars and an ambulance outside of the building. Ten or twelve curious people were milling about, none of whom would have been there but for the flashing lights. I explained to one of the officers that I was the victim's attorney. I showed him my bar card and explained that Detective Harms had called me over to identify the body. With that, I was allowed to cross the police line.

Detective Harms greeted me once I was inside the front door of Cardarelli's second-floor flat. He asked me to take a seat at the kitchen table, and for the next half hour he grilled me in detail on everything I knew about Cardarelli, taking copious notes all the while. Only at the end of this process did Harms lead me into Cardarelli's bedroom to undertake the grim identification task, something I had done before, but only for older, familyless clients who had died a natural death. At first I saw nothing; the bedroom seemed in perfect order, the single bed neatly made. It was only when Harms and I rounded the open door of the room's closet that I came upon as sad a sight as I had ever seen in person. Poor Paul Cardarelli was seated on the floor of his closet, or nearly so, because in fact his weight was suspended by a noose made out of his necktie, the other end of which had been tied in a knot around the clothes-hanging bar. For police purposes, I identified that this was indeed my client, Paul Cardarelli; for my own purposes, I identified the tie as the one he had worn to the deposition. I asked the officer if they had affixed a time of death.

"Clearly a number of days ago," was his response.

I told the officer that I needed to leave the room, but that I might be able to give him useful information about what had motivated the suicide, and its likely timing. He asked me to take a seat in another room and wait until he completed some paperwork.

In a state of shock—I actually felt quite dizzy—I stumbled my way into the living room and sat down heavily in a burgundy-colored leather easy chair. It was a good ten minutes before I even looked up, allowing my eyes for the first time since entering the flat to focus on my surroundings and take them in. I was bowled over by what I saw. This wasn't really an apartment at all, not in the usual sense. It was a library. Every single wall was covered in floor-to-ceiling bookshelves. In the large living room, Cardarelli had created additional shelf space by building two double-sided bookcase horseshoes that extended out from one wall, leaving only a small passage on the other side of the room.

I rose from my chair to explore, absolutely amazed by what I was looking at. The second and third bedrooms turned out to also be set up to maximize shelf space. In fact, it would have been essentially impossible to install any more shelves in the apartment; even the entry hallway was narrowed by one wall being given over to ceiling-height shelves of books. And every shelf of every case was completely full of books; there didn't appear to be any empty spaces whatsoever. Mesmerized, I began to examine how the thousands and thousands of volumes were organized, which of course brought to mind how Cardarelli had looked so carefully at the spines of the books in my office, now so many months ago.

The library was separated into sections, each neatly labeled on the shelving. I had, for example, been seated facing "European History." In the corner was a set of antique oak card catalog boxes, neatly stacked on a small table. I opened one drawer enough to see that inside there were alphabetically arranged three-by-five index cards categorized by "Author(s)." When I looked at one random card, I could see that it had been neatly typed, and there were hand-penciled entries on the card cross-referencing the book to three other books in the collection in which it was cited, or to which it was related. I was stunned, completely taken aback. When I closed the drawer, I wandered into the two additional rooms of the apartment, each of which was an additional wing of the library. Even Cardarelli's kitchen and bathroom each had a full wall of books.

I have asked myself many times since whether it was by chance, or whether I had searched for the section of shelves in the hallway that held Cardarelli's collection of Latin American magical realist literature. I actually have no memory of how it happened. But sure enough, there was his copy of Mario Vargas Llosa's *Aunt Julia and the Scriptwriter*, which I took down from the shelf. I opened it to the story of the truck driver who had the roadway accident that Cardarelli had so accurately described to me in our very first meeting. As I turned the pages of the chapter to its next to last page, where the mystical cure is described, it became clear that Cardarelli had reread the chapter after he and I had spoken about it because I came upon a marginal inscription that Cardarelli had written in neat, librarian-like pencil script at the end of the story. It simply said, "No such magic for me."

I had just finishing reading the inscription when Detective Harms tracked me down. I tucked the paperback under my arm as the detective led me into the kitchen. As we passed by them, I could hear the paramedics discussing the logistics of how they were going to remove the body through the hallway that had been so significantly narrowed by the addition of bookshelves on one side. Apparently their gurney couldn't pass through.

Once seated at the kitchen table, I described how, three days earlier, Cardarelli had been deposed in the wrongful death case, and how his feelings about killing a young woman in the accident may have triggered his suicide. Given that he had hanged himself with the very necktie he had worn to the deposition, I explained to the police that their laboratory investigation might well establish the time of death as the afternoon or evening of that same day. I also confirmed to the officer that Cardarelli had described to me that he had no family left whatsoever. In any case, I certainly knew of none for the police to inform. Detective Harms took all this down in his written notes and plied me with one question after another for a full hour. Finally, I was allowed to leave the apartment.

And, yes, I did pinch Cardarelli's Vargas Llosa book to replace my missing copy, and to remind me of this fascinating man. From time to time, I take it down and reread Cardarelli's sad marginal notation, still wondering whether there was something more I could have done or should have done. But I never end up with any more insight than the time before; even after decades have passed, I don't have any more answers than I did that first evening.

Driving back to Boston, wending my way through traffic, I absent-mindedly turned on the radio, pondering what I was going to tell Wilkins, when I landed on one station that was playing the all-too-appropriate refrain of a Beatles song: "All the lonely people, where do they all come from?"

IV

Professor Henry Huddleston and the History of Love

A number of years ago, I received a call from Henry Huddleston, professor of history at Harvard University. He had been referred to me by Professor Arnold Craft, who had taught me civil procedure when I was a law student, and who had since become my client and friend.

Professor Huddleston called to discuss, as he phrased it, "a rather unusual piece of estate planning." When we met five days later, he captivated me immediately. While he was built like an NFL linebacker, he spoke in one of the gentlest tones of voice I have ever encountered. The years—or perhaps it was some medical condition—had bent his massive frame forward somewhat, but he was still striking looking, in part because he wore his straight, snow-white hair pulled back in a soft-looking ponytail that trailed down over the collar of the black turtleneck shirts he invariably wore.

We spoke for a moment or two about the onset of winter that was more apparent day by day and then chatted about several people we knew in common. When the conversation turned to Professor Craft, who had recently passed away, my new client glanced out my office window at the view over Boston Harbor and went silent for a few moments.

Then he sighed, turned his face toward me, and simply said, "Thinking about mortality. Let's get down to business."

With that, we were off and running into what was to prove to be the most interesting estate planning case that ever came my way—by far.

"First, Counselor," the professor began, "you need to know that I have never married and have no children. I also have no other family whatsoever, save for one uncle. Second, fairly soon I am apparently going to inherit a tidy sum of money from this uncle of mine; he's quite elderly, and not well. Third, I would like to describe to you an unusual trust I want you to draft for me."

"Just like that, Professor?" I asked. "Don't you want to know a bit about my practice, and something about my experience and all that kind of information?"

"No, no." He chuckled. "I want you to do this work for me because of what Arnold told me about you. He said to me some time back that you did his and Sandra's estate planning work. Enough said. But it's more than that. Arnold told me you had been a university professor over at BU before law school. And that happens to be *exactly* what I need: an attorney who used to be an academic. Why? Because I need my attorney to serve as a trustee of this trust I want to create, and the trust will be deeply involved in academic life. I need a trustee lawyer who can navigate academe. You're perfect. Shall I get down to details?"

"Sure, why not. I have no idea where you're going with this." I laughed.

"Just you wait; you won't be disappointed, I promise you. But, listen, can you tape record what I am going to say? I want you, and future trustees, to have a permanent tape recording of what I have to say. Can we do that?"

"The idea makes perfect sense, Professor. But the way to do it is to give me a week to arrange for a licensed videographer and a court stenographer. That way, we would have admissible evidence of your 'testamentary intentions,' just in case there were ever a challenge to your will or trust. The original tapes are catalogued and kept off-site, and we keep only a copy in your file. On top of that, we would have the stenographic record. Is it okay to wait a week and do it the right way? That way it will have some real teeth."

"Of course, of course. That makes perfect sense. Let's do it just that way."

"Okay, great. I'll set that up for a week from now, same time, same place. But a question for you, sir. Can I get a brief description of what in the world you intend to do with the trust? You've piqued my interest, to say the least."

"Sure thing. Let's see, where to start . . .? Well, as I told you, I have no family whatsoever, outside of the aged uncle I mentioned and a couple of very distant second cousins I don't know from Adam. On top of that, I've never spent much time developing friendships—or let's put that this way: I haven't become close enough to any friend to leave him an inheritance. So there you go. I plead guilty, Your Honor, to having devoted my entire life to my academic work. It feels a little odd saying that out loud, but it's the simple truth, and as my attorney you need to know that."

I nodded and waited for the professor to continue his story.

"So since I don't have family or close friends to leave an inheritance to, I've been spending a considerable amount of time thinking about what to do with the money I'm going to inherit, plus my own savings. And I have to tell you, Counselor, I haven't been this excited about *anything* in years. Here's my idea: I want to create a fund, or trust, or . . . whatever you advise, that during my life, and after I'm gone, will benefit young scholars and graduate students who work in my area of interest. The more I've thought about this idea since I came up with it, the more certain I am it's what I want to do. You see, there are only a few score of professors who work in my little corner of academic history, and the area of our interest generates no research funding whatsoever. So my intention is to use my inheritance and my savings to fund the research of graduate students and young professors in my field. Pretty cool, *n'est ce pas?*" he concluded in French with a big, handsome smile.

He paused to take a somewhat raspy breath. I could both see and hear that whatever health issues the professor was dealing with, they were taking their toll.

"Very cool indeed. *Super cool*," I replied enthusiastically. "I can see why you're so excited about the idea. Tell me one thing, Professor, what subfield of history do you specialize in?"

He hesitated, for dramatic effect. "I am a student of the history of love."

My face must have betrayed my incredulity. He smiled broadly.

"You heard me right. Throughout my career, I have studied the effect of romantic love on historical events."

I remained silent, so he continued.

"Counselor," the professor said, using the term he was to address me by throughout our relationship, "I want you to know something personal about me from the start, in case you're finding it a bit strange that I'm unmarried and childless and yet a specialist in the history of romantic love. You see, I'm only unmarried and childless as a product of bad luck, not by choice. I set out to find love and to have a family, and I once did find love, when I was a much younger man. For ten years, I lived with a literature professor, whom I adored." He choked up a bit at the memory. "Sorry," he added, clearing his throat. "I just wanted you to know that I'm not someone who studies love in lieu of loving. I had my decade in the sunshine, and just happened to never refind it."

I nodded in acknowledgment, encouraging him to continue. But only silence followed, so I continued on with a question about what the academic study of love entailed and whether or not romantic love had changed over time. And I was amazed to hear myself ask these questions. The odds of anything interesting happening or being said while working on an estate plan are close to zero. Yet here I was, already asking a question about the history of *love*; this was mind-boggling.

"Most people assume that 'love' as we know it has always been a part of human life, but that is not at all what the historical record tells us," the professor began to answer. "A great deal of my personal research and writing has involved studying just this issue, trying to fathom how love functioned in the ancient world. My language skills are in Latin, ancient Greek, Aramaic, and Hebrew, and a great deal of my work has involved analyzing and writing about what early texts tell us about the development of romantic love and how these developments were to change the history of the Western world in a number of ways. Does that give you an idea?"

"Amazing. Sure, that gives me some idea," I replied. "So tell me about your expectancy with respect to your uncle's estate. What's the deal?"

"Well, here's what I know at this point: On my most recent yearly visit to see him, he told me that he thinks the inheritance should amount to at least a million dollars, if all goes well. The uncertainty arises because apparently there is oil under his eighty-acre farm up in Montana. He told me that he had long since entered into an oil lease or contract or something like that with an oil company. Apparently they've told him it could be quite a while before they could give him any kind of estimate of what his royalty stream would amount to. If I understood him correctly, this will depend not only on how much oil is found but also on the price of oil over time and the costs to the company of extracting it. What happens to our project, by the way, if my uncle is wrong and the amount is far more modest than his million-dollar estimate?"

"At the magnitude of money you are talking about, it doesn't sound like we would need to create a fancy, expensive-to-run entity like a foundation. We could probably favor the students you talked about by using an irrevocable trust, I should think. This would work whether you inherit a hundred thousand dollars or ten million. Such trusts are beautifully simple to set up and administer. There are some tax consequences we would need to discuss, but let's leave that for another day. What about your personal assets? You said they're going in as well, right?"

"Yes. Everything I have will go into the same trust. I suppose my savings and retirement account together are worth something like another million, maybe even a bit more. And I own a sweet little house within walking distance of your old law school. From what I hear, even modest real estate around the university has become quite valuable.

So my total net worth should be roughly two million dollars—something like that. Is that still appropriate for the kind of trust you have in mind?"

"Absolutely, although in the process, I will want to consult with my partners here at the firm who specialize in estate tax issues. We should consider the pros and cons of what we would need to do to achieve a tax-favored status—but all that for another day."

"Great," he said. "So then, are you intrigued enough to take on this long-term project?"

"I might well do it," I said, in a joking tone. "But only on one condition."

"What's that?" replied Professor Huddleston with a note of concern in his voice.

"No, no. I'm just kidding about having a condition. Of course I'll take this on, unless I'm not qualified enough on the academic side of things; I'm certainly no historian. But for today, since our substantive meeting is more or less over, I was wondering if there was any way I could get you to tell me in a bit more detail about just what historians study when they study the history of love. I mean, above and beyond what you told me about your own work."

"Would you really like to hear something about that?"

"I sure would. Otherwise, what a waste it would be for you to have come all the way downtown for such a short meeting."

"Right now?"

"Right now. And frankly, you'll be doing me a great service, because if you leave this room, I need to open that fat folder you see on the corner of the desk there and review a draft commercial building lease for a client. I'll bet you serious money you haven't read anything as dull as a commercial lease in years and years—maybe ever. So if you can't save me from my eventual fate, can you at least delay it?"

A big, bright smile broke out across the professor's face. "Well, given that my doctor told me two weeks ago that my appointment at the pearly gates has been rescheduled for earlier than I would have wanted—that's why I have finally gotten serious about my estate planning—I'm trying like mad to rack up all the Good Samaritan points I can. And I assume I would get at least a few for delaying your sad fate, don't you think?" We both had a laugh at his retort. Then he added, "But you need to make a choice. I can tell you about some of the main academic debates currently in vogue about the history and sociology of romantic love, or I can just tell you an actual love story that had an effect on world history. Which would you prefer?"

"That's easy. I'll go with the dry, academic analysis," I replied without hesitation.

Looking puzzled, the professor questioned me: "Really?"

"Of course not. I hope you wouldn't hire anyone who would take *that* option. No, tell me a love story. Tell me a love story I will never forget, and tell me one that will teach me a history lesson to boot."

He laughed. "Okay, okay. But as you can imagine, after a career of gathering and reading colleagues' collections of historically significant love stories, I am familiar with hundreds of them. So let's do this. You think about a fictional love story, say in a film you saw, that particularly touched your heart, and I'll see if it cues up a historical tale that matches your criteria."

I thought for a moment and, much to my surprise, a film actually came to mind. "Okay, Professor, I've got one. I was definitely charmed and even moved by Julia Roberts and Richard Gere's film *Pretty Woman*."

"Why do you suppose you liked it?" he shot right back at me. Damn, I felt like I was in class again.

"Oh . . . good question. Let me think." I clearly had to come up with something well north of how great Roberts looked in those outfits Gere's character kept buying her. I took a moment or two to gather my thoughts and then gave it a shot. "I guess it had to do with how Roberts's character—a prostitute—blossomed in the sunlight of the respect she got from Gere's character. And it was captivating to watch her transform herself. But I guess the moment that really bowled me over was when she tears up listening to the final aria of *La Traviata*, and Gere's character looks over and grasps what a full woman she has become. I guess the film said a lot to me about the power of love and connection."

"Well done!" the professor replied.

Phew, I'd passed. "B, maybe B plus?"

Huddleston ignored my quip and shifted into professor gear. "That movie is what we call a Pygmalion love story. According to Greek myth, Pygmalion, the king of Cyprus, was a master sculptor. At one point, he carved a statue of a woman that was so beautiful that he fell completely in love with it, even to the point of kissing the cold marble. In desperation, he prayed to Aphrodite, the goddess of love, and she was so moved by the beauty of the king's love for the statue that she turned it into a living flesh-and-blood woman. This mythical theme has reappeared over and over again in literature and music for over two thousand years. You find it in Ovid's *Metamorphosis*, in George Bernard Shaw's *Pygmalion*, and of course in Lerner and Lowe's brilliant Broadway musical *My Fair Lady*. It's also told to children: think about *Cinderella*, and her prince. Actually, you couldn't possibly have made a better choice of theme. You see, the irony of this classical theme that touched your heart in *Pretty Woman* is that *by far* the greatest of all Pygmalion stories was absolutely historical. One hundred percent historical. And one thousand percent grander in scope than any of the authors of the fictional treatments dared dream. Now that's a big claim, isn't it?"

I responded with enthusiasm. "That's a *really* big claim all right. A thousandfold grander in scope? You've set yourself quite a challenge. So let me get this straight: The story I'm about to hear is completely factual—historical, I should say. It's not a tale, and it's not embellished in any way?"

"Correct. And by the way, we have impeccable historical resources that describe in detail the life of our real-world Cinderella who rose up from being a guttersnipe to being one of the most remarkable women in all of European history, arguably the greatest empress the Roman Empire ever knew. And just to seal the deal, we know for certain that she was far, far more beautiful than your Julia Roberts. Are you ready?"

"Are you kidding? Absolutely. . . . What are we betting?"

Huddleston's warm laugh rang out. "Beer in Harvard Square, at the establishment of the winner's choice. And you, Counselor, *you alone* get to be the judge of whether she outshines her fictional competition by a factor of a thousand."

I just smiled, leaned back in my chair, and put my feet up on the file with that dreadful, inch-thick lease I would have to suffer through at some point. The professor cleared his throat, adopted what I was to learn was a tone of voice he reserved only for storytelling, and launched into it.

"The story begins in the year 500 in Constantinople—today's Istanbul. In the early 300s, Constantine the Great had reunited the divided territories of the Roman Empire and declared Christianity to be its official religion. For a variety of reasons, he simultaneously moved the capital of the empire from pestilential Rome to the small town of Byzantium on the Bosporus straights. He renamed it after himself: hence, Constantinople. Major public work construction projects quickly turned the town into the jewel of Eastern Europe, and so it remains today.

"In the city center there was an enormous stadium, the Hippodrome. It was used to stage a perpetual circus that entertained the masses and the elite alike. Like the Colosseum in ancient Rome, the Hippodrome often presented gladiatorial battles involving wild beasts that were brought from throughout the empire. Among these wild creatures were massive bears, and one of the bear keepers, a man named Acacius, had a daughter just before the turn of the sixth century. It was this lowly born girl who, in the fullness of time, would become the heroine of our story.

"Now when Acacius died in 503, the burden of raising their three daughters was left to his penniless widow. The task, however, was nearly hopeless: circus performers and animal keepers were at the very lowest of the fixed ranks of Roman culture—just above slaves. The girls were literally urchins, playing in the streets with male children; in contrast, girls from proper families were kept home in *gynocia*, completely and at all times segregated from boys and men.

"Now, at the same time, a young man of relatively humble birth, one Flavius Petrus Sabbatius, was invited by his uncle to take up his studies in Constantinople, the Paris of its day. Fate would smile on this particular young scholar, for in due course his uncle, an officer in the palace guard, would be crowned emperor. Better still, this childless uncle would appoint this nephew as his successor. It would be many years, however, before the future emperor would fall head over heels in love with our heroine, Theodora, and make her his empress.

"We know that by 512, Theodora joined her older sister as a stage actress, and performers and actresses, by the standards of the time, were considered courtesans. But that is a generalization, and we actually have historical specifics, as I promised you, because the great historian Procopius lived in Constantinople at this time and devoted an entire book to the life and times of our heroine. He writes that in her youth, this stunningly beautiful woman specialized in dancing in gossamer, see-through gowns and that she was available as a courtesan. We also know from multiple sources that she had a daughter out of wedlock in 515, a girl who was also to play an important role in the history of the Roman Empire, but that's another story. The only place the historical record falls short for us is that we only have one likeness of Theodora's legendarily beautiful face: the famous marble mosaic that stares out at us in the church of San Vitale, which you can visit in Ravenna, Italy."

The professor paused. "I fear I'm going into too much detail for you. Shall I just summarize the story?"

"Good God, no," I called out. "Tell it in Technicolor."

My bard laughed out loud at my nonsense and then took up his tale again.

"So Theodora's legendary beauty began to attract men of standing to court her as a mistress; some things never change. And one particular love affair was to transform her life. She became concubine to a powerful man named Hecebolus, who soon thereafter was appointed governor of the five great Roman cities of North Africa. He took her with him to the provincial capital of Apollonia, in modern-day Libya. But like so many affairs, then and now, this one didn't last, and our heroine found herself dismissed from the governor's palace about a year after she'd arrived. Theodora then traveled east along the Mediterranean coast and came to the second greatest city of the Eastern Roman Empire: Alexandria, Egypt. At the time, Alexandria was the most important center of learning and enlightenment in the empire. It possessed one of antiquity's most important libraries, and many of the great minds of the ancient world had studied in this remarkable metropolis on the shore of the Mediterranean, where the Nile flows north into the sea. We're talking about Homer, Pythagoras the mathematician, and Herodotus the historian, they—amongst others—had all graced its lecture halls and intellectual circles. Alexandria had a mysterious side to it as well: it had the reputation of changing the lives of even the emperors who visited there. The lives of no lesser historical figures than Alexander the Great, Julius Caesar, and Mark Antony were all influenced by their endeavors in Alexandria. Theodora was no exception: her life would be completely altered by her experiences there as well.

"Think about Roberts's character learning which fork to use in *Pretty Woman* or Eliza Doolittle being schooled in proper English pronunciation by Professor Henry Higgins in *My Fair Lady*. Theodora had clearly been through this type of transformative undertaking, but not even Procopius tells us where or when or how that happened. But what we do know is that by the time our heroine arrived in Alexandria, she was clearly at ease in high social circles. But it went much further than that. She did what other women in her era didn't even dream of doing: she became a public intellectual. If Alexandria was North Africa's Paris, she became its Simone de Beauvoir. She was in attendance and at the forefront of soirées and seminars and convocations where the learned issues of the era were debated by the greatest minds of the time. She met and became particularly close to two theologians of extraordinary stature, Severus and Timothy the Patriarch of Alexandria. These two men were at the very center of the great debate that was tearing Christianity in two. Remember, Christianity at the time was still young and struggling with how to handle basic tenets of its core theology. Perhaps the biggest issue of the time—no matter how arcane it may sound to us—was whether Jesus was of one nature, indivisibly man and God, or of two natures, fully capable of suffering as a man completely apart from his divinity. This dispute was more than theoretical; it actually moved armies and was soon to lead to the permanent division of the Roman papacy from the Eastern Orthodox Church. Amazingly, our Theodora became involved at the very heart of this debate.

"On another level, Theodora's stay in Alexandria was to forever change her life because she met and greatly impressed a noblewoman named Cesaria, a descendant of Emperor Anastasius. We know this because we actually have the letter of introduction that Cesaria gave to Theodora; this letter was to grace her entrance into the highest reaches of society in the great city of Antioch, in what is now Turkey, through which Theodora would travel on her way back to Constantinople.

"I should mention that women of her era seldom traveled *at all*, and they certainly didn't travel unescorted. But our Theodora seemed to be practically unrestrained by the norms of her epoch. One example of this I personally love is that Theodora was a sort of self-made sociologist. We know that she took active steps to learn about the everyday lives of common people in the lands she passed through on her travels across Egypt and north into Palestine, through Syria and up and through the whole of the Levant, modern-day Turkey, on her way back to Byzantium. We know she learned Latin, Coptic, and Aramaic to complement her mother tongue, Greek. And all of this remarkable self-education was to have quite a significant effect on how our Cinderella would govern when, later in her life, her prince made her his empress.

"Needless to say, these experiences seasoned our Theodora. The woman who arrived in Antioch, the capital of Anatolia, was far more sophisticated than the beautiful courtesan who had followed Hecebolus to North Africa. By the early 520s, Theodora had a reputation as a learned, self-confident force of nature. She was by this time entirely comfortable socializing with persons of the highest social, political, or ecclesiastical rank, and her reputation preceded her. The only thing unchanged was her extraordinary beauty; on that all contemporary commentators agree."

The professor paused for a rest; his breathing was becoming labored. The light over Boston Harbor was just starting to fade into twilight, and he asked if we might turn off the awful glare of the florescent office lights and allow the clear natural light of the winter sky to fill the room. I took a minute to fix us each some tea, threw my feet back up on that damnable lease, and allowed the professor's tale to wash over me once again.

"Well, let's see, where were we?" the professor mumbled. "Ah yes," he said, modulating to his storytelling voice. "Let's pick up the story after Theodora has traveled north through modern-day Syria and arrived in Antioch, the most cosmopolitan city of the Levant. Antioch of the early 520s had quite a reputation for its hedonistic lifestyle—sort of the Las Vegas of its day. Circuses were held almost daily, mostly for affluent young gentlemen, and the city's hippodrome and amphitheater were open three or four times a week, providing extravaganzas for the plebeians. This was not at all Alexandria, where intellectuals held sway; here, it was actors and actresses who were the local influential personages. And none amongst them was more celebrated than a prominent female entertainer and dancer called Macedonia, who we know was absolutely bowled over by the beauty and the presence of our Theodora. But Macedonia was not just an entertainer; she was part of a group of superstars who were at the center of the wild life of Antioch—sort of the Rat Pack of 1950s Las Vegas.

"Now enters the role of chance in life—think Puck's magic potion in *A Midsummer Night's Dream*. It turns out that Macedonia had a second career that no one around her knew anything about: she was an agent, a spy really. She reported by secret courier directly to the consul, Flavius Petrus Sabbatius, who by this time had taken the name Justinian to honor his uncle, the Emperor Justin, supreme ruler of the Byzantine Empire. Amazingly—at least as a historian I find it amazing—we actually have the original letter in which Macedonia recommends to Justinian that he give an audience to a remarkable woman called Theodora. I've actually read the original letter in the university archives in Istanbul. I find that *so* incredible. Anyway, the effect of that letter was like Shakespeare's magic potion: 'The juice of it on sleeping eyelids laid / Will make or man or woman madly dote / Upon the next live creature that it sees.'"

The professor fell utterly silent, taking a break to sip at his tea. It was nearly dark now in the office, and a wonderful calm had settled over the room. And then, as if some switch had been flipped, he was off and running again.

"When I was in Istanbul, I was also able to read with my own eyes a copy of the return letter to Macedonia in which Justinian granted Theodora an audience. He would have been about forty when they met, and he was undeniably the most eligible bachelor in all of the late Roman Empire. We know precisely what this tall, handsome man looked like because we have an exact likeness of him in a sculpture that stands today in Saint Mark's Basilica in Venice. But above and beyond being movie star handsome, Justinian was a Renaissance man nearly a thousand years before the Renaissance. He was a student of history, politics, and geography, as well as being a well-trained and extremely resourceful commander of the Roman legions. During his reign he would re-expand the borders of the empire to what they had been under Constantine the Great and make contributions to law and culture that were of an even greater scale. But most importantly for our story, at very first sight, as Puck and his magic potion would have it, Justinian fell head over heels in love with Theodora. Even Procopius, the contemporary historian who wrote a somewhat scathing book about the couple, had to admit in his narrative that theirs was 'an over-powering, extraordinary love.'

"Now mind you, this was no average couple. They were remarkably forward thinking for their times. Within months of meeting, Theodora moved into the imperial palace to live with Justinian, which was abso-lutely unheard of at the time. And she did this despite the fact that it was seen as entirely improper by Justinian's aunt, the empress. But, like your Richard Gere, resourceful Justinian was not to be stopped: he pre-pared and had the emperor sign an official decree explicitly designed to allow him to marry Theodora. The new law, called *On Marriage*, set the legal basis whereby a reformed actress who has led an hon-orable life could petition for permission to wed a nobleman and be granted the title of patrician. And guess what," the professor added with a smile, "the statute was quite explicit that children born to the reformed actress prior to her marriage would also become patricians. It certainly helps to have friends in high places, doesn't it?" he added with a little chuckle.

"So in the year 525, Justinian, who was only two years from becom-ing Emperor himself, proposed to our Cinderella. And you can imagine what a grand affair this wedding was! We have detailed accounts of the glorious ceremony that was held in the Hagia Sophia cathedral, built two hundred years earlier by Constantine the Great. Even today when you visit the Hagia Sophia you can catch a sense of the grandeur of their wedding day. Theodora was twenty-five years of age and dressed in gold. She was gloriously beautiful, but she was *so* much more than that. By this time, she had turned herself into one of the most fully realized women of her time. And we know that Justinian was well aware of the breadth of her capacities, because almost immediately after he became emperor, he declared his beautiful empress to be a full Augusta, or co-emperor of the realm. They ruled, as a couple, for nineteen years before Theodora's untimely death. After that, Justinian remained on the throne for another seventeen years, completing numerous projects that they had conceived together. There were dozens of these under-takings, but I only need to give you an account of just one of these remarkably humanistic and progressive projects to reach that 'thou-sandfold' claim that lies at the heart of our wager.

"At Theodora's initiation, the couple had done everything they could to try to convince the ecclesiastical luminaries of the era to settle the theological disagreements that were leading toward the division of the Church into its Roman and Eastern Orthodox factions. While Theodora ultimately failed in this effort, she succeeded in convincing the opposed parties to refrain from calling on the armies that they could have rallied, and instead to try to settle the matter by rational debate before their court. Get it, Counselor? Think of the words I've used, and of your legal training: *Rational debate before the court.*

"Roberts's character in *Pretty Woman*, Cinderella, and Eliza Doolittle brought beauty and brightness and charm to their princes, but Theodora brought so much more to hers—and in real life. For it was in these debates that Theodora arranged to have held in Justinian's court that the basis of law as we know it was first born. In other words, by getting the opposed parties to agree to abide by the imposition of procedural rules that would ensure rational debate, the concept of the rule of law was first put into practice. This concept became a key ele-ment of Justinian's scholarly research into and his revision of ancient Roman law, culminating after Theodora's death in his promulgation of the Justinian Code. And this codification of law a millennium later formed the basis of the Napoleonic Code, which, as you must know from your law school studies, forms the basis of all current European legal systems.

"If I had more time I could describe to you the many inclusions in the Justinian Code that we owe directly to Theodora. Let me just mention one: she used her position to champion the cause of women, which so far as I know, was completely unprecedented. In the code, for example—for the very first time in Western history—the law recognized the rights of women to inherit wealth and lands, to be financially protected by a deceased husband's estate, to enter into contracts, and to be financially autonomous."

The professor paused once again, sipped his tea, and looked over at me in the dim light of the darkened office. "Allow me just one final example of the strength of this woman and the power of this couple's love for one another. In about 545, the bubonic plague began in Egypt and spread quickly throughout the Middle East and into Europe. It was to kill twenty million citizens of the Roman Empire—roughly half the population. Justinian himself fell ill and was expected to die. Theodora, however, refused to cease personally nursing him. Since the couple was childless, court advisers suggested that plans be made for her to prepare an immediate marriage with a general upon the emperor's death. But, at risk of her life, the empress quashed all such efforts, staking her personal survival on Justinian's recovery. Remarkably, he pulled through; very few stricken people did so. And remember, people had a prescientific mind-set in the ancient world: this was still an era where natural events such as the earthquakes, and the great plague itself, were seen as signs of God's displeasure. So Justinian's unlikely recovery was perceived as a miracle, and the royal couple came to be experienced as something even greater than the remarkable secular rulers they clearly were. It was John and Jackie Kennedy a thousand times over; Constantinople as real world Camelot."

The professor took in a huge breath, and exhaled slowly before winding up his tale. "After Theodora's death, Justinian lived and reigned for another seventeen years, but he never remarried. Theodora was the only woman he ever loved." Now the professor looked over at me, and modulated from his bard's storytelling voice to the tone he used in everyday conversation. "So this ends my story of the courtesan who became a lady, an empress, and a world historical figure. Now,

Counselor, you know what we study when my colleagues and I look back at the role of romantic love in the history of civilization."

I was speechless. After quite a while, all I came up with was, "You're right. You made the thousandfold threshold with plenty to spare. Beer's on me; you choose when and where." I stood up, suddenly somewhat embarrassed that the room at this point was almost entirely dark. I flicked on the glaring neon lights, which instantly dissolved the almost mystical mood the professor's story had created. We arranged to meet the following week to further the project, and before I knew it, I stood alone in my office overlooking twentieth-century Boston with all its lights and busy streets. But there still was some little part of me back in the sixth century, amazed at what the story had to say about the power of love and connection.

*

Professor Huddleston returned a week later, and no doubt about it, I was eager to see him. It was such a treat when the occasional case came along that promised to be a learning experience. This one met that standard far more than I yet understood.

I met with the professor for the better part of an hour to go over the concept he had in mind for his estate plan. We reviewed the options available to him, and I explained how my tax partners recommended we structure the trust so as to minimize gift, estate, and income taxation as far as possible. We then turned to review what he intended to say during the videotape session, and I suggested a few elements of legal phraseology I wanted to have the professor include, and passed him a few notes with appropriate legal terminology for him to read into the record. We then went into a conference room where the videographer had set up impressive quantities of sound and camera equipment. Off to the side sat the court reporter, with her stenography machine. As soon as the professor was seated and the videographer had introduced him on tape, the session began.

"My purpose in making this videotape recording and legal transcript is twofold: First, and most importantly, I want the trustees of the trust I am settling, especially the successor trustees who will never meet me, to understand both my personal background and my goals in leaving all my worldly assets to encourage research in my subfield of academic history. Second, I want to discuss how I would like the trust to be run. So let me start at the beginning.

"I grew up as an only child in an empty little farm town in western Wisconsin. By the time I was about ten, I knew that I desperately wanted to leave rural life as far behind as I possibly could. I just wasn't built for it. My father had died when I was quite young, and my mother worked at the town's little general store to support the two of us. I well understood that my only hope of escape was to excel at school, and I can't imagine a child working more diligently at his studies than I did. With some combination of hard work and dumb luck the effort paid off, and I was admitted to the University of Wisconsin with a full scholarship. I majored in history, minored in Latin, and read everything about the ancient world I could get my hands on.

"I returned home after my freshman year and found a summer job working on a local farm. But in July of that fateful summer, my mother had a stroke, and by the time the farmer's wife could get me off the fields and drive me to the hospital, she had passed away. The only family left to me after that was my mother's brother, an uncle who lived in Montana, and some second cousins whom I had only met once as a very young child. After services for my mom, I cleaned out the little wooden house we rented and sold the furniture, plates, and glasses for the grand sum of twenty-five dollars. I packed my worldly belongings into two small suitcases and took the bus back to Madison. That was that. I was on my own.

"Back at college, I became even more devoted to my studies. I read and studied everything that was assigned—and a lot more that wasn't. By the time I wrote my senior paper, which was called 'Everyday Family Life in the Roman Empire,' I was able to list over a hundred books and academic articles in its bibliography, several of which I had read in Latin. Of course, not having a home to go back to over holiday breaks made life a tad lonely, but it also had its advantages: I had a lot more time to work on my studies than did my fellow students. So in the end, I did rather well, I suppose, because following graduation I was admitted with a full scholarship into the doctoral program of the Department of History of Yale University.

"At Yale, I came under the influence of a series of truly great professors who affected my future academic career by insisting I needed to become fully proficient in the ancient languages I would need to read the original texts of the sources I was most interested in. In the six years it took me to earn my PhD, I brought my Latin up to a professional level of competency and added ancient Greek as well. My doctoral dissertation, which was later published as a book, was called 'Love and Marriage in the Ancient World.' I mention this because I want it to be clear to my trustees that my academic interests had not changed in the six years between my undergraduate thesis and my doctoral dissertation, nor have they changed much since. All three of my books, and something like twenty-five of the approximately thirty articles I have published in academic journals, treat this same subject matter or very closely aligned topics.

"All right. So that is my personal background. Now let me turn to the specifics of the estate planning that I am undertaking with my attorney. I mentioned earlier that my only relative was, and still is, an aged, childless uncle, my mother's only sibling, her brother Louis Pennington. Today he resides in an assisted-living facility in Delphia, Montana, and at ninety-one years of age, his health is failing him. When I visited him about six weeks ago, he spoke to me in some depth about his own estate planning. Apparently, some years ago he purchased an interest in a Montana oil field ten miles or so from where he lived, and over the years he twice heeded capital calls to prevent his modest interest from being overly watered down as additional rounds of private equity were arranged for the venture. He also told me that he had drawn up a will at some point that left everything to his living trust, but that since his wife, my aunt, had passed away, and since his only sibling, my mother, was also deceased, whatever went into the trust would eventually be coming to me.

"Given this, and given some health issues of my own that have only recently been brought to my attention by my doctors, I thought it prudent to prepare for this inheritance, especially given what I have in mind to do with my own assets after my death. That's why I am making this videotape.

"And I want to add one more historical tidbit. Almost the last words my uncle said to me as I left on my most recent visit to him were, 'Henry, figure out some creative way to use the money. Don't just buy some big house with it or something.' I think he would be pleased indeed with what I am about to say."

The professor paused to take a drink of water, and then continued. "Okay. When both my uncle and I are deceased, there will be no immediate family to inherit our assets. Accordingly, I have instructed my attorney to draft for me a trust into which I will transfer any and all assets I have or that come my way. It is my intention that my trust be designed to benefit the research of young scholars in my field of academic history. These future unnamed beneficiaries shall be selected by my trustees, whose determination on all such matters shall be at their unfettered discretion and shall expressly be final and not reviewable by any court, academic entity, or other authority."

Again the professor took a short break and sipped some water. After reading some of the suggested written legal language I had supplied him with, he continued. "I will be asking my attorney to join me as the other initial trustee of the trust. It is my intention to appoint two additional trustees who shall be professors of history whose field of expertise is the same, or similar, to my own. One of these I shall appoint during my life, and the other I shall appoint by instrument upon my death. Should I predecease the funding of the trust, or for any reason fail to validly appoint such additional trustees for any reason, my trust calls for my surviving cotrustee or cotrustees to appoint one or two successor trustees, as the case may be, consistent with my intentions. If for any reason my cotrustees fail to validly so appoint, I hereby ask any court reviewing my will and trust to accept this videotape I am making today into evidence in any such proceedings and to then appoint appropriate successor trustees consistent with what I have said herein. The terms of the trust provide that after my death or incapacity, each of these three trustees shall have the right and power to appoint their own successor trustee when for any reason any of them can no longer serve.

"At this point, I would like to thank in advance anyone and every-one who is involved with my estate or my trust for acting consistently with the goals I have set forth today in this videotape recording and in my trust instrument itself. Thank you, and good-bye."

*

As it turned out, Professor Huddleston had been correct about his uncle's frail state of health; about eight months after the testamen-tary instruments were prepared and signed, he called to say that his uncle had passed. He had learned this in a phone call from an attorney named Tom Riggins, who was his uncle's estate planning counsel in Montana. Huddleston asked me if I would call attorney Riggins and coordinate whatever needed to be done.

Within days I spoke with Mr. Riggins, who seemed a very capa-ble attorney and a personable fellow. He confirmed that his client, Louis Pennington, had indeed named Professor Huddleston's mother and her issue as the sole remainder beneficiaries of the trust. The only other beneficiaries named in the will were the second cousins the professor had referenced: each had been left a specific bequest of $25,000. Mr. Riggins also mentioned that he had received a call from an attorney named Ned Owens, who was representing all four of the second cousins. Riggins knew Owens all too well, and described him as "a Hollywood casting director's image of a plaintiff's tort lawyer: two hundred and twenty pounds of pure greed, who still wears white bucks and, even more amazing, a white belt he must have inherited from his grandfather." I laughed out loud at the image.

"Has he been hired to challenge the will?" I asked.

"Very likely. I certainly wouldn't be surprised to see Owens file an appearance for the beneficiaries and at least threaten to challenge the will," Riggins replied. "His goal wouldn't be to prevail; that's essentially impossible under our case law, given the facts. But he's very much the type who would try to jerk us around enough to get us to negotiate a higher number for his clients."

"So if I understand correctly, he wouldn't have much traction under Montana law?"

"Right. Almost none. The instrument was properly executed, which makes it self-authenticating. And I'd be glad to testify that there are no facts that even remotely support an argument of undue influence. On top of that, the will has been in place for many years, and an earlier version had the same beneficiaries. As for these second cousins, the decedent had very little to do them, and by leaving them a specific bequest of twenty-five thousand dollars each, he clearly demonstrated that he recognized their existence and treated them as he saw appropriate. So no, no traction unless there is some set of facts I'm not aware of."

I asked counsel if in Montana there was an in terrorem clause, and whether there was one in the uncle's will. These clauses typically state that if an heir challenges a will and does not prevail, his original bequest lapses.

"We do indeed," Riggins said. "And you'll have no problem with the language in the decedent's will. I don't think you can draft it any stronger."

It was several weeks before I next spoke with Attorney Riggins. He told me excitedly that a representative of the oil company estimated that with any luck at all, there would be an income stream in the magnitude of $15,000 to $25,000 *a month* and that production from the well could easily carry on for many years.

I immediately called Professor Huddleston with the good news. He was so quiet on the other end I had to ask if he was still on the line.

"Hot damn!" he finally called out. "And I have equally good news for you, Counselor. Professor Mary Sanderson just agreed yesterday to become a trustee. She is a professor of ancient European history at Wellesley College and a very significant contributor to our field. Now that we are going to have some money in the trust, if it's okay legally, I would suggest that you draft up the appointment paperwork as soon as possible and we get on with the fun part of all this. Does that make sense legally? Can we get this thing operational soon?"

"It makes perfect sense. The appointment instrument is a one-paragraph paper; I'll have it over to you by messenger later today," I replied, growing nearly as excited as the professor with the thought that this dream of his was becoming a reality.

"Okay, send me whatever I need to sign. Any idea when we might get some money to work with?"

"If Montana practice works like its Massachusetts equivalent, there should be no problem with your receiving a preliminary, partial distribution, if the Montana court allows it. You would then gift that into the trust. I'll get Riggins to file a motion asking the court to allow that. And I suppose we need to start thinking about how to generate grant applications, no? There could be some significant lag time getting the application process up and running, don't you think?"

Huddleston's voice lightened, "Now you're talking, Counselor! Let's get the ball rolling. Goddamn it, this is going to be fun!"

I laughed out loud. "I have to tell you, Professor, I'm getting as excited about this project as you are. I so miss my academic days—especially the teaching. I'm totally looking forward to reading the candidate proposals. I can't thank you enough for this opportunity."

"I promise you," was his response, "You're going to meet some *fabulously* talented young academics. I don't know how much history you read as a social psychology professor, but I've always found it downright *fun* to keep reading and learning. To be frank with you, I never could believe I was being paid a salary to read and write history. I always found it too much fun to consider it work; it was more like getting paid for doing my hobby. It's been a great career for me, Counselor, and by coming along for the final chapter, you're going to experience just why that's so."

*

I was so busy with an upcoming trial in federal district court, and everything was progressing so well with the professor's initial ideas for stimulating grant applications that I hadn't spent a moment thinking about Attorney Riggins's warning about Attorney Owens. But just as Riggins had feared, Owens indeed filed an objection to the petition for allowance of the will. This blocked any chance of a quick preliminary distribution of cash to the trust, and hence we had to put on hold our efforts to invite young scholars to begin filing funding applications with the trust. The objection claimed that Professor Huddleston had visited "undue influence" on his uncle during the yearly visits he had made during the last decade of Mr. Pennington's life. Owens also argued that his clients—the second cousins—were much closer to the decedent than the distant cousin who had long since fled the state and never returned. He argued that the only reason Professor Huddleston visited was to continue his campaign of pressuring his ever-more-frail uncle. Attorney Owens had also filed supporting affidavits signed by each of the second cousins. As far as I could tell when I read them, there were no relevant facts whatsoever in them, and while I knew nothing about Montana practice and jurisprudence, I couldn't see how the objection could prevail without a significantly more robust demonstration of undue influence.

Professor Huddleston was visibly saddened when I next met with him and relayed the news.

"Tell me, Counselor," he said slowly in a low voice, "assuming you've had experience with such rubbish in the past, when families go at each other like this in lawsuits, do they tend to get beyond it when some court figures out a fair resolution?"

"Honest answer?"

"Yes, give me the honest answer."

"No, not in my experience. Lawsuits are rough-and-tumble adversarial affairs. Typically, when the process finally plays out, one side ends up enormously upset about the outcome. And worse, the losers tend to remain convinced of the merits of their case. In my experience, it's tough to put Humpty Dumpty back together again."

The professor contemplated what I had said. "I guess that doesn't surprise me. Damn it, man, these are the last living blood relatives I have. Absolutely the last. What do you suggest?"

"Well, there's a clause in your uncle's will, we call it by its Latin name, an in terrorem clause, that means—hang on, you're the only client I ever had who can do his own translation. Anyway, the way it operates is that if a named beneficiary brings a challenge against the allowance of the decedent's will and fails to prevail, his original bequest lapses. So we have a stick to work with, as well as a cash carrot."

"I still want your advice, Counselor. Carrot or stick?"

"I'd go with both. I'd start with the carrot—for a modest amount. If it works out, at least it leaves you a *chance* of reviving contact with your cousins. After all, the greed and toughness could be coming more from the attorney than the cousins. Attorney Riggins says their attorney is a professional SOB. He absolutely predicted this, knowing the guy. So that's my advice."

The professor sat perfectly still for the better part of a minute. Then, in a sad, almost plaintive voice I hadn't heard before, he said, "These people are the last relatives I have on the face of the Earth, and they *sue me*? Or sue my uncle, or whatever it is. It hurts, Counselor, it really hurts." He paused again. "Look. Here's what we're going to do. From this point forward, it's yours to handle. Go ahead and spend some money to settle this, if that's what it takes to get our trust funded without delay. Or threaten them with that in terrorem clause—or both—your call. But whatever you do, do what's best for the trust. I wash my hands of these people from this point on; I haven't seen them since I was a little child, and I don't really give a damn about them. I care much more about the kids we're going to help with the trust; that's my new family. So you handle it, and please don't check back with me again. I don't want to hear about this, or about them, ever again."

*

It took nearly three weeks before Owens finally returned my call. He was exactly as Attorney Riggins had described: brash and oppositional, with no interest whatsoever in constructing a cooperative, working relationship. When I asked him what evidence he had of undue influence, his response was simply, "Let's just talk about money. That's what this is all about."

Toward the end of a painful conversation, I reluctantly offered him an extra $10,000 per beneficiary, plus $10,000 toward his legal bills.

His reaction was blunt: "You're crazy if you think this matter can be settled for an extra fifty thousand dollars. Do you have *any* idea of the value of the oil rights the old man owned?"

"No, actually, I don't," I responded. "Do you?"

"Millions, many millions. So this fifty-thousand-dollar settlement offer is an insult. The five cousins should each get an equal share. That's our position."

"Counselor," I replied, "This is not a fifty-thousand-dollar issue for you to take to your clients: it's a one-hundred-fifty-thousand-dollar issue, because if your clients don't prevail on the objection you filed, they can each kiss good-bye their twenty-five-thousand-dollar specific bequest. Have you told them about the in terrorem clause? I trust under Montana law you're required to take my settlement offer to your clients. It's their decision to make, not yours, correct?"

"Don't you dare try to tell me how to practice Montana law. I looked you up—that's the fucking Harvard Law in you, and it pisses me off. You handle your side of the case, and I'll handle mine," he snapped.

"Mr. Owens," I said quietly, ignoring his agitation, "this offer is open for forty-eight hours from this moment, after which it will be withdrawn. If I don't hear from you in two days' time, I'll have Montana counsel mark up a hearing on the petition, and we'll argue your evidence-free objection to the court. Who knows, maybe I'll even show up myself. And mark my words, if I come out there and we prevail, your clients will take nothing. And tell your clients about the offer I made today. Try to keep in mind that they're my client's cousins, and avoiding litigation might help leave intact the very little family connection there seems to be. Do you at least agree with that last statement?"

"These cousins don't even know each other, and don't give a damn about each other. So your point is irrelevant. We'll see you in court unless your client adds a zero to the current offer." With that he hung up.

Attorney Owens never called back. Just over three weeks later, I flew out to Montana the afternoon before the hearing. Attorney Riggins picked me up at the airport and took me out to dinner. Over a really quite remarkable barbeque meal, he prepared me on the differences between Montana and Massachusetts probate court procedure, and reassured me that he would be by my side if I faltered on Montana practice.

First to be heard was my motion to appear pro hoc vice; this motion allows an out-of-state attorney to argue before a court so long as there is an associated in-state counsel at his side. This was allowed—if over

Attorney Owens's gratuitous objection. The objection to the petition to allow the will was next to be heard, so Attorney Owens had the floor. He was a tall, overweight, powerful man, with extraordinary multicolored brown hair of a dozen different shades. His voice was an operatic bass-baritone that careened off the walls of the small courtroom. But he had an insurmountable problem: his stentorian resonance couldn't begin to atone for the complete absence of evidence supporting his claim of undue influence. He put each of the four cousins on the stand, two of whom managed to squeeze out a few tears for their dearly departed uncle, and all four of whom testified about how lovingly close they had been. It was third-rate acting, visibly coached by a fourth-rate attorney, and the judge's furled brow gave me reason to believe that he found it as disingenuous as I did. I couldn't see any reason to risk granting any gravitas to their testimony by deigning to cross-examine them.

So when it was my turn to argue Professor Huddleston's case, I simply called Attorney Riggins to the stand. Riggins testified that he had had numerous discussions with the decedent, and that there had never been any change whatsoever in beneficiaries, dating back twenty years. He also testified that Mr. Pennington was enormously fond of his nephew and immensely proud that Huddleston had become a full professor at Harvard University. Most impressive to the court, I thought, was Attorney Riggins's description of how his client had consistently spoken in glowing terms of the professor's yearly visits.

It didn't take any more evidence or argument for the court to rather abruptly stop me. "Thank you, Counselor, I have a full sense of your case." He turned toward Mr. Owens. "Counselor, for your objection to survive the evidence I just heard, you need to point out some significantly meaningful evidence as to undue influence or argue how you might develop such evidence during discovery. If you don't, I'm going to allow the petition to allow the will into probate and appoint the executors named by the decedent."

"Well, of course, I don't have any evidence yet, Your Honor," Owens shot back. "That's the point of discovery, to turn up evidence."

"No, Mr. Owens, that's not how it works," the judge said, looking down over the top of his glasses. "Are you telling me you filed the objection without any information whatsoever that there was undue influence? Do you understand that you could be subject to disciplinary procedures for doing that? I am asking you one last time: Do you or do you not have any information whatsoever at this point—admissible or not—that there were any actions that might constitute undue influence?"

"Well, Judge, you heard the testimony of my clients. That's information."

The judge responded in an unperturbed, even-toned voice that I certainly would have failed to accomplish in his place. "Mr. Owens, even if I take the testimony of your clients at face value that they loved and had a great relationship with their uncle, *do you understand* that that in no way constitutes evidence of undue influence on Mr. Huddleston's part?"

Owens, down to his last card, resorted to his imposing voice and physical stature. Drawing himself up to his full height and speaking twice too loudly, he let the court know his view of the case. "Judge, I do not see why you are making this matter so complicated, when it is a simple case: there are five cousins, and they should each take one-fifth of the estate."

The judge finally looked flabbergasted. I'd have written a decent-sized check to know what thoughts ran through his mind, but all I was to learn was that he was a jurist of quite remarkable restraint. "Mr. Owens, I'm going to take that as a no."

The judge then spent several minutes writing, without looking up at any of us. When he finished, he raised his head and, in a quiet tone of voice, read from his papers. "The objection to the allowance of the will is overruled, and the petition to allow the will into probate is allowed. Henry Huddleston and Tom Riggins are hereby appointed as temporary coexecutors of the decedent's estate, pending their full appointment on their submission of a bond in a penal amount of no less than one million dollars. Now, is there anything else before the court today?"

"Your Honor," I offered, "the will contains an in terrorem clause, and there is a motion before the court for a declaratory judgment on the clause. My client is not in Montana today, and I am wondering if the court would allow a recess so that I might call him to confirm that he wishes me to ask the court to rule on this motion."

"Counsel to side bar," the judge said sternly, waving away the court reporter. When he had us alone, he was firm. "Gentlemen, I want you to go out in the hallway to discuss this matter and *get it resolved*. Mr. Owens, are you familiar with how little latitude I have on this motion under controlling case law? Have you thought about the fact that if your clients lose their specific bequests based on advice from you to challenge the will despite having zero evidence of undue influence, they could come back at you with malpractice actions? Did you warn them about the presence of the clause, and explain to them how it works? Have you thought any of this through?"

"Well, Your Honor, I don't agree that—"

The judge cut Owens off, and his squint said everything. "I want you attorneys back here at two o'clock, and either you will have resolved this matter between you, or I will rule from the bench. Am I clear, gentlemen?"

"Yes, Your Honor," we intoned in unison, at which point the judge stood up and left the courtroom for his chambers. I motioned Riggins off for the moment, and led Owens into the empty jury box to talk. Each of us took a seat.

"Mr. Owens," I began, "you have one more chance: thirty thousand dollars for each of the four beneficiaries, which is five thousand dollars more than the decedent intended, and an additional ten thousand dollars toward your fees. Your clients will be thrilled. Hell, you'll be a hero since they won't have to pay your fees out of their inheritance. What do you say?"

Owens glowered at me. "No *fucking* way, Harvard. I don't know how you come out here all the way from Boston and mess with a local judge. The two of you are like a fucking tag team in the ring against me. That oil is worth a fortune, and these four cousins get peanuts while one cousin gets it all. Does that sound fair to you? You need to talk your people into real money, or this case won't settle. I'll find a way to get back in court—in front of a different judge."

I actually had no intention of calling Professor Huddleston, given what he had said to me. After the break, I told the clerk that we had no agreement and that we needed to go back before the court. He went into the judge's chambers, and ten minutes later the court was back in session. To his credit, the judge listened with exemplary patience to every baseless argument Attorney Owens could cook up about how the professor's yearly visits constituted a manipulative intent to influence the decedent, until at a certain point even this most tolerant of judges ran out of patience and cut off Owens by thanking him profusely.

I had been planning my response, but the judge didn't even glance my way as he ruled from the bench, ending with words that were sweet music to my ears: "Because all four of the specific bequest beneficiaries filed objections to the will, thereby triggering the in terrorem clause contained in the decedent's will, and because I hereby find said objections to be completely without basis, I hereby order, decree, and declare that the coexecutors of the estate shall act in accordance with said clause and with this order, and shall treat all four of the listed specific bequests as having lapsed."

"Note my objection, and my intention to appeal this order," belted out Attorney Owens, waving his arms for effect.

"So noted. Is there anything else before the Court today, gentlemen?"

"Yes, Your Honor," I answered. "There is a motion to allow a preliminary distribution to be made from the estate to the beneficiary. Given that there is a good deal of cash in the estate, and given that the beneficiary intends to gift the entirety of this distribution into a trust that will support graduate students in their academic research, I would argue that the motion should be allowed to permit timely use of these funds. There is a copy of the trust appended to our motion. Finally, I would also argue that no one would be prejudiced by allowance of this motion."

The judge turned to opposing counsel. "Mr. Owens, ignoring for the moment the interesting procedural question of whether after my previous ruling your clients have any standing left in this matter to object, shall I presume you oppose this motion on their behalf?"

As the dejected, somewhat diminished-looking Attorney Owens shook his head yes, the judge simultaneously shook his head no, speaking volumes with the look he shot at opposing counsel over his eyeglasses. "The motion is allowed." With that the judge sprang from his chair with an almost athletic grace and receded into his chambers.

"See you in the appeals court, Harvard. This isn't over yet." Owens scowled.

"Oh, you won't see me, Counselor. I don't do appellate work," I retorted. "You'll have to deal with a partner of mine, who, compared with me, is truly one tough son of a bitch."

"Fuck you," Owens blurted. Those were the final words I ever heard from this charming gentleman. There never was an appeal, so all I could do was hope his clients had taken action against his outrageous malpractice. On our side of the case, I never again heard the professor refer to his cousins. Sad business.

Just over six weeks later, Professor Huddleston received a preliminary distribution of $100,000 from his uncle's estate, plus the documentation assigning to him his uncle's interest in the oil rights. He in turn gifted the funds and interest into the trust, and just like that, we were in business. And there was soon an additional piece of good news: no more than a month after the trust's name was entered on the oil company's books, a consortium approached us with a buyout offer of $1.2 million. Tempting though this was, we rejected the offer based on the predicted long-term viability of the oil field, and the negative tax consequences that would have resulted from a lump-sum buyout. About a year later, Tom Riggins filed a final accounting of the decedent's estate along with the final state and federal estate tax returns and closed the matter out. The remaining assets in the estate made their way through Professor Huddleston to his trust, and we were then in high gear to find deserving candidates and fund their projects.

*

During what turned out to be the final two years of his life, Professor Huddleston, Professor Mary Sanderson, and I met each month at the Harvard Faculty Club in Harvard Yard to review the funding applications that now came flowing in. The club is housed in a gorgeous federal-style building, and the study where we met was beautifully appointed with burgundy leather chairs surrounding an antique writing table. The walls were paneled in cherrywood that over the centuries had developed a remarkable patina, and the white book shelves were filled with leather-bound volumes. I cannot imagine a lovelier setting in which to consider the topic of love, which of course was raised in one way or another in each and every application or grant request we reviewed. It was perfectly clear that Professor Huddleston enjoyed every moment in the process we developed to give his money away: the perusing of the intriguing research proposals, the interviews with the bright young applicants, the awarding of the grants and stipends, and of course, the flood of gratitude from the successful recipients. All of it, every moment of it, visibly brought great pleasure to a man who otherwise would have been alone in his office, lost in ancient texts, doing yet another study on pretty much the same topic he had always written about. I have no reason to doubt that the energy he absorbed from the young and vital applicants was the best tonic for the illness that ailed him.

And, to be honest, it wasn't only Professor Huddleston who was refreshed and rejuvenated by our contact with these capable and spirited young scholars. For a recycled academic like myself, encountering and listening to these graduate students and youthful assistant professors was a welcome bridge back to my abandoned career as a university professor. My wife picked up on the energy I apparently exhibited on my trustee days. As she quipped one morning: "Since you're so young today, could you *please* rake up the leaves on the porch before it snows again."

I suppose all jobs, all professions, have their pros and cons. As for being a university professor in our era, while the biggest con (literally) is dealing with the bloated and overpaid administrations that now dominate each university campus, the biggest pro is working closely enough with graduate students to absorb some of the intellectual excitement they invest in mastering their field and striking out on their own research ventures. I kept pinching myself to see if I was just dreaming that I had a law case that put me back—if only part time—on a university campus.

But it was more than that. The topic here, after all, was love. Suddenly I was surrounded with glorious stories, fascinating studies, and innovative thinking, all about love. The contrast between this and what I otherwise read and talked about in the law office could not have been sharper.

The stream of proposals grew as word of the trust spread, so each month there were more proposals to review and discuss. Many were irresistibly fun to read—some were downright mesmerizing—so when a new one arrived in the mail, there was no way to keep myself from diving in. I read them on the T on the way downtown; I read them walking along the sidewalk on the way to my office; I read them in court when I should have been listening to opposing counsel; I read them while eating a sandwich on my favorite bench on Boston Harbor. There was always at least one, and usually several, in my briefcase. I was hooked on them and just *barely* able to struggle through the bone-dry legal documents associated with my routine law cases.

The proposals came in from history departments across the country, and we even began to receive a few from abroad. To my nonhistorian's eye, the majority of the submissions seemed like entirely deserving topics for master's theses or doctoral dissertations, so at any given time, I had no idea how we were going to select between them. But of course, that was really up to the two professional historians, so I had no real worries along those lines. I was entirely free to enjoy reading each one on its own merits.

One proposal that definitely caught my eye was submitted by a graduate student who was proposing to research the affective element present in the connection between master and apprentice. Her thirty-page précis and plan of research contained fascinating references to where and how she intended to locate medieval European guild data on the topic. But what was especially captivating in her proposal was her plan to relate this to what remains in the modern era of what was once such a remarkable institution. Her plan included research into a number of relatively contemporary apprentice relationships of particular interest. By far the most colorful case study she proposed was that of a woman named Conchita Cintrón and the man who dared take her on as an apprentice in a field theretofore absolutely barred to women: bull fighting. Apparently, in the 1930s, the impossible once again came true, and Cintrón not only became a famous "matadora" throughout the Spanish-speaking world, but simultaneously maintained a full and loving home life as a wife and mother. The grant application quoted Orson Welles, who wrote about Cintrón: "Her record stands as a rebuke to every man of us who has ever maintained that a woman must lose something of her femininity if she seeks to compete with men."[12]

Actually, I had to formally recuse myself from the trustees' considerations about this application to study the master-apprenticeship relationship because twice in my life, once in each career, I had been an apprentice, and since I had myself greatly benefited from each relationship, I was entirely biased on the topic. As a young assistant professor at Boston University, a shortage of offices led to my being asked to share for two or three years the office of E. V. Walter, easily the most erudite and scholarly senior professor in the department. What great good luck! There was so much to learn from him that had never been discussed in graduate school, and just as this grant applicant predicted would happen in an apprenticeship, a warm friendship indeed developed between us that lasted throughout the rest of Walter's life. And then, nearly fifteen years later, I left the security of one of Boston's largest and best law firms to become the apprentice of a master attorney who had an overflowing practice in a far smaller firm. Never did I make a better decision: Robert Silver taught me by guiding me through scores of cases and was always available when I found myself puzzled. He'd been an air force pilot before going to Harvard Law on the GI bill, so he had a very serious sense of training an apprentice. He showed me the importance of connecting with court clerks to learn about a judge's procedural preferences, he revealed how an argument to a jury needs to paint colorful images that flow as pictures into the jurors' minds—way above and beyond the words you use—and, most importantly, he unveiled to me the secret of how to make clients feel well served and confident that their best interests were in safe hands. And, as this young grant applicant's proposal envisaged, once again a warm friendship developed, lasted, and meant a lot to both of us until the day Silver's health failed and required his precipitous retirement from the practice.

---

12. Orson Welles, introduction to *Memoirs of a Bullfighter*, by Conchita Cintrón (Dumfries, NC: Holt, Rinehart and Winston, 1968).

But it didn't stop there. It wasn't long at all after my mentor's forced retirement before I hired my own apprentice, and the cycle of master-apprentice transfer of knowledge and experience was renewed. I thought the applicant was spot-on when she wrote in the abstract of her submission, "The relationship is symbiotic: the mentee receives invaluable know-how from a seasoned professional, and the mentor receives unlimited admiration and much-needed rejuvenation from his apprentice." Everybody wins. Why wouldn't an affective relationship develop?

Another application that caught my attention was submitted by an assistant professor from the University of California at Santa Cruz who wanted to further investigate the nature and dynamics of cross-cultural friendships that had had historical impact. I thought this was such an interesting take on love, which we all too often tend to think of only as romantic love, when of course there are so many other modes: love between friends, parent-child love, and so on. The application discussed a number of fascinating instances of love between friends (*philos* not *eros*, the applicant reminded us) that she intended to study. The one that really caught my eye was her interest in a remarkable friendship from the thirteenth century between Genghis Khan, the ruler of the Mongol Empire that stretched from the Middle East to the China coast, and Ch'ang Ch'un, the leading Chinese Taoist monk of the era. She described how the great Khan of Khans was searching for a modern religion for his people in a time before Islam had penetrated to the East, and he had heard tell of the remarkable senior monk and his religion. Ch'ang Ch'un, well into his seventies, not only accepted the great Khan's invitation, but rode by horseback from an area near modern-day Beijing all the way to Samarkand, in what is now Uzbekistan. To complete the twenty-six-hundred-mile journey, the monk's caravan crossed some of the most severe terrain imaginable. The expedition took over a year to arrive and culminated in three summer months of meetings between the ruler of the secular world and this sage of the sacred world. The trust applicant's description of these meetings was absolutely spellbinding: day after day, the two men met on the banks of a flowing river, and discussed—through interpreters of course—the Taoist perspective on *wu-wei* (effortless action where big outcomes are accomplished with modest means by acting in harmony with the prevailing conditions), strategic retreat (how yielding in the face of greater force can later lead to victory), and why trade mastery trumps superficial intellectualism (why it is more rewarding to spend an evening with a master thief than with a mediocre philosopher). Apparently by the time the summer ended and the great Khan's army broke camp for the season, the astonishing relationship of mutual respect between the two accomplished men had developed into a close friendship that was to endure, if by messenger, for the remainder of the monk's life.[13]

Another request to fund doctoral dissertation research came from a Yale PhD candidate who proposed to study same-sex relationships in historical perspective. According to the essay portion of his application, and as one would expect, there is nothing new about men loving men and women loving women, but of course the social reaction to homosexuality has changed greatly over time and has varied widely between cultures. This young scholar was proposing to research and write about how some historically interesting same-sex relationships deeply affected the lives of those who ruled over nations and empires, and he had an impressive set of language skills with which to read ancient texts. In his essay, he outlined ten world historical figures he intended to study. The one that struck me as particularly fascinating was a relationship from the second century involving the Roman emperor Hadrian. While Hadrian is best known for his military campaigns that secured the peripheries of the Roman Empire, he is less well known for having ushered in a period of relative peace and stability within the realm. The proposed study, however, was not about the martial or social accomplishments of the emperor but about his having fallen head over heels in love with a handsome boy named Antinous. The applicant stressed that this was Rome, not ancient Greece with its well-known liaisons between gentlemen and their boyfriends. On the contrary, Hadrian's homosexual relationship was as frowned on

---

13. "The Travels of Ch'ang Ch'un to the West, 1220–1223, Recorded by His Disciple Li Chi Ch'ang," in *Mediæval Researches from Eastern Asiatic Sources* by Emil Bretschneider (New York: Barnes & Noble, 1888). This publication includes a translation by Bretschneider of Genghis Khan's letter of invitation.

then as it would have been in Victorian England. The emperor, however, stood firm even in the face of considerable social approbation, openly loving and living with Antinous for a decade. Then, in the year 130 CE, when the great emperor and his lover traveled to Egypt, tragedy struck: Antinous drowned in a boating accident on the Nile. The remaining eight years of Hadrian's reign were marked by an almost obsessive focus on his grief. Hadrian had the youth worshipped as a god, founded the city of Antinopolis on the banks of the Nile in his honor, constructed temples and altars to the boy, established schools and Panhellenic games in his name throughout the empire, commissioned nearly two thousand stone likenesses carved (many of which survive to this day), and arranged for Antinous's handsome young image to be imprinted on official Roman coins—the only nonimperial image *ever* so used.

All of these mesmerizing proposals—and so many more—were candidates to be funded by the ongoing flow of barrels and barrels of black Montana oil. And since the flow and the price of oil had both recently increased, we were easily able to afford flying in candidates to meet with us. We immediately realized that interviewing candidates in person gave us a much more accurate understanding of how they intended to go about their research and a far better chance of correctly assessing the likelihood of their achieving what they set out to accomplish.

Meeting the applicants in person had another advantage: it permitted us to experience firsthand the level of youthful exuberance exhibited by them, and that, after all, was part of what was so appealing about the enterprise I had lucked into. Of course, there were times when the unlimited energy of the young mind ran aground on the shoals of feasibility, and several of the proposed studies were funded only after the two history professors succeeded in convincing the applicants that research practicality was a major consideration for us. But, as you might imagine, reining in youthful enthusiasm was not always so easy. Take, for example, the Yale PhD candidate mentioned above who planned to research and write about the details of ten instances of historical figures whose homosexuality figured into their public lives. During the trustees' preliminary discussion about the proposal, the two history professors, while finding the project promising in many ways, planned to suggest to the candidate that perhaps he should think about reducing the number of such personages to be covered in his dissertation to a more manageable set. Then we met the young man.

Lawrence Kaplan was fascinating to listen to from the moment we finished our meal with him at the Faculty Club and got down to hearing him out on his proposal. Kaplan was a nice-looking blue-eyed young man whose blond hair had not forsaken him for light brown, as mine had at his stage of graduate school. He was five foot two, maybe five foot three, and he couldn't possibly have weighed more than 120 pounds. But notwithstanding his stature, Kaplan had as deep and resonant a speaking voice as you can imagine. He discussed the specifics of history the way a natural musician plays an instrument above and beyond what composer's write: it's no longer about the notes, it's about the music. I had the distinct impression that the young man had never forgotten any historical accounting he had ever read, and my professional historian colleagues later expressed almost identical reactions.

Late in the interview, the two history professors were visibly exhausted by their still-unsuccessful effort to get the candidate to trim down the vast scope of his proposed study. Almost casually, probably intending to take a break from his pruning effort, Professor Huddleston asked the candidate why he had decided to focus exclusively on same-sex love relationships for his study.

Mr. Kaplan replied, without the slightest hint of being taken aback by the question, that there were two reasons: First, we are living in an era when social norms about same-sex sexuality are being reformed at an almost unprecedented rate. And part of the task of historians, he went on to somewhat sternly lecture the three of us, is to fulfill their "duty," as he phrased it, of enlightening contemporary social change on a particular issue by exposing for popular consumption the historical context of the evolving norms on the matter. He then described an impressive study he had undertaken for his master's thesis that, to his mind, clearly demonstrated how academic history departments were failing in this regard. He had ordered up the course catalog book from the top 100 US four-year colleges and universities. Once he had these, he perused the course offerings for any course that pertained in any way to LGBT issues. He then wrote to the professors teaching these courses asking for a copy of their course reading lists, and had received just over eighty to review. His data showed that the substantial totality of these courses were offered in sociology and psychology departments, with only a handful being offered by history departments. Moreover, from his review of the reading lists, it was clear that when LGBT issues were offered by sociology and psychology professors, there were almost no readings required of the students that would serve to place the contemporary status of LGBT issues in historical perspective. We were impressed.

Kaplan paused for a moment. "The second reason is personal," he said in a much slower, even deeper tone of voice, looking down at the floor. "I don't know if it's appropriate to bring up."

We all assured him that that was entirely his decision, but that there would be no prejudice in his discussing it—or not—as he chose. He hesitated, but then decided to share with us what was on his mind. His voice and demeanor filled with emotion. "I had a brother—a fraternal twin, in fact—who for the first ten or twelve years of my life was never more than five feet from me. We even looked so much alike that people always assumed we were identical twins. For years and years we actually had no idea what that meant and couldn't have cared less." He paused again, and the tiniest quick smile shot across his face the way a falling star shoots across the sky and then is gone. "But when puberty hit us, our differing genetics divided us from one another as definitively as a big kitchen knife slices through a cucumber. Mark was gay from the first moment he had a sexual thought; I was straight. We argued, we fought, we stopped playing together, and we went our separate ways, each into his own circle of friends. Within a year, Mark came out to our parents as gay, and they were horrified and entirely unsupportive. To their credit, I have to say, within a few months, half a year maybe, they began to become more understanding and to accept Mark for who he was. They were making strides, bold strides. But I was not. Not when they did. Not until it was too late.

"I did a great deal of damage to my relationship with my brother. And there are wounds in this world that never heal. At school, Mark had been tormented and teased, even bullied, and it was only in the final few months that I even began to stand up for him. But it was too late. One day, without warning and without any precipitating event that we could identify, Mark went home alone from school and swallowed every pill in our parents' medicine cabinet. Every single pill."

There was complete silence in the room when Lawrence stopped speaking. Both historians shot me a look that I could read as easily as a cue card: "You've got the fucking social psychology degree; use it and deal with this." So I did, after a pause meant both to celebrate the solemnity of what we had been told and to give me a moment to figure out what I could possibly say.

"Lawrence," I tried to intone in a respectful tone of voice, "thank you for sharing something so personal with us. I can't speak for my cotrustees, but I can tell you that you have my vote to fund this project—though this is contingent on your taking seriously the advice you are hearing today about trimming back the scope of your project. But I want you to understand that I am voting to fund this research based on your academic record and the proposed project, not because of what you just revealed to us about your family history. That being said, this dissertation topic is wonderfully well chosen. While the topic is clearly of interest to anyone trying to fathom the extraordinary amount of social change we have all witnessed on LGBT issues in the past several decades, the research and reflection you will do on the topic will serve you well on a personal level. There is probably no better way for you to expiate the trauma you must have experienced than to put your brother's homosexuality, and your initial reaction to it, in perspective. I don't doubt for a moment that your dissertation will make an eminently publishable book, and I think there is a good chance you will feel much more whole, and much more healed, when your work sees the light of day. And can I add something personal?" I asked "I hope you dedicate the book to your brother, openly and proudly."

The young man looked up, directly into my eyes, and smiled, not with his lips, really, but with his eyes.

*

All good things come to an end, and in the third year of royalty checks and titillating grant proposals, the professor learned from his doctors that he had only three or four months of vigor left before he would likely experience a rapid decline in his strength. With respect to the trust, he told the two of us at the meeting his grim news, but followed by saying that he was completely confident we could carry on without him. He also reported that he was appointing as his successor trustee a professor named James Howland, an expert in Roman and Middle Eastern History at the University of Chicago. Finally, he also announced that he wanted to hold one more annual dinner, even if it would have to be a few months earlier than it otherwise would have been.

Ah, those annual dinners! To my mind, these affairs had been the top moments of the first years of the trust. Huddleston had designed them to be sumptuous and memorable, and that they certainly were. They were held in the private dining room of the Harvard Faculty Club, and each had included all of the year's successful applicants. For this particular evening, however, Professor Huddleston had decided to invite the fourteen previous awardees plus the current year's two successful candidates—Lawrence Kaplan being one of them. The affair was held as a black-tie event, and the passed hors d'oeuvres, the French meal, and the well-selected wines lived up to the Faculty Club setting. Conversation was stopped at intervals by Professor Huddleston to introduce the newly successful applicants who then each gave a fifteen-minute summary of what his or her research entailed. The practice was that other recipients would follow on by articulating any research or conceptual suggestions they might have on the topic. This meant that after each presentation, there was a flood of discussion about possible directions to head with the undertaking, about relevant sources to take a look at, and about suggested subtopics that might be covered. All of this was recorded, transcribed, and subsequently sent to all participants. I always found it astonishing that these young, top-notch scholars not only had firm control of their own topic area, but were also very often able to make valuable contributions to their fellow awardees who were working on completely unrelated matters. And I greatly admired the insight of Professor Huddleston in establishing the collectivity of our awardees as a community of connected scholars.

Needless to say, since it was known to all that this was going to be Professor Huddleston's swan song, everything was done to make it an entirely memorable evening. Our incoming trustee, Professor Howland, whose best-known book was on the history of "courtly love," which was such an important element of the code of chivalry of medieval Europe, was also in attendance. When I first met him at the festivities, I was relieved to learn that, above and beyond his professional skills, which I had no reason to doubt were any less prodigious than Professor Huddleston had described, he was also a man who clearly enjoyed life. Howland's girth rendered him a suspender man, and his infectious laugh gathered the young scholars around him as if he were the pied piper. It was crystal clear that it was going to be a delight to work with him.

All of our awardees were able to attend the gala affair, save one. This single past grant recipient who had to miss the evening did so only because she had given birth to her first child only about three days before our convocation. To Huddleston's visible delight, he received a call from her during our celebration announcing that a healthy Henry Brian Nicholson had entered this world, "a product of a great deal of loving." The professor clearly was moved by the choice of first name.

It could not possibly have been colder outside—on the drive over I had heard that the temperature was to drop to minus three during the night. But it could not possibly have been warmer inside. This contrast between the bitter cold winter weather and the evening's celebration of love was so stark that I thought about it throughout the evening. I certainly had never attended an event that was more centered on love; each and every person in the room was a scholar of the subject, except for yours truly, local attorney. And, of course, on top of their shared academic area of expertise, all of the young scholars also had in common that they were beneficiaries of the generosity and munificence of Professor Huddleston. As you might imagine, if I've been at all able to give you a flavor of the man, Professor Huddleston wasn't at all hard to like, even to love.

At the conclusion of the fifteen-minute presentations by the two new awardees and the discussions that followed, Professor Huddleston asked if the past grant recipients present in the room could each take five minutes to present to others a quick review of what they were working on and the status of their research and writing. As I listened to each young scholar, I couldn't help but notice the contrast with the news broadcasts I had listened to while snaking my salt-encrusted car to the evening's event through the snowbank-narrowed roads from Boston to Harvard Square in Cambridge. The nightly news was, as always, a litany of horrors: three or four different wars, racial and religious strife on every continent, record-breaking droughts, and on and on and on. It was so grim, in fact, that when I finally arrived and parked, I had literally had to spend a minute or two just sitting in silence in the underground parking garage, trying to let my mind clear so that I could begin the transition to the delights of the celebratory event that awaited. The bracing winter air and the walk through historic and unchanging Harvard Yard certainly helped still more, and entering into the demure Faculty Club put the evening's news still further away. But there was still part of me caught up in the frenzied world of contemporary life—until the young scholars began to present the themes of their research. How incredibly uplifting it was to hear these brilliant young people, one after the next, remind us that while the world has always had its wars, its religious conflicts, and its patterns of oppression and domination, it has also always had love—in all its varied forms.

But the highlight of the evening came after dinner, when there was a round of toasts to Professor Huddleston, followed by chants of "speech, speech, speech!" The unpretentious and amiable professor asked if we minded if he sat as he fulfilled his final duty as trustee. Imagine the occasion. Think of its weight. It was the final moment of an intellectual life that began in the professor's teenage years, and of an academic career that had spanned half a century. A chair was brought forward, around which we formed a semicircle, each of us facing this venerable man whom we so respected.

"Thank you all so much for taking time out of your busy lives to join me this evening, and thanks for understanding that this annual gala dinner of our trust had to be a bit earlier than 'annual' would normally imply. I didn't have a hell of a lot of choice, because as you know, I have an upcoming appointment that apparently I need to keep." There was a warm and gentle wave of laughter at his ironic remark.

"Seriously though, I do want to take a few minutes to talk about why I created this trust and what I hope you, as the trust's emissaries, will help the trustees accomplish for years and years to come. As many of you know, I figured out the secret of how to become terribly wealthy: I left the matter entirely to chance." Again, the room filled with warm laughter. "An uncle of mine just happened to have no children, just happened to be predeceased by his wife, and just happened to have the foresight to make a very clever investment in what was then an unpromising Montana oil field. So as long as that black goo continues to come out of that field, the trust will continue to be funded, and our work—your work now—in researching what I like to call the history of love can be supported.

"But I claim no credit and deserve no praise for recycling my uncle's petro dollars into your projects and careers, for it is I who am blessed to have academic heirs to pass these funds on to. And please, don't make too much out of what I have done: what may appear to you to be generosity is in fact once again the product of pure chance. The love of my life just happened to die too young for us to have had children, and I happened to have never met another woman who could tolerate me."

The professor paused for a few moments repose, and then continued. "As I see it, modern science can explain a great deal about the physics that underlies inorganic chemistry, and about the inorganic chemistry that underlies organic chemistry, and about the organic chemistry that underlies the biochemical processes necessary for life, and about the evolutionary forces that through hundreds of millions of years developed ever more complex forms of life until *Homo sapiens* first appeared on Earth. Building on these hard sciences, the social sciences have advanced our understanding of how human patterns of social organization have developed through thousands of years from the simple communal groupings of tribes to the complex, postindustrial societies of our era. But when in all this development did love first appear? Where and why and how did it first develop? What was its evolutionary or social purpose? Where is that explained?"

Huddleston looked around at the young scholars, who were transfixed. "I, like you, am a historian and not an evolutionary theoretical bioanthropologist. But here's my guess—and that's all it is; it certainly doesn't merit being called a theory. It seems to me that as evolution has developed the phyla over the eons, animals have taken increasingly better care of their young. The link to evolutionary success seems obvious: it's got to be a clever genetic edge on the competition for parents to protect their young while they are still small and vulnerable. A small percentage of fish protect their eggs and their young, but a far higher percentage of reptiles do. Amphibians by and large do still better, and then along came mammals, who not only protect their young but, to varying extents, add an element of tenderness as they nurse and shelter their offspring.

"And then humans entered the scene. While other young mammals are relatively viable vis-à-vis their predators in a matter of months, young humans take far, far longer to arrive at this state. Just look at the average college freshman," the professor added, giving us all a laugh break. "So what is clear, it seems to me, is that early human mothers living in the face of nature would have had to hold their children in their arms for years—even longer and more often than we do now, I should think—since there were more risks to shelter them from. My best guess is that, at some point, the expanding mental capacity of *Homo sapiens*, which, of course, literally means 'he who knows himself,' allowed the human mother to perceive and contemplate how she *felt* about the child she was holding, nursing, nurturing, and protecting.

"So here's my very unscientific leap from anything I've ever read, including what I could find in the anthropological literature, about how love developed in history. May I?" Lots of nods, lots of smiles, and not a few tears around the semicircle. "My guess is that early human mothers at some point in the development of language named what they felt for the children they labored so hard to birth, nurse, nurture, and protect. And they named that feeling *love*. Once they did that, the rest followed: When they asked themselves how they felt about what their own mothers had done for them when they were young and helpless, they called that love. And the feeling they had for the men who kept them and their children safe, who foraged and hunted for them? That feeling they also called love. And what they felt for those around them who joined forces with their immediate family and struggled with them against the wild forces of nature? Well, that too they called love."

The professor took the better part of a minute to catch his failing breath, then started up again. "I remember to this day the undergraduate biology course where I learned my first fancy academic phrase: 'ontogeny recapitulates phylogeny.' This means that the development of the human embryo goes through stages that reflect the evolutionary development of humans. Allow me to use this as a metaphor for the development of the capacity to love in each individual human child. When a human child is born, its physical attachment to the mother is cut, and its emotional attachment is begun. The mother is the child's safe harbor in every way, and within months the emotional attachment to her is well advanced. Then the newborn becomes a bit more exploratory, and it begins to become attached to its father, then later to its siblings, then to its grandparents and extended family, then to its neighborhood friends, and so on. It's just a metaphor, but to some extent it does seem that the development of each child's capacity to love recapitulates how the social evolution of the human capacity to love might have developed among early humans."

The professor paused once again, and as he rested, he looked from left to right around the semicircle, favoring each of us with the warmth of his smile. Then, in a voice that was audibly tiring, he broached one final topic. "Finally, I have one last train of thought for you. Over the years, people have asked me, even reproached me with the question, 'Why do you study the history of love?' I sometimes responded with, 'Why do others study the history of war?' But, of course, there certainly has been cause to study the history of war: it's abundantly clear that violence and war, and the indifference to the human suffering they generate, have always been present. But isn't it just as clear that love has been present just as long as war? So how can it be frivolous to study love, when love is one of the quintessential human qualities? Perhaps you and I study the history of human love because, in the final analysis, to study love is to affirm it." He paused one final time, and only barely caught the breath he needed to say, "Good-bye and good luck to each and every one of you, and thank you so much for what you bring to our joint venture."

With this, each of us in turn passed by our seated and quite exhausted host and said our good-byes.

*

I had grown so fond of Professor Huddleston after all we had done together over the better part of four years that it was my pleasure to visit him at his home once a week for what turned out to be the remaining six weeks of his life. He had chosen to have in-house hospice care, and like Camus's Meursault, the nearer the end drew, the clearer he became. Most of our discussions were about additional proposed research projects, but there was one final conversation I will always remember. It occurred on my last visit to the venerable scholar's house.

That evening, I fought my way through a nor'easter snowstorm to get to the professor's home, which was walking distance from Harvard Square. I was so cold that I didn't warm up right away, even after entering into the relative balminess of the small antique house, with its walls of books, low ceilings, and wide-plank pine floors. There was no way to speed the process. It was just one of those winter evenings when, even after coming inside, you only take off your coat and sweaters one layer at a time.

No longer able to mount the stairs, Professor Huddleston was confined to a rented hospital bed in his converted first-floor study. His abandoned desk now sat in the dining room pushed up against the wall; it reminded me of President Kennedy's sailboat, forever up on land at the Kennedy Museum on the Boston waterfront. There was a hospice nurse on duty, and she suggested that I wait about fifteen minutes for my visit, as she needed a bit of time with the professor to prepare him. I'd been to the house a considerable number of times during the past four years, especially during these recent endgame visits, but I had never poked around. Huddleston's house, like many of the eighteenth-century homes in and around Harvard Square, was a tiny affair; people were smaller then, and heat was hard to come by. But there is a real charm to these survivors of another era. Not surprisingly, I could see the hand of a bachelor decorator in what art hung on the walls and what objects were displayed. The art choices, it seemed to me, were concentrated on events from ancient history—no surprise there. But the selection of events was even more telltale: no battles, no war, no bloodshed. Clearly Huddleston had the theme of love up and running once again, although I got the impression it wasn't an easy theme to decorate with. There was a wonderful Honoré Daumier etching of the moment when Aphrodite turned Pygmalion's statue into the flesh-and-blood Galatea. And another wall held a beautiful framed photograph that I recognized from the historical events the professor had narrated on the very first day I met him: the remarkable love story of Justinian and Theodora. The photograph was a close-up of the face of Theodora, taken from the marble mosaic of her found in Ravenna, Italy. Here was the one and only likeness we have of this beautiful woman, and he was right: she did indeed put Julia Roberts to shame, looking out at me from fifteen hundred years ago. And on a coffee table, there was a small replica of the famous Rodin statue, *The Kiss*.

But then it came to me. There were no photographs. None. I looked around the entire first floor, and unabashedly continued my search in the second floor's two bedrooms. Not a single photograph in the house. I had never thought about it, but of course it made sense: no family, no photographs. The idea tore at my heart and almost brought tears to my eyes. Like so many others, I have and treasure an ever-expanding collection of family snapshots. As I write this sentence in my home office in 2016, if I look up, I peer into the unthinkably deep dimples in the cheeks of my then-four-year-old son. On the file cabinet behind me, the same boy can be found naked as a one-year-old, hugging pals at day care as a five-year-old, batting as a seven-year-old, skiing as a nine-year-old, and getting married in his thirties. We all do this. People run into their burning houses to grab their family photos and tell news reporters at flood scenes about what it feels like to lose these links to the past. But in Huddleston's case, there was no family, and there were no photographs. Sad. So sad.

Just as I came downstairs, the nurse rounded the corner and told me it was okay to enter the study and visit with the professor. I was still deeply chilled from the winter storm that howled outside and whistled its way through the clapboards of the old house, so I asked the professor if he wanted me to build a fire at the end of his bed in the old fireplace that graced the room. He was so enthusiastic about the idea that I didn't even mind going back out into the storm to retrieve logs from his backyard shed. The professor didn't say a word through all my Boy

Scout efforts to get the kindling arranged, place the logs, and light the fire. I thought maybe he had dozed off, but when I finally succeeded in rousing flame, I turned and could tell that he had watched the entire production.

After still another considerable period of peaceful silence—save for the storm's raucous sounds and the fire's gentle crackle—I asked if there were any final legal issues he wanted to discuss.

"No, not at all," Huddleston replied. "Everything's the way I want it. And Counselor, thanks for all you've done to make that happen, and another thank you for coming over in this awful storm to visit me. It's above and beyond the call of duty."

We both grew silent again, each of us staring into the fireplace, allowing the crackling to tell us its story, as fires have no doubt seized and held the attention of people from the earliest of times. Ten minutes or so passed, and when I looked over, I could see that now the professor's eyes were closed. His breathing seemed shallow and raspy, and it was clear how little strength was left to the man. I didn't know what to do, so I just turned back to the fire. I looked back a little while later and was pretty certain that the professor had fallen asleep. I stood and started to leave, but the two-hundred-year-old floorboards creaked loudly, and when I looked over at him again, his eyes were wide open.

"Leaving?" he asked.

"Sorry, I thought you were asleep. Are you okay? Is there anything I can—"

"Yes," Huddleston interrupted. "Sit down."

I did, of course, and waited. He took half a dozen breaths, each audible, each slower and hoarser than the last. Finally, looking back at the fire, he spoke. "There aren't any more stories."

It took me a moment to reply. "I understand. Just rest. There's no need to speak, no reason to tell another story."

"No. You *don't* understand."

Now I was puzzled and at a loss as to how to respond. The new silence that fell on us was different; it was thick and ponderous and uncomfortable.

Finally, he explained. "I don't mean there's no more stories because I'm out of time to tell stories to *you*." Another long pause followed.

"What I mean is that there's no more time for me to tell *myself* stories, to fill my emptiness with yarns and tales instead of facing what I need to face."

The silence now was even heavier, and then came a new kind of sound, weeping; quiet, deep, weeping. Why not? It had to be hard to be so near the end.

But that wasn't the issue at all. Another minute passed, and then the professor spoke from his heart. "It's like my father and his father and his father and *his* father are all crying out inside my chest: 'Henry, what have you done?'" The crying now was accompanied by moans, moans that went deep down into the soul of this man.

I sat silently, hoping my presence was some kind of comfort. I thought again of Camus's *The Stranger*, and how Meursault blossomed as he watched his gallows being built, and how he denied the priest's offered absolution—the morphine of the soul.

"While I'm delighted you're here, Counselor, your presence doesn't make me feel any less alone—you can't fill that role. I see that now. The only people who could have done that for me aren't here—because I never allowed them to exist: no wife, no child, no grandchild, no future. What was I thinking? I wasted so many years that needed filling up with *my life*, not with stories about the lives of others. *What was I thinking?*" And with this unburdening, the tears and sobs increased fivefold.

With all my heart and soul, I wanted to leave that room and get out into the sideways snowstorm that would cleanse me of what I was hearing, what I was witnessing. But it was not my time, not yet. It was still his time.

Again the words came back, spoken so slowly, and in a voice that couldn't have been more different from the professor's storytelling tone. "Yes, she was dead, but I was still alive, and there were other loves to find, other lives to build. How could I have failed to understand . . . a thousand stories of love, and never their lesson learned."

Then there was only raspy breathing, and there were no more words. A troubled sleep had snuck up behind the professor and taken him into its embrace.

I left the room, told the hospice nurse that the professor had fallen asleep, and walked back to my car without putting on my hat, beseeching the windblown snow to cool my burning face and soothe my aching soul. And when I finally arrived home after a torturous drive, I took my sleeping child up into my arms, brought him into bed with me and my wife, and slept as closely bundled against the two of them as I possibly could.

EPILOGUE

In this book, I posit that loneliness is not an emotion, but a sensation: it is simply the perception of inadequate connections to others. And like other bodily sensations, such as hunger and thirst, it can be experienced at any stage of life. Seth Doe felt irredeemably isolated, a social outcast as a child in the springtime of his life, while Sidney Rittenberg suffered agonizing loneliness through fifteen years of solitary confinement in the summertime of his years. Paul Cardarelli saw no further purpose to his lonesome life in the autumn of his days, and Henry Huddleston, professor of the history of love, first discerned how lonely he was only on the wintery day on which he died.

Admittedly, the first two of these law cases were exceptional in that unusually powerful external social forces were at play. Seth Doe was born into the wild vortex of normative forces that surround the incest taboo; his tragic loneliness was largely determined at the moment of his incestuous conception. Sidney Rittenberg did everything he could to forge strong connections in revolutionary China, without any possible way of foreseeing that these bonds would be torn apart by the onset of Cold War international politics. The endeavors of both men to avoid loneliness were hopeless. Each swam in waters where the current was far stronger than their stroke.

But the remaining two cases we examined were of a different nature. They show us that while the ever-increasing isolation of individuals in contemporary society is progressively more threatening to the connections that protect each of us, loneliness need not prevail. We can and we do take steps to stay linked to family, friends, and colleagues; we just need to work harder to do so in a social environment that is characterized by the eradication of the multigenerational family, the vanishing of traditional communities, and the uprooting effect of geographic dislocation. And similarly, we can and we still do reach out to others to form new connections; but again, it takes more effort to succeed given the hectic pace of urban life, the confusion of media personalities with actual acquaintances, and the increasing presence of strangers in an ever-more-populous world.

In the context of the evolving social world, think about the final two cases I shared and how both clients paid so dearly for their failure to reach out and connect with others. Paul Cardarelli left his family and community at age eighteen, determined to never return. But then he failed to connect with anyone else, mistaking the heroes and characters in the books he read for the flesh-and-blood connections he would need for support and nurturing when trauma struck. And Henry Huddleston, also alone in the world at age eighteen, doomed himself to loneliness with two similar faux pas. First, he indulged himself for forty years in continuing to actively mourn the death of his lover instead of striking out to find someone new. And, tragically, he allowed his fascination with the love stories of history to blind him to the fact that he didn't have one of his own. Admittedly, he made a fascinating effort to make new connections late in his life, but the new relationships, despite all their warmth and charm, were still centered on his work and failed to provide him with anyone to hold his hand as he lay dying.

There are legions of Cardarellis and Huddlestons among us, for there is a crisis of loneliness that plagues postcommunal urban life in our country. Recent studies have shown that by 2010, more than a third of American adults led chronically lonely lives. And we know this number has been rapidly increasing; ten years earlier, only 20 percent of Americans experienced such tragic isolation. Given that seclusion and disconnection from others are such powerful predictors of functional decline and early death,[14] certainly we can say that chronic loneliness is one of the great public health crises of our times. Such is the conclusion of another powerful study on the topic titled *The Lonely American: Drifting Apart in the 21st Century*.[15] Consider this revelation from the study: just under half of older American adults who relocate to a new address score as chronically lonely on the UCLA Loneliness Scale.[16] So think twice about this statistic before you sell your house or give up your own apartment late in life to move to a retirement setting, for you may well be moving into loneliness.

But I do not mean to say that we are helpless in the face of those aspects of contemporary society that increasingly generate and intensify mass chronic loneliness. On the contrary, the life stories we have examined reveal that even in the face of powerful, grand-scale social forces, we can each take steps to lower our risk of succumbing to loneliness. We just need to be more actively aware of the need to actually take these steps, just as we increasingly do in other spheres of life. For example, we expend considerable time and effort avoiding malnutrition by trying to eat wisely, which is no easy task: it means confronting head-on the massive corporate forces that fill our grocery stores with unhealthy, highly processed food. We also, in increasing numbers, take action to avoid musculoskeletal deterioration by exercising in defiance of the sedentary culture of our era that is engendered by desk-bound work and couch-bound entertainment. And in recent years, many have recognized the importance of purposefully staying mentally active to offset the vacuity and triviality of corporate mass culture. Given that chronic loneliness has been found to be as powerful a health risk as

---

14. Perissinotto MD, Carla M., Irena S. Cenzer MA, and Kenneth E. Covinsky, MD, "Loneliness in Older Persons: A Predictor of Functional Decline and Death," *Journal of the American Medical Association for Internal Medicine*, Vol. 172, no. 14 (July 2012); see also John T. Cacioppo and William Patrick, *Loneliness: Human Nature and the Need for Social Connection* (New York: W. W. Norton and Company, 2008), and the additional reported research of professor Cacioppo and his colleagues cited in the Bibliography.
15. Jacqueline Olds and Richard Schwartz, *The Lonely American: Drifting Apart in the 21st Century* (Boston: Beacon Press, 2009).
16. Ibid.

obesity, sedentary lifestyle, and smoking,[17] it clearly merits counter-measures that are as vigorous as those we take in these other aspects of our lives.

Concretely then, what are the prophylactic measures we can take to avoid becoming just another statistic in the chronic loneliness that increasingly plagues our country? To me, the four lives we have followed speak volumes about two general strategies available to each of us in our personal struggle against loneliness. First, the stories illuminate the importance of being *aware* of when we feel lonely or when we are making poor choices that expose us to loneliness, and second, they tell us to be *active* in nurturing our existing connections and daring in creating new ones.

Being Aware of Being Lonely

Action begins with *awareness*. Think back about the role that awareness—or more accurately the lack of awareness—played in the cases we studied so closely. Seth Doe should have become aware of the power of the incest taboo and foreseen the consequences of his continued relationship with his sister, given that he experienced firsthand the hard and sudden criminalization of his incestuous parents. Sidney Rittenberg should have become aware of the danger of his visibility and vulnerability in revolutionary China after his first six-year stint in solitary confinement. Paul Cardarelli should have been aware of the importance of seeking out clinical counseling after his deadly highway accident, especially given his recitation to me of the Vargas Llosa story and the explicit and repeated advice he heard from both Rhonda Wilkins and me to seek treatment. And Professor Huddleston—the ultimate student of love—should certainly have been aware that after grieving the loss of his fiancée, he needed to set out to find another companion on life's otherwise lonely journey.

---

17. Sonya Brownie and Louise Horstmanshof, "The Management of Loneliness in Aged Care Residents: An Important Therapeutic Target for Gerontological Nursing," *Journal of Geriatric Nursing* 32, no 5 (2011): 318–325.

So the first message from the stories is how important it is to have our eyes wide open about the health and viability of our existing connections, for it is only these connections that hold loneliness at bay. We each need to think proactively about the status of our connections, and fashion strategies about what we can do to strengthen and expand them. Part of this process involves being honest with ourselves about which of our connections are in fact no longer functioning or viable. It's far too easy to be in denial about such matters and to assume that old friends are still friends or that past colleagues still care.

Nurturing and Creating Connections

The four lives we have studied also counsel us to *stay connected and make new connections*. But what does that mean? Our earliest connections—our families—are given to us, and we have no choice but to make do with the cards we are dealt. Doe was born into a tragically flawed family, Rittenberg was raised by a single father who died young, Cardarelli came from a hellishly oppressive home life that he couldn't wait to escape, and Huddleston hailed from a simple home that evaporated with complete finality after his first year of college. But later in life, they each had opportunities to make new connections that *could* have been taken and that *should* have been taken. Seth Doe balked at connecting to his preadoptive parents because he still mourned the loss of his birth mother. A wiser path would have involved a realistic assessment of his need to disconnect from his past and connect to his future. Sidney Rittenberg allowed all of his connections to the United States to wither and die, so there were none to save him from a second long, dark term of solitary confinement in Mao's prisons. Paul Cardarelli never undertook to make connections with anyone, seeing himself as being above his working-class origins but inadequate to meet anyone from more educated strata. And Professor Huddleston never recovered from the death of his fiancée to strike out and find another woman to love. Each and every one of them failed in the art and science of maintaining and creating connections, and each of them paid dearly for their failure.

Everyone reading this epilogue has experienced moments of disattachment and loss: they are part of life. We each endure the death of grandparents and then parents, the empty nest when children grow and move on, the broken heart when a lover leaves, and the disappearance of friends and colleagues when we or they leave a community or a school or a team or a job. What is needed after such loss is a recognition of *the necessity of reconnecting to others.* Of all the sad and plaintive voices that my career in the law brought to my ears, none matched the moans of poor dying Henry Huddleston as he mourned his failure to do just this. The challenge each of us faces after endings is to create beginnings. The *only* option is to strike out with determination to make new friends when old ones move away, to join new teams as old ones disperse, to take the time to become involved in voluntary communities to replace the organic communities of yesteryear, and yes, to find a new lover after grieving the loss of one who is gone.

At the end of his classic work on loneliness, Albert Camus has Meursault, enlightened at last by his impending execution, reflect on the situation of his mother in her home for aged persons:

> For the first time in a long time I thought about Maman.
> I felt as if I understood why at the end of her life she
> had taken a "fiance," why she had played at beginning
> again.[18]

Perhaps the final challenge to be garnered from our four stories is to go even further than Meursault does and to dispute with him his use of the verb "to play" (*jouer*). No, Monsieur Meursault—your mother was not *playing*; she was just living. And it was irrelevant that she was at life's end: living without loneliness is about connecting each and every day, and that very much includes the final day.

*

---

18. Albert Camus, *The Stranger*, trans. Matthew Ward (New York: Random House, 1989: p. 122).

There's good news, however. While the antidote for many ailments is hard to find, the antidote for loneliness is readily available: *connections*. In a 2010 landmark survey by the AARP entitled "All the Lonely People," there is a brief list of how to become and remain connected; none of its suggestions will surprise you: nurture your personal relationships, don't substitute electronic communication for face-to-face contact, take the time to volunteer, join a social club or community, and stay in touch with former colleagues after you retire.[19] While every entry in the list is common sense, what matters is whether or not each of us actually gets active and takes these steps. As the four lives we have witnessed make clear, you must either take care of your connections or risk suffering the dire consequences of slipping into loneliness.

*

Connections are not possessions; they are active, living, dying, dynamic processes. Assessing our connections, nurturing our connections, making new connections: all this takes time and effort and even courage. But all this hard work needs doing today, and a whole new round of the same work will need our attention tomorrow, and the next day, and down the weeks, and years, and seasons of our lives.

J. W. Freiberg
Boston, 2016

---

19. Brad Edmondson, "All the Lonely People," *AARP The Magazine*, November/ December (2010).

ACKNOWLEDGMENTS

Helena Evans. My wife and partner and friend who has taught me so much about connection and love; without you, I would have been able to write only half this book.

Jeanne Fagnani. As brief as this book is, it took a solid five-year effort to write, and Jeanne, my dear friend of forty years, you would not let me stop when discouragement tempted me. You were so wonderfully encouraging and convincing through all that time; *merci tellement.*

Justin and Sarah Freiberg and Luke Hunsberger. Thank you, my children, for your confidence and your valuable critique of earlier efforts; in so many ways I could not have done this but for you three.

The Harvard Law School. I am still amazed that you admitted a thirty-six-year-old academic on his promise to meld his legal education and his social-psychology background in order to pursue a career that would benefit from the double training. My gratitude to the law school, to its legal aid bureau (of which I was honored to be president), and to my remarkable fellow students—then and through the years—is boundless.

The Home for Little Wanderers, the Italian Home for Children, Child and Family Services, the Stevens Children's Home. These extraordinary children's social service agencies, along with numerous smaller-scale adoption agencies, paid me the extraordinary honor of naming me their general counsel over nearly three decades. So did scores of psychiatrists, psychologists, and licensed independent clinical social workers with private practices. My gratitude to the administrators of these agencies, and especially to the many hundreds of clinical professionals with whom I worked over all these years, cannot be exaggerated. It was in the almost daily case consults with these professionals that I learned a great many of the real-world fact patterns that underlie the case stories that are presented in *Four Seasons of Loneliness.*

Anna M. Leroy. I shall never forget the two weeks on rue de l'Arbalète where we worked, hacking away at a great forest of words and ideas to find the book that lay hidden within. You were amazingly helpful.

Amanda O'Brien. Your copyediting of this book was immeasurably important; without you, a great many participles would still be dangling. Thank you ever so much.

Shannon O'Neill. Your developmental editing of this work was one of the most solid performances I have ever seen any professional deliver—in any line of work. I cannot thank you enough for your insights throughout the process.

Emilie Sandoz-Voyer, Meghan Harvey, and the rest of the Girl Friday team. Your coordination of the editing and publishing of this small book was impeccably handled. It was a delight and pleasure to work with you.

Alain Touraine. I learned so much from you, both in my work under you on my doctoral dissertation and then in the ten years that followed in my association and occasional presence at your Centre d'Études des Mouvements Sociaux in Paris. But what this particular book owes especially to you is your advice in 1979 when I told you I was resigning my professorship to go to law school, and you replied, "Keep your sociological eyes open, Terry, and someday you will write a book for us on what you have learned as an attorney."

APPENDIX

UCLA Loneliness Scale Version 3

Reference:

Russell, D. (1996). UCLA Loneliness Scale (Version 3): Reliability, validity, and factor structure. *Journal of Personality Assessment, 66,* 20–40.

Description of Measure:

A 20-item scale designed to measure one's subjective feelings of loneliness as well as feelings of social isolation. Participants rate each item on a scale from 1 (Never) to 4 (Often).

This measure is a revised version of both the original UCLA Loneliness Scale and the Revised UCLA Loneliness Scale. The first revision was done to make 10 of the 20 original items reverse scored. The second revision was done to simplify the scale so less educated populations could comprehend it (see other UCLA Loneliness Scale pages on this website).

Abstracts of Selected Related Articles:

Russell, D, Peplau, L. A., & Ferguson, M. L. (1978). Developing a measure of loneliness. *Journal of Personality Assessment, 42,* 290–294.

Research on loneliness has been hindered by the lack of a simple and reliable assessment technique. The development of the UCLA Loneliness Scale, a short, 20-item general measure of loneliness is reported. The measure has high internal consistency (coefficient alpha = .96) and a test-retest correlation over a two-month period of .73. Concurrent and preliminary construct validity are indicated by correlations with self- reports of current loneliness and related emotional states, and by volunteering for a "loneliness clinic."

Russell, D, Peplau, L. A., & Cutrona, C. E. (1980). The Revised UCLA Loneliness Scale: Concurrent and discriminate validity evidence. *Journal of Personality and Social Psychology, 39,* 472–480.

The development of an adequate assessment instrument is a necessary prerequisite for social psychological research on loneliness. Two studies provide methodological refinement in the measurement of loneliness. Study 1 presents a revised version of the self-report UCLA (University of California, Los Angeles) Loneliness Scale, designed to counter the possible effects of response bias in the original scale, and reports concurrent validity evidence for the revised measure. Study 2 demonstrates that although loneliness is correlated with measures of negative affect, social risk taking, and affiliative tendencies, it is nonetheless a distinct psychological experience.

McKenna, K. Y. A., Green, A. S., & Gleason, M. E. J. (2002). Relationship formation on the Internet: What's the big attraction? *Journal of Social Issues, 58,* 9–31

Self Report Measures for Love and Compassion Research: *Loneliness and Interpersonal Problems*

We hypothesized that people who can better disclose their "true" or inner self to others on the Internet than in face-to-face settings will be more likely to form close relationships online and will tend to bring those virtual relationships into their "real" lives. Study 1, a survey of randomly selected Internet newsgroup posters, showed that those who better express their true self over the Internet were more likely than others to have formed close online relationships and moved these friendships to a face-to-face basis. Study 2 revealed that the majority of these close Internet relationships were still intact 2 years later. Finally, a laboratory experiment found that undergraduates liked each other more following an Internet compared to a face-to-face initial meeting.

Scale:

INSTRUCTIONS: Indicate how often each of the statements below is descriptive of you.

Statement	Never	Rarely	Sometimes	Often
*1. How often do you feel that you are "in tune" with the people around you?	1	2	3	4
2. How often do you feel that you lack companionship?	1	2	3	4
3. How often do you feel that there is no one you can turn to?	1	2	3	4
4. How often do you feel alone?	1	2	3	4
*5. How often do you feel part of a group of friends?	1	2	3	4
*6. How often do you feel that you have a lot in common with the people around you?	1	2	3	4

7. How often do you feel that you are no longer close to anyone?	1 2 3 4
8. How often do you feel that your interests and ideas are not shared by those around you?	1 2 3 4
*9. How often do you feel outgoing and friendly?	1 2 3 4
*10. How often do you feel close to people?	1 2 3 4
11. How often do you feel left out?	1 2 3 4
12. How often do you feel that your relationships with others are not meaningful?	1 2 3 4
13. How often do you feel that no one really knows you well?	1 2 3 4
14. How often do you feel isolated from others?	1 2 3 4
*15. How often do you feel you can find companionship when you want it?	1 2 3 4
*16. How often do you feel that there are people who really understand you?	1 2 3 4
17. How often do you feel shy?	1 2 3 4
18. How often do you feel that people are around you but not with you?	1 2 3 4
*19. How often do you feel that there are people you can talk to?	1 2 3 4
*20. How often do you feel that there are people you can turn to?	1 2 3 4

Scoring:

The items with an asterisk are reverse scored. Keep scoring on a continuous basis. This scale is provided only for Researchers.

BIBLIOGRAPHY

Brontley, Jeffrey, and Wendy Millstine. *True Belonging: Mindful Practice to Help You Overcome Loneliness, Connect with Others and Cultivate Happiness.* Oakland, CA: New Harbinger, 2011.

Cast Away. Directed by Robert Zimeckis. By William Broyles, Jr. Performed by Tom Hanks, Viveka Davis, Michael Forest, Helen Hunt, and Nick Searcy. Los Angeles: Twentieth Century Fox Film Corporation, DreamWorks, SKG, 2000. DVD.

Brownie, Sonya, and Louise Horstmanshof. "The Management of Loneliness in Aged Care Residents: An Important Therapeutic Target for Gerontological Nursing." *Journal of Geriatric Nursing* 32, no. 5 (2011): 318–325.

Cacioppo, John T., William Patrick. *Loneliness: Human Nature and the Need for Social Connection.* New York: W. W. Norton & Company, 2008.

Cacioppo, John T., Hughes, M.E. et al. "Loneliness and Risk of Alzheimer's Disease." *Archives of General Psychiatry* 64, (2007).

Cacioppo, John T. and Stephanie Cacioppo. "Social Relationships and Health: The Toxic Effects of Perceived Social Isolation." *Journal of Social and Personality Psychology Compass* 8, no. 2 (2014): 58–72.

Cacioppo, John T., Louise C. Hawkley, Greg J. Norman, and Gary G. Berntson. "Social Isolation." *Annals of the New York Academy of Sciences* 1231 (2011): 17–22.

Cacioppo, John T., and Louise C. Hawkley. "Social Isolation and Health, with an Emphasis on Underlying Mechanisms." *Perspectives in Biology and Medicine* 46, suppl. 3 (2003):S39–S52.

Cacioppo, John T., and Louise C. Hawkley. "People Thinking About People: The Vicious Cycle of Being a Social Outcast in One's Own Mind." In *The Social Outcast: Ostracism, Social Exclusion, Rejection, and Bullying,* edited by Kipling D. Williams, Joseph P. Forgas, and William Von Hippel. New York: Psychology Press, 2005.

Cacioppo, John T., Louise C. Hawkley, Gary G. Berntson, John M. Ernst, Amber C. Gibbs, Robert Stickgold, and J. Allan Hobson. "Do Lonely Days Invade the Nights? Potential Social Modulation of Sleep Efficiency." *Psychological Science* 13 (2002): 384–387.

Camus, Albert. *The Outsider.* New York: Penguin Books, 1961.

Cattan, Mima, Martin White, John Bond, and Alison Learmouth. "Preventing Social Isolation and Loneliness Among Older People: A Systematic Review of Health Promotion Interventions." *Ageing and Society* 25, no. 1 (2005): 41–67.

Defoe, Daniel. *Robinson Crusoe.* Black and White Classics, 1719.

DiTommaso, Enrico, Cyndi Brannen-McNulty, Lynda Ross, and Melissa Burgess. "Attachment Styles, Social Skills and Loneliness in Young Adults." *Personality and Individual Differences* 35, no. 2 (2003): 303–312.

DiTommaso, Enrico, and Barry Spinner. "The Development and Initial Validation of the Social and Emotional Loneliness Scale for Adults

(SELSA)." *Personality and Individual Differences* 14, no. 1 (1993): 127–134.

Dumm, Thomas. *Loneliness as a Way of Life.* Cambridge, MA: Harvard University Press, 2008.

Dykstra, Pearl A., and Tineke Fokkema, T. "Social and Emotional Loneliness Among Divorced and Married Men and Women: Comparing the Deficit and Cognitive Perspectives." *Basic and Applied Social Psychology* 29, no. 1 (2007) 1–12.

Dykstra, Pearl A., Theo G. van Tilburg, and Jenny de Jong Gierveld. "Changes in Older Adult Loneliness: Results from a Seven-Year Longitudinal Study." *Research on Aging* 27, no. 6 (2005): 725–747.

Edmondson, Brad. "All the Lonely People." *AARP The Magazine* November/December 2010.

Elliot, Elisabeth. *The Path of Loneliness: Finding Your Way Through the Wilderness to God.* Grand Rapids, MI: Revelle, 1998.

Ernst, John M., and John T. Cacioppo. "Lonely Hearts: Psychological Perspectives on Loneliness." *Applied and Preventative Psychology* 8, no. 1 (1998): 1–22.

Feldon, Barbara. *Living Alone and Loving It.* New York: Fireside, 2003.

Gardner, Wendi L., Cynthia L. Pickett, Valerie Jeffries, and Megan L. Knowles. "On the Outside Looking In: Loneliness and Social Monitoring." *Personality and Social Psychology Bulletin* 31, no. 11, 2005.

Hawkley, Louise C., and John T. Cacioppo. "Aging and Loneliness: Downhill Quickly?" *Current Directions in Psychological Science* 16, no. 4 (2007): 187–191.

Hawkley, Louise C., Mary H. Burleson, Gary G. Berntson, and John T. Cacioppo. "Loneliness in Everyday Life: Cardiovascular Activity, Psychosocial Context, and Health Behaviors." *Journal of Personality and Social Psychology* 85, no.1 (2003): 105–120.

Holt-Lunstad, Julianne, Timothy B. Smith, Mark Baker, Tyler Harris, and David Stephenson. "Loneliness and Social Isolation as Risk Factors for Mortality: A Meta-Analytic Review." *Perspectives of Psychological Science* 10, no. 2 (2015): 227–237.

Houllebecq, Michel. *The Elementary Particle*. Translated by Frank Wynne. New York: Vintage, 2001.

Keegan, Marion. *The Opposite of Loneliness: Essays and Stories*. New York: Scribner, 2014.

Laing, Olivia. *The Lonely City: American Adventures in Being Alone*. New York: Picador, 2006.

Lauder, William; Kerry Mummery; Martyn Jones; and Cristina Caperchione. "A Comparison of Health Behaviors in Lonely and Non-Lonely Populations." *Psychology, Health and Medicine* 11, no. 2 (2006): 233–245.

Lieberman, Matthew D. *Social: Why Our Brains Are Wired to Connect*. New York: Crown Publishers, 2013.

McGuire, Shirley, and Jeanie Clifford. "Genetic and Environmental Contributions to Loneliness in Children." *Psychological Science* 11, no. 6 (2000): 487–491.

Moustakas, Clark E. *Loneliness and Love*. Upper Saddle River, NJ: Prentice-Hall, 1972.

Narang, David S. *Leaving Loneliness: A Workbook: Building Relationships with Yourself and Others*. Encino, CA: Stronger Relationships LLC, 2014.

Olson, Kimberly L., and Eugene H. Wong. "Loneliness in Marriage." *Family Therapy* 28, no. 2 (2001): 105.

Peplau, Letitia Anne, and Daniel Perlman. "Perspectives on Loneliness." In *Loneliness: A Sourcebook of Current Theory, Research and Therapy*, edited by Letitia Anne Peplau and Daniel Perlman. New York: John Wiley and Sons, 1982.

Perissinotto MD, Carla M., Irena S. Cenzer MA, and Kenneth E. Covinsky, MD. Loneliness in Older Persons: A Predictor of Functional Decline and Death. *Journal of the American Medical Association for Internal Medicine* Vol. 172, no. 14 (July 2012)

Pinquart, Martin. "Loneliness in Married, Widowed, Divorced, and Never-Married Older Adults." *Journal of Social and Personal Relationships* 20, no. 1 (2003): 31–35.

Olds, Jacqueline, and Schwartz, Richard. *The Lonely American: Drifting Apart in the 21st Century*. Boston: Beacon Press, 2009.

Ong, Anthony D., Bert N. Uchino, and Elaine Wethington. "Loneliness and Health in Older Adults: A Mini-Review and Synthesis." *Journal of Gerontology* November (2015): 1–7.

Putnam, Robert. *Bowling Alone: The Collapse and Revival of American Community*. New York: Simon and Schuster, 2000.

Reisman, David, and Nathan Glazer. *The Lonely Crowd*. New Haven, CT: Yale University Press, 1989.

Rittenberg, Sidney, and Amanda Bennett. *The Man Who Stayed Behind*. New York: Simon and Schuster, 1993.

Rook, Karen S. "Promoting Social Bonding: Strategies for Helping the Lonely and Socially Isolated." *American Psychologist* 39, no. 12 (1984): 1389–1407.

Rotenberg, Ken J. "Loneliness and Interpersonal Trust." *Journal of Social and Clinical Psychology* 13, no. 2 (1994): 152–173.

Rotenberg, Ken J., and Kmill, J. "Perception of Lonely and Non-Lonely Persons as a Function of Individual Differences in Loneliness." *Journal of Social and Personal Relationships* 9, no. 2 (1992): 325–330.

Russell, Daniel W. "UCLA Loneliness Scale (Version 3): Reliability, Validity, and Factor Structure." *Journal of Personality Assessment* 66, no. 3 (1996): 20–40.

Savikko, Niina, Pirkko Routasalo, Reijo S. Tilvis, Timo E. Strandberg, and K. H. Pitkälä. "Predictors and Subjective Causes of Loneliness in an Aged Population." *Archives of Gerontology and Geriatrics* 41, no.3 (2005): 223–233.

Schnittiker, J. "Look (Closely) at All the Lonely People: Age and Social Psychology of Social Support." *Journal of Aging and Health* 19 (2007): 659–682.

Seeman, Teresa E. "Health Promoting Effects of Friends and Family on Health Outcomes in Older Adults." *American Journal of Health Promotion* 14, no. 6 (2000): 362–370.

Shankar, Aparna, Anne McMunn, James Banks, and Andrew Steptoe. "Loneliness, Social Isolation, and Behavioral and Biological Health Indicators in Older Adults." *Journal of Health Psychology* 30, no. 4 (2011): 377–385.

Shaver, Phillip R., and Cindy Hazan. "Being Lonely, Falling in Love: Perspectives from Attachment Theory." *Journal of Social Behavior and Personality* 2, no. 2 (1987): 105–124.

Taylor, Shelley E. *The Tending Instinct: How Nurturing is Essential to Who We Are and How We Live.* New York: New York Times Books, 2002.

Turkle, Sherry. *Alone Together: Why We Expect More from Technology and Less from Each Other.* New York: Basic Books, 2011.

U.S. Census Bureau Report. *America's Family and Living Arrangements.* Washington, DC: US Census Bureau and US Department of Commerce, 2012.

Welles, Orson. Introduction to *Memoirs of a Bullfighter*, by Conchita Cintrón. Dumfries, NC: Holt, Rinehart and Winston, 1968.

Weiss, Robert S, ed. *Loneliness: The Experience of Emotional and Social Isolation.* Cambridge, MA: MIT Press, 1973.

White, Emily. *Lonely: Learning to Live in Solitude.* New York: Harper Perennial, 2010.

Wilson, R. S., K. R. Krueger, S. E. Arnold, J. A. Schneider, J. F. Kelly, L. L. Barnes, Y. Tang, and D. A. Bennett. "Loneliness and Risk of Alzheimer's Disease." *Archives of General Psychiatry* 64, no. 2 (2007): 234–240.

Worland, Justin. "Why Loneliness May Be the Next Big Public Health Issue." *Time Magazine*, March 18, 2015. http://time.com/3747784/loneliness-mortality.

ABOUT THE AUTHOR

J. W. Freiberg holds a BA from the University of California, Berkeley, an MA and PhD from UCLA, and a JD from Harvard Law School. He was formerly Assistant Professor and Director of Graduate Studies in the Department of Sociology at Boston University, and a member of the Centre d'Études des Mouvements Sociaux in Paris, where he taught Sociology and Social Psychology at the École Pratique des Hautes Études en Sciences Sociales. In addition to having held positions at several of Boston's oldest and most prestigious law firms, he is the author of the highly acclaimed books *Critical Sociology: European Perspectives* and *The French Press: Class, State and Ideology*, as well as over thirty-five articles, book introductions, and other scholarly works on social psychology and legal issues. His writings have been translated into French, Italian, and Japanese. During his career, Freiberg was awarded a Woodrow Wilson Dissertation Fellowship, a National Science Foundation Research Fellowship, and a Centre National de la Recherche Scientifique Fellowship. He continues to practice law, serves as a Justice of the Peace for the Commonwealth of Massachusetts, and lives in Boston with his wife, near their children.

Made in the USA
Middletown, DE
11 June 2017